MASTERS OF MAYHEM

MASTERS OF MAYHEM

Lawrence of Arabia and the British Military
Mission to the Hejaz

JAMES STEJSKAL

CASEMATE

Philadelphia & Oxford

Published in Great Britain and the United States of America in 2018 by
CASEMATE PUBLISHERS
1950 Lawrence Road, Havertown, PA 19083, US
and
The Old Music Hall, 106–108 Cowley Road, Oxford OX4 1JE, UK

Hardback Edition: ISBN 978-1-61200-574-4
Digital Edition: ISBN 978-1-61200-575-1

A CIP record for this book is available from the British Library

Printed and bound in the United States of America

For a complete list of Casemate titles, please contact:

CASEMATE PUBLISHERS (US)
Telephone (610) 853-9131
Fax (610) 853-9146
Email: casemate@casematepublishers.com
www.casematepublishers.com

CASEMATE PUBLISHERS (UK)
Telephone (01865) 241249
Email: casemate-uk@casematepublishers.co.uk
www.casematepublishers.co.uk

Front cover image: The Hejaz Armoured Car Section and RFA 10-Pounder Motor Section in Wadi
Rum. Mar–April 1917. (Harry Chase, Photographer, James A. Cannavino Library, Archives & Special
Collections, Marist College, USA)

Back cover image: Buxton, Brodie, Marshall, Stirling, in mufti, head out to reconnoitre Mudowarra in
one of the RFA Talbots. (Edward Metcalf Collection, The Huntington Library, San Marino, California.)

To those who went before us
and those yet to begin the journey.

"They were not soldiers, but pilgrims, intent always to go the little farther."

T. E. LAWRENCE AFTER JAMES ELROY FLECKER

Contents

Author's Note

It has been one hundred years since the Great War of 1914–18 took place. Although recent events have brought some place names back into focus, many of the locations and borders mentioned in the book have long ago changed or been forgotten. So too, have the geopolitical players changed. Both the Austro-Hungarian Empire and the Ottoman Empire disappeared after the war to be replaced by new states.

The Ottoman Empire was founded by the Osmanli Dynasty circa 1299 and was built by the Turkman peoples. But the Ottoman Empire comprised a vast territory and incorporated many of its subject peoples into its government and army, including the Kurds and the Arabs.

In this work I refer both to the Ottoman Empire, its proper name, as well as the more commonly used name of Turkey. As Edward Erickson pointed out in his book *Ordered to Die*, the enemies of the Ottoman Empire usually referred to their opponent as *Turks*.

Accordingly, I also refer to the Ottoman Army as the Turkish Army, whether its units and soldiers were of Turkish, Arab, or Circassian origin.

*

My thanks go out to Valerie Gilman who was of great assistance sharing the stories and photos of Leofric Gilman, John Ansley and his staff at Marist College, Stephen Tabor and his staff at the Huntington Library, Katrina DiMuro and Lianne Smith at King's College London Archives, as well as the invisible people behind the online archives at Kew (The National Archives), and the British Library.

I am also indebted to fellow historians Philip Walker, Joe Berton, Charles Eilers, and Kerry Webber; as well as conflict-archaeologists John Winterburn (and John Pascoe) and Neil Faulkner for their help. The people at Casemate Publishers in Oxford including Ruth Sheppard, Clare Litt, Tom Bonnington, Isobel Nettleton, and Katie Allen deserve a great deal of credit for supporting this project.

Most of all, this book would never have been possible without the help, patience, and counsel of my wife and best friend, Wanda.

Introduction

Surveyor-General's Office, Cairo – 1914

A shadow momentarily blocked the light streaming in through the doorframe. Ernest Dowson looked up to see the outline of a diminutive man in a rumpled uniform. He couldn't tell if it was regulation uniform or just a khaki suit, but what he could divine was the man seemed half amused, half embarrassed to be interrupting the operations of the office. Dowson would later remember that impetuous grin as well as the man himself. At that moment, however, he just thought, "Whoever can this extraordinary pipsqueak be?"

The man turned out to be Thomas Edward Lawrence. He was part of a team enlisted by the British government to survey the area in anticipation of possible, future enemy action against Egypt. Lawrence had spent much time in the region and spoke Arabic and several dialects used by the local populace.

In 1909, he made a personal pilgrimage to Palestine and Syria to survey Crusader castles. He used the notes and sketches he wrote and drew on that trip to write a thesis for his final history examinations at Oxford University. He returned in 1911 to work on the British Museum's archaeological excavations at Carchemish, Syria, under the tutelage of David Hogarth. During his last trip to Carchemish, he had worked with C. Leonard Woolley, who described Lawrence as impish and disdainful of work he felt could be done differently and more efficiently. What impressed Woolley was Lawrence's ability to work with the locals on the dig. His language skills were buttressed by his empathy for the indigenous peoples. Sometimes, at the expense of the dig, he would sit for hours with the workers and talk about customs or language.[1]

Lawrence's first foray into intelligence work began shortly thereafter. In December 1913, Captain Stewart Francis Newcombe, Royal Engineers, was tasked to conduct a survey of Palestine near Beersheba, an area that was mostly unknown to British mapmakers. Newcombe was an experienced military engineer and adventurer and had already surveyed railway routes in Abyssinia, Sudan and Egypt. Ostensibly, the survey was for archaeological purposes and conducted under the auspices of

---

[1] It was a talent that would later serve Lawrence well and one he described in his 'Twenty-seven Articles'. (Appendix 2)

the Palestinian Exploration Fund (PEF) in the northern Sinai and southern Negev deserts. In reality, however, the survey was to service War Office needs for up-to-date maps of the region; they would be critical to the defence of the Suez Canal. The inclusion of Woolley and Lawrence in the expedition lent a fig-leaf of cover that actually resulted in a well-respected study called *The Wilderness of Zin*, published by the PEF as its annual for 1914/15. Lawrence wrote in a letter home that they (he and Woolley) were meant to be "red herrings" for what was basically "a political job".

Through the first months of 1914, Woolley and Lawrence assisted Newcombe. After Woolley independently surveyed the northern section of the area, Lawrence travelled with Newcombe to survey the southern portion. The trip would prove valuable to Lawrence for two reasons: he acquired more experience as a surveyor and map-maker and he travelled and gained familiarity with an area that would prove pivotal to his later military career – the overland approach to the port city of Akaba.

Once the survey was completed, Woolley and Lawrence returned to Carchemish to finalize their work on the dig and write up their findings. In May, they were visited by Newcombe whose interest in the area was piqued by their reports of the Berlin–Baghdad railway being constructed by the Germans nearby. Newcombe concluded his visit to the dig site and made his way home to England hoping to follow the railway's route into the Taurus Mountains to collect information on its course and construction. After he returned home, Newcombe wrote back to tell his comrades he had been unsuccessful in gathering the information and asked that they try their luck. Woolley and Lawrence set out in June 1914 for England on a summer holiday and, as luck would have it, they were able to elicit the needed details about the railway from a disgruntled Italian engineer who had recently been fired from the project.

Back in England they set about finishing their work for the PEF while watching anxiously as war broke out. Lawrence knew he wanted to contribute to the war effort, but was told by Newcombe to wait before volunteering. Newcombe knew that Lawrence's knowledge could best be used in the Middle East and, until Turkey entered the war, he should hold back or risk being sent to Europe. Besides, he was too short for the army's height standards.

Once the survey work and book were finished, Lawrence obtained a job as a civilian working in the military's map section in London where he focused on Ottoman territory. When war with Turkey was declared in October 1914, he would be transferred to Cairo. Little did he realize the skills learned during his travels would soon be put to the test in ways he never imagined.

Southern Jordan – November 2012

I was standing on the parapet of an old Ottoman fortification looking down into a valley called Batn al Ghoul or Belly of the Beast. To the south stretched mile after mile of red and ochre sand, punctuated by rock outcroppings and the trace of

Highway 5 that ran down to the Saudi border at Hallat Amar. From my vantage point on the Ras al Naqb escarpment, I could see a train station, or more precisely, the remnants of one. The Hejaz railway once ran though this desolate valley along the ancient path that merchants, travellers, and the pilgrims of the Hajj had used for centuries. The railway connected Damascus to the north with the Holy City of Medina far to the south.

The Wadi Rutm station below was destroyed during the Great Arab Revolt in 1917. Since that time, it had lain derelict, assailed by sandstorms and locals who constantly dug holes in and around its few buildings, looking for the Turkish treasure rumoured to be hidden there. The rails were long since gone, recycled for their good German, Belgian, or American steel, or just used by a local in some construction project.

I had been to Jordan before, the first time just after the first Gulf War in 1991. I was working in Damascus and, although I enjoyed the Grand Souk with its pervasive aromas of roasting cashews, *qahwah,* and garbage, I needed an escape. It was Christmas Day and, on a whim, I grabbed a taxi at the bus depot and headed for the border. Renting a car in Amman, my trip continued to Akaba, stopping at Wadi Rum and Petra on the way.

Remnants of Wadi Rutm station. (Author)

Modern replacement for Hejaz railway culvert bridge near Wadi Rutm. (Author)

Akaba, now a bustling seaport, was a lost cause for me. The port was cloaked in a cloud of gypsum dust coming from the ships being loaded with one of Jordan's only sources of revenue. The historical vistas and sites were mostly gone and Wadi Itm was now a paved road, not the treacherous gorge it once was.

Wadi Rum, on the other hand, was a place where I was able to contemplate the echoing canyons, red sand, and the wide expanse of the valley. It mirrored the scenes I had seen in David Lean's movie, *Lawrence of Arabia*. I had read *Revolt in the Desert*, the much attenuated version of T. E. Lawrence's *Seven Pillars of Wisdom,* and I spent a lot of time trying to correlate the vistas I saw with what the movie and the book depicted. The vast quietness gave me a feeling for what the protagonists of the time experienced. Since that time, I've read the longer version of Lawrence's opus and many of the companion books that sought to tell aspects of Lawrence and the campaign.

I returned to Jordan in 2012 to work with the Great Arab Revolt Project, a project that was following Lawrence's trail from World War I in an attempt to determine how accurate (or truthful) he was in telling his personal history. To paraphrase Huckleberry Finn, Lawrence was a man who may have stretched his role in history, but generally told the truth.

The organizers and participants were mostly a cerebral lot who called their work "conflict archaeology". First developed in the study of the battlefield at Little Big Horn, it is a sub-discipline of archaeology that deals "with technological, social, cultural, psychological aspects of modern conflict". The twenty of us were mostly English, with

Looking at Wadi Rutm station from Ras al Nagb fort. (Author)

a Scot or two, an Australian whom I kept mistaking for Crocodile Dundee, a Belgian woman in love with either Lawrence or Peter O'Toole, and a couple of American vagabonds, of which I was one. It was my first trip with the group. Many of the others had spent all seven of the previous, twenty-day 'seasons' in Jordan chasing Lawrence.

The project was coordinated with the Jordanian authorities who were amused to hear that poking around a 100-year-old battlefield could be called 'archaeology'. The 120-kilometre drive down from our hospice at Wadi Musa served to highlight their view. On the first day of the expedition, we were driving to our 'dig' site. We passed a tumble-down pile of huge stones, an ancient village. One of the veterans responded to my interest by pointing out a stone with an 'X' carved into it: the barracks of the Roman Tenth Legion, he said, adding that it was a rather recent addition to the neighbourhood. I understood the Jordanian's point.

Our group was made up of specialists. Half the team were professional archaeologists, including a site manager, photographers and recorders, three metal detectorists, and the rest, including me, amateurs with an interest in Lawrence or the Arab Revolt. Before long, I realized I did have a useful skill besides digging and sifting sand: my military experience. While on top of a ridge overlooking Batn al Ghoul and the steep descent of the Hejaz railway towards the valley below where the remains of a railway station stood, one of the learned bunch came up to me while I was gazing out over the quiet expanse of the desert and asked, "What purpose do you think this place served?" We had found Turkish tent rings, discharged Mauser rifle cartridges and British artillery shrapnel around the walls of the fort. I told him my impressions about the site, and later I found the war diaries of the British mobile artillery unit that had shelled the fort, which confirmed much of what I thought.

While we were working that site, Neil Faulkner and Nick Saunders, the leaders of the project, took a couple of the team and headed south. There was a great deal of suppressed excitement as they were chasing tidbits of information that pointed to a site of great interest. Up to that point, the only physical evidence of the Arab guerrillas and Lawrence that the expedition found had been the few rifle bullets and artillery shell fragments littered around the Ottoman-Turkish positions. That was until one of the archaeologists working in the British archives between trips found a sketch map drawn by a Royal Flying Corps pilot during the war. It showed a prominent geographic point the pilot used as a guidepost for his route, called 'Tooth Hill'. That name rang a bell and a subsequent reread of *Seven Pillars* led to Lawrence's description but not the location of the site. It had been used as a camp and staging base for attacks on the Hejaz railway several times during the campaign. There was also a photo taken by a British officer who worked with Lawrence that showed the hill, their camp, and several of the Rolls-Royce armoured cars involved in the raids.

Armed with the map and photo, the small team sought out the site and amazingly stumbled onto an undisturbed, old campfire pit surrounded by the shards of a ceramic British military jug. It was the Tooth Hill camp, the first physical signs not only of British occupation of a site but also evidence that Lawrence's account was accurate. Several days of searching, digging, and recording ensued, now with the whole team involved.

At one location near the fire pit, a cluster of British ammunition was found, around 80 expended rifle cartridges, but among them several misfires – cartridges with primers that had been struck by a firing pin but had failed to fire. The boss asked me for my opinion about the pile. I reflected for a moment and, remembering the picture, the answer was apparent. There had been no battle at Tooth Hill – the battles took place miles away. The ammunition was a particular type, Mark VII .303 calibre with a 'spitzer' pointed bullet, a type preferred for use with the Vickers-Maxim and Lewis machine guns.

I surmised that an armoured car crew had fired its Vickers machine gun in one of the battles that took place along the railway line as described in *Seven Pillars*.

Tooth Hill camp. (John Pascoe & John Winterburn)

Tooth Hill today. (John Winterburn & Great Arab Revolt Project)

Afterwards the cars returned to the camp and, during the subsequent clean-up, the crews swept the spent cartridges out of the car into the desert. Hence, a mixed pile of fired and misfired rounds, which had lain undisturbed for nearly a hundred years. And now, my interest was piqued by the armoured cars.

In my studies, the Rolls-Royce armoured cars had shown up in the World War I campaigns in German South-West Africa and German East Africa. In the Hejaz, I was seeing the cars used for the first time as part of an irregular warfare operation to support guerrillas behind the lines on long-range raids. There were also mobile artillery platforms, along with air and naval assets and an imperial corps of Australian and New Zealander cameliers, who did yeomen's work alongside the Arab rebels.

Type 65 fuse from British 10-pounder shell found at Ras al Nagb fort. (Author)

Type 65 fuse from British 10-pounder shell found at Ras al Nagb fort. (Author)

Lawrence was among the first to 'advise' a *foreign* irregular force, and one of the first to document his experiences. What I realized was that this 'sideshow' of a sideshow in the Great War, which secured General Allenby's right flank as his army fought its way into Syria, was one of the first modern examples of combined special operations. 'Combined' in that it employed many different arms of the military: air, sea, and land elements, and 'special' in that irregular forces – the Arab tribes – advised by foreign military officers fed with the best intelligence available, fought an asymmetrical campaign of guerrilla warfare against a stronger military: the Ottoman Army.[2]

There have been many books about Thomas E. Lawrence, the man known as 'Lawrence of Arabia'. Lawrence was an anomaly – an amateur officer who eschewed British military traditions and discipline and who loathed its seemingly mindless adherence to rules, regulations, and conventions. Yet, when needed, he embraced

---

[2] Combined operations are those "in which two or more of the fighting services co-operate to strike the enemy with the maximum effect at a chosen place and a chosen moment".

its leadership, organization, and resources to achieve the ends he desired. This work is neither a hagiography nor calumny of Lawrence. Although he plays an important role in this history, Lawrence is not the primary subject. I must add, however, that Lawrence's fame, bolstered by the propaganda that Lowell Thomas spread with his book *With Lawrence in Arabia* and lecture tour, means that Lawrence intrudes into nearly every discussion of the Arab Revolt, this one included.

There have also been many books about World War I – the Great War – in the Middle East and its campaigns: from the Ottomans and Gallipoli to the Arab Revolt and Allenby. This book does not aspire to tell the detailed history of the war in the Middle East, the Arab Revolt or Allenby's success. For that, I suggest any one of the many books listed in the bibliography, especially *Seven Pillars* as well as Neil Faulkner's *Lawrence of Arabia's War*.

Writing about the Middle East is complicated and the transliteration of words, names, and places can be confusing. I have elected to retain spellings used in contemporary texts and have also chosen to use the bare minimum of footnotes to enhance readability.

What follows is the story of the campaign as it evolved. From its unstable beginnings, its faltering initial campaigns, to irregular warfare, and finally conventional operations with its inevitable conclusion. The leaders who inspired the revolt and shaped its tactics and strategy are discussed along with the roles of the special men and units who made up the British Military Mission and fought alongside the Arabs.

The first chapter deals with the global and regional situation up to the outbreak of the Arab Revolt in the Hejaz. It is a very superficial account but presents the pertinent information that impacted the revolt. The treatment of the revolt itself is episodic and I describe many but not all of the operations that took place. I also have avoided dealing with the political aspects of the Arab Revolt (especially Sykes-Picot and the Balfour Declaration) as well as Grand Sherif Hussein's internecine squabbles with ibn Rashid and ibn Saud, other than in passing. In the background of this telling, one must remain constantly aware that the Great War raged in Europe and elsewhere. Because it was far away, the destruction, the horrific noise and terror are not apparent. But it was always there, affecting every decision and action, even in the Near East.

While there are many excellent books that recount Lawrence and his operations in totality, my rendering looks at the specific operations which demonstrate how British tactical methods evolved, the contributions of 'Hedgehog' – the British Military Mission to the Hejaz – and how they influenced later leaders and operations. Not all the engagements that Lawrence or the British Military Mission took part in will be discussed; there are far too many for a short book, and several have been covered in detail elsewhere. I have selected others that demonstrate British operational planning both for guerrilla raiding, as well as direct action by combined operations forces.

With this work, I hope to show that this campaign was one of the seeds – an inspiration – for British special operations that followed.

Prologue

An Alliance Leads to War

When Gavrilo Princip fired his pistol in Sarajevo, he probably had no idea that he would be the cause of World War I. His two bullets killed Archduke Ferdinand, the presumptive heir to the Austro-Hungarian throne, and dragged the nations of Europe into a bloody, mud-slogging war of attrition that stretched across the face of the continent. On one side initially was the Triple Entente: the United Kingdom, France, Russia, and soon Italy. On the other were the Central Powers of Germany and Austro-Hungary. It was late summer in 1914.

That monstrous conflict had its origins in the complex changes to Europe's balance of power that had taken place in the previous century. But, although the focus of the war was in Europe, many of the factors that pushed the protagonists towards conflict were to be found elsewhere. Indeed, the first shots of World War I were exchanged not in Europe, but in Africa. These campaigns, called by some 'sideshows', to divest Germany of its colonies would occupy the Entente, or Allied Powers, until after the armistice in 1918.

Another 'sideshow' was about to begin in the Middle East, the consequences of which remain with us to this day.

Prior to World War I, the Ottoman Empire was in a tight spiral of decline. The Ottoman-Turks needed a patron to help protect their territory, but no European power was willing to be their ally. Rather, the great powers of Britain, France, Germany, and Russia sat like vultures above a dying man waiting for their opportunity to rip the cadaver apart. Everyone expected the empire to succumb quickly and, when it did, the Europeans would be there to grab the pieces.

Britain had spent much of the 1800s ensuring its own empire was secure from two principal enemies: France and Russia. In Afghanistan and Persia, much blood and gold was spent trying to secure the northwestern approaches to the Raj – British India – from a possible Russian invasion. And, as the scramble for Africa ensued, Britain was among the first nations to expand its imperial ambitions onto the 'dark continent'. By the 1880s, she had gained control over the Sudan and Egypt and confronted France at Fashoda. All the while, Britain continued to prop up the Sublime Porte – the Ottoman government at Constantinople – in order to block Russian influence in the region. It was all part of the 'Great Game' played to determine "the question of Russian or British supremacy in the world".

But alliances changed as the new century loomed. Russia's revolutionary unrest and its stunning defeat at the hands of Imperial Japan at the Battle of Tsushima in 1905 combined to lessen the threat Russia posed to the United Kingdom.[1]

Additionally, the 1904 Entente Cordiale between Great Britain and France alleviated nearly a thousand years of rivalry. The treaty settled many of the colonial frictions that had arisen in the 1800s and gave Britain freedom of action in Egypt while France got a free hand in Morocco. Thereafter, London had little reason to fear French encroachment on the Nile. That said, British officials in Egypt and India continued, not without reason, to be concerned about French and Russian intentions in the Middle East.

Years before, a popular uprising in 1882 in Egypt led Great Britain to occupy and take control of that country, nominally part of the Ottoman Caliphate, in order to protect British interests in the Suez Canal and the short route to India.[2] While parliament lambasted the corrupt regimes of the Middle East, many of which had been supported by London to block Russian encroachment, the new prime minister, William Gladstone, denounced atrocities against Christians in the region and withdrew his country's strong support of the Sublime Porte.[3]

The Ottoman Empire had its own territorial concerns, among these was the defence of the Bosphorus Straights. During the 'Scramble for Africa', it lost its provinces in North Africa – Tunisia and Morocco – to the French, and would soon lose Libya to another European power, Italy. Having lost London's support and feeling threatened by Moscow, the Ottomans sought a new protector.

Germany meanwhile had only recently become a truly great nation of Europe. Starting in the 1860s, Prussian Minister President Otto von Bismarck and Field Marshal Helmuth von Moltke, Chief of the Prussian General Staff, had fought a series of wars that successfully welded a hodgepodge of Teutonic kingdoms and principalities into a single German state (minus Austria). Following the defeat of France in 1871 and with the annexation of Alsace-Lorraine, Bismarck was able to unify the loosely confederated states and create the German Empire.

---

[1] Foreign Secretary Sir Edward Grey concluded that Russia was no longer a threat, which resulted in a 1907 treaty, 'The Convention between the United Kingdom and Russia relating to Persia, Afghanistan, and Tibet'.

[2] In 1882, Britain annexed Egypt as 'a veiled protectorate'. This lasted until November 1914 when Egypt was formally proclaimed a protectorate following Britain's declaration of war with the Ottoman Empire.

[3] "British government pronouncements suggested that Britain's occupation was temporary, its intention being to 'rescue' Egypt from 'disorder' and the Egyptian throne from a nationalist movement, dubbed a 'military mutiny', and then to 'retire'. There was in reality neither general agreement nor clearly conceived policy. British rule in Egypt was as authoritarian as that of the Khedives. For Imperial Britain, the occupation provided a naval base and strengthened control of an indispensable passage [the Suez Canal] to Asia." – Afaf Lutfi Al-Sayyid, 'The British Occupation of Egypt from 1882', *The Oxford History of the British Empire: Volume III: The Nineteenth Century*, ed. Andrew Porter, Oxford: Oxford UP, 1999.

The 'new' Germany came late to the European scramble for colonies and territory, primarily because Bismarck wisely felt the *Deutsches Kaiserreich* was large enough already. Within Germany, however, a call for what would later be termed *lebensraum* (living space) was beginning to be heard from all levels of society. Bismarck, who became the Chancellor of the German Empire under Kaiser (Emperor) Wilhelm I, did not relish the prospect of expanding the nation's borders and, further, did not wish to upset either Great Britain or Russia. Nevertheless, he was persuaded to accept colonies, East Africa, South-West Africa, Cameroon and Togo on the 'dark continent' and several remote islands in the Pacific as territories that were to be exploited by German émigrés.

Some Germans saw the Ottoman Empire, Mesopotamia, and Persia as a natural extension of a Greater Germany that would provide both expansion and raw material wealth for the homeland. General Moltke, who had visited eastern Turkey as a young army officer and seen its potential, was among them.

After being snubbed by Britain, the Ottoman Empire's autocratic leader, Sultan Abdulhamid, turned to Berlin for help. Bismarck responded positively by sending a commission of military advisors but he hedged his bets: each would have to be employed by the Sultan and have no visible connection back to Germany. At the head of this commission was Colmar Freiherr von der Goltz, a Prussian infantry officer, theorist, and instructor at the Potsdam military academy.

Thus began a relationship that would worry London even more than the Russians. Germany had come a long way since Bismarck had uttered the words, "The entire Eastern Question is not worth the healthy bones of one Pomeranian grenadier." Germany hoped to profit from the relationship in ways beyond its martial ambitions. Industrialists won contracts to provide arms and material and others began to look beyond Turkey's eastern borders into Persia and even further, towards India.

In 1888, Wilhelm II took the throne when Wilhelm I died. Unlike his predecessors, Wilhelm II was expansionist, bull-headed, and thought he could run Germany without advice. He dismissed Bismarck and then proceeded to render worthless the former Chancellor's complex system of alliances and counter-alliances that had helped to maintain the peace in Europe. Wilhelm II was persuaded that vast rewards awaited the German people in the East. Turkey would be the target, not only for increased marketing of Germany's goods, but for reaping its material wealth. Wilhelm II sought to slowly and quietly take control of the Ottoman Empire.

The new Kaiser placed himself on a course to affront most every European sensibility when he extended his friendship to the Sultan during a visit to Constantinople in October 1898. There he and the Sultan exchanged ostentatious gifts. He then continued on to Jerusalem. Never a modest man, he entered the city riding a black charger and wearing a tropical uniform he had designed himself. He passed through a breach in the city's wall cut especially for him. Although the Kaiser attempted to show humility – at one point he dismounted, kissed the ground and prayed before continuing – he was mocked by the press throughout the visit.

It was after all a time when every country in Europe was discussing the Ottoman Empire and how they were going to divide it up among themselves when the 'sick man' died. Wilhelm II had beat them to the punch by befriending Sultan Abdulhamid when the Ottomans most needed it. Great Britain, France, and Russia were probably as envious as they were alarmed.

He capped off his visit with a trip to Damascus where he visited the tomb of the warrior An-Nasir Salah ad-Din Yusuf ibn Ayyub, better known as Saladin, the first sultan of Syria and Egypt. At a dinner, Wilhelm II gave a speech that further alarmed the monarchs of Europe in which he declared himself to be the protector of Islam and Muslims worldwide. Naturally, the rulers of the other European nations were enraged. They all had large Muslim populations in their empires while Germany had none.

Although the Sultan regarded the German Emperor warily, Wilhelm II achieved what he had sought: a concession for a railway had been given to Germany and its influence would grow; the Berlin–Baghdad railway would be built by German engineers with German steel.[4] At the same time in Berlin, the Secretary of State of

---

[4] Although Belgium and the United States also provided steel rail.

the Imperial Naval Office, Grand Admiral Alfred von Tirpitz, pushed his emperor to build a naval fleet that would counter the Russian and French fleets and rival that of the world's preeminent sea power: Great Britain.

Both of these aims, along with an increasingly powerful German industrial base and Wilhelm II's miscommunication and braggadocio, raised Britain's fear of the danger Germany posed. And, although Tirpitz slowed the rapid pace of building his mega-fleet, analysts decided his smaller fleet still posed a direct threat to a Great Britain that jealously guarded its naval supremacy.

The project to build a railway from Berlin to Baghdad, with its intended terminus at a new port to be built south of Basra on the headwaters of the Persian Gulf, especially alarmed Lord Curzon, the Imperial British Viceroy in India. In 1904, Curzon dispatched a political officer to parley with the Emir of Kuwait to ensure the Turks and Germans did not gain a foothold on the Gulf. In this role, Colonel Malcolm Meade persuaded the Emir that England's guarantee to safeguard his borders and throne was worth a pledge not to cede his lands to the Turks, whom the Emir didn't like anyway. This effectively forced the railway to end in Baghdad, but did little to assuage British disquiet. Many saw the railway as a dagger pointed straight at India.

Britain now viewed Germany as the preeminent threat. Driven by nationalist desires, a burgeoning industrial capacity, and its emperor's swagger, it was a power to be reckoned with.

Sultan Abdulhamid saw Germany as his empire's saviour. But the Turks would give Britain one more chance before the world fell into the abyss of the Great War.

In 1908, the Sultan was forced to restore the constitution he had suspended in 1878. An uprising by a group of revolutionaries, mostly military officers stationed in Ottoman Macedonia who opposed the suspension, quickly spread throughout the province. When the military threatened to march on the capital, the Sultan relented and restored the constitution. Parliamentary control was reestablished over the empire and the second constitutional era was born. Parties emerged in the parliament, among them the Liberals, but one in particular dominated: the Committee of Union and Progress (CUP) and its core leaders who were known as the 'Young Turks'. For the moment, they were content to leave actual governance of the empire to the Grand Vizier (prime minister). The CUP merely oversaw his and the Sultan's activities.

Germany, having supported Abdulhamid, was left out in the cold by the Young Turks who wanted little to do with the Kaiser at that point. The British could have stepped back in to fill the void, but was indefensibly ignorant of the true nature of the revolt. At first sympathetic to the Young Turks who now controlled parliament, the British ambassador to the Sublime Port, Sir Gerhard Lowther, was convinced that the Turks were being led by a cabal of Jewish Freemasons intent only on grabbing power.[5] This was because the embassy lacked good access to the Sublime Porte

---

[5] A belief echoed years later by Ronald Storrs in his biography, *Orientations*.

and relied on an advisor who detested the Young Turks. That mistake would have far-reaching consequences, among these a reluctance to work with the new power in Constantinople and a susceptibility to judgements based on wholly inaccurate or biased information.

The revolution had left the Ottoman Empire vulnerable and its outlying provinces felt the time for independence had come. Bulgaria declared itself free of Constantinople's rule, Albania would follow later.

Sultan Abdulhamid bided his time, turning to the religious community and opponents of the CUP opposed to its secular nature to launch a counter-coup. In April 1909, Abdulhamid launched his counter-stroke, but it was quickly quashed when the Third Macedonian Army returned to the capital and seized control once again. Abdulhamid was replaced by his more malleable brother, Mehmed V and the Young Turks were reestablished in parliament.

Sensing Ottoman weakness, Italy chose this moment to seize the North African regions known as Tripoli and Cyrenaica (today's Libya). The various factions in Constantinople reacted with confusion and division about how to prosecute the war that arose with Italy. The government wanted to abandon its North African possessions, but the Young Turks in parliament wanted to fight on. With few means to resist and its garrisons in Libya quickly overwhelmed, the Turks began a guerrilla war by surreptitiously sending military officers as advisors to rally and train the local tribes, including the Senussi. The Italian offensive was stymied. In response, the Italians expanded their campaign by attacking other Ottoman territories and then rallying the Balkan states of Montenegro, Greece, Bulgaria, and Serbia to their side. The Turks, who were now hopelessly outnumbered, quickly lost most of their remaining Balkan territory.

The Liberal-led government now contemplated the pursuit of peace. When the CUP opposed this and criticized the government's prosecution of the war, Grand Vizier Kamil Pasha cracked down on newspapers that supported the CUP and arrested some of its members.

It was the siege of Edirne (Adrianople) that changed the Ottoman government's plan completely. Edirne, a fortress city in Thrace near Turkey's western border with Greece, was surrounded by Bulgarian forces. In January 1913, it appeared the government was about to surrender the city. In frustration, several CUP members broke into the Sublime Porte and seized full power, killing four men in the process. Despite taking control of the government, the CUP was unable to stop Edirne's capture and was forced to sue for peace. The Ottoman Empire surrendered most of its European possessions along with the people who lived there, and lost its Libyan territory in North Africa to Italy.

The Liberal Party blamed the CUP for the loss of Libya, which led to an attempt to push the CUP out of government. This time, the CUP reacted by eliminating its rivals in parliament. Three CUP members, Mehmed Talaat, Ahmet Djemal, and

Ismail Enver, were promoted to the senior rank of 'Pasha'. Known as the 'Triumvirate', they would lead the party and promised to revitalize the economy, rebuild the military, as well as restore the constitution and national pride. But their rule became autocratic as they centralized the government and reasserted control over its outlying provinces, which had been granted a great deal of autonomy by Abdulhamid. This in turn would lead to some groups, notably the Armenians and the Arabs, to seek greater autonomy within the Ottoman Empire. The consequences would be deadly.

All the while, the CUP Triumvirate realized that the predatory desires of their larger neighbours like Russia were more aroused than ever before and, after seeing what Europe had done to Africa during the 'Scramble', the fear of dissolution and partition led them to seek a strong patron.

The CUP's innermost circle of leaders fanned out to search for a benefactor in the European diplomatic corps. Mehmed Djavid, the new Minister of Finance, was pro-British. He approached the British ambassador for support but was sent packing. Ahmet Djemal, now the Minister of Marine, received the same treatment from the French, as did the new Minister of the Interior, Mehmed Talaat, who approached (oddly enough) the Russians. All of these countries were disinclined to sign a treaty, anticipating the Ottoman Empire would soon crumble and they could pick up the pieces for themselves.

Then came the Second Balkan War. The Ottoman Empire was able to recover much of the territory previously lost to Bulgaria. Ismail Enver, called 'the Liberator' for recapturing Edirne from the Bulgarians during the Second Balkan War, approached the German envoy to propose a mutual defence treaty. Enver believed that Germany had the strongest army in Europe and that an alliance would keep the empire alive. Initially, Germany kept its distance.

All the while, despite their misgivings over an alliance, the Europeans still vied for influence with Constantinople. A British naval mission and French and German army missions were engaged in the modernization of the Ottoman military services. Clearly, they were seeking to position themselves in anticipation of a collapse. Meanwhile, Europe moved towards war.

The Ottomans tried to stay out of the fray, but events would conspire to bring them directly into the line of fire. The Turkish need for a European ally was the first of these.

Talaat later justified the search for an ally, saying, "Turkey needed to join one of the country groups so that it could organize its domestic administration, strengthen and maintain its commerce and industry, expand its railroads, in short to survive and to preserve its existence." The Ottoman Empire was still in freefall. It was early 1914.

As the clouds of war gathered over Europe, Winston Churchill, First Lord of the Admiralty, played a crucial role in forcing the Sublime Porte's decision. Believing that the Ottoman Empire would ally itself with Germany, he ordered two Turkish warships being built in British shipyards seized on 31 July 1914. The ships, the *Rashadieh* and *Sultan Osman I*, were the most modern Dreadnought-class ships yet built. And, although they had been paid for, Churchill thought they would end up in the hands of the Germans if they were delivered to Constantinople. The Turks were incensed.

In late July 1914, the Turks pressed German ambassador Hans von Wagenheim for an alliance, but Berlin was not convinced. It was only when the Kaiser himself spoke up that a crucial condition was posed: an alliance would be entertained if the Ottoman Empire would commit to war against Russia. A secret alliance was signed on 2 August 1914 but, even so, due to the document's poor wording, its obligations to support Germany were unclear and still being discussed by the Ottoman government.

When the war in Europe began, the German Mediterranean Squadron, consisting of two warships, the SMS *Goeben* and SMS *Breslau* under Admiral Wilhelm Souchon, opened hostilities by shelling several ports in French Algeria in an effort to disrupt the transport of colonial soldiers to France. After a short engagement, the two ships escaped eastward, pursued by the British fleet. Under orders, they sailed for the Dardanelles, knowing that if they reached Constantinople, the ships would be interned for the duration if Turkey declared itself neutral in the coming conflict. Germany reasoned that was better than being sunk by the superior force chasing them.

When the Turks learned of the Germans' plight, they understood they held the high cards and laid out a series of extortionate demands for the German ambassador that, if refused, would have left the ships to their fate before the British guns. The Germans accepted the conditions and the ships at arrived in port on 10 August without being engaged by the British. Once safe in harbour, the Turks proposed to 'buy' them for the Ottoman Navy and then made it a fait accompli by simply issuing a declaration that the sale was done. The Germans had little choice but to go along. Admiral Souchon and his German crews changed into Turkish uniforms and became the new Ottoman Navy. The British government mistakenly believed the Kaiser had turned the two ships over to compensate Turkey for the loss of the *Rashadieh* and *Sultan Osman I*.

Meanwhile, a true conspiracy was under way. Enver Pasha believed Germany would win the war, but he could not convince his fellow CUP members to support him. Failing all else, he tried to provoke the Russians into declaring war on the Ottoman Empire by secretly dispatching the newly acquired, German-crewed Ottoman ships along with several other naval vessels into the Black Sea to 'be attacked' by the Russians. Although Enver and Souchin were colluding, the Admiral took the idea one step further to make absolutely sure the Turks would be brought into the war. His fleet proceeded to sink several Russian ships and shelled Sevastopol and several other towns on Russia's Black Sea coast. The Allies immediately severed relations with the Ottoman government.

When the news of Souchon's activities reached Constantinople, yet another crisis erupted in the Turkish parliament. The Grand Vizier ordered Enver to have Souchon

xxvi • MASTERS OF MAYHEM

stand down. Enver's coalition was on shaky ground and he found himself isolated when the cabinet decided to issue an apology to Russia for the German admiral's actions. Enver did so, but then stuck his thumb in Russia's eye by inserting a phrase that blamed the incident on a Russian provocation, knowing the apology would be rejected. Russia declared war on the Ottoman Empire on 2 November and, with that, Enver got his wish. Turkey had a powerful patron as its ally and the empire was at war.

After the Turks failed to respond to a British ultimatum to expel the German ships and the German Military Mission, Winston Churchill ordered the fleet to shell Turkish coastal installations. In early November, Royal Navy ships destroyed the fortress at Seddulbahir and damaged three other batteries. It was the precursor of bigger things to come.

The Russians quickly followed with a ground attack on the Ottoman Empire. Driving west deep into the Caucasus Mountains, they were initially successful. The Russian commander, optimistic because of the enemy's apparent weakness, decided to continue his push forward beyond his assigned objective. This time, his forces were met by a reinforced and determined defender. The Turkish Third Army halted the advance and forced the Russians to retreat into a defensive position in the rugged mountains. Then came the snows and both sides warily went into winter quarters.

The British also opened their ground offensive in the Persian Gulf. Anticipating they would occupy Mesopotamia and its newly found oilfields when the war ended, the British Government of India (GOI) at Simla directed its army to secure the port of Basra. In November 1914, the commander of the Mesopotamian Expeditionary Force, Lieutenant-General John Nixon, landed two brigades and seized the port. Then he pondered his next move. The decision he made would prove to be one of the costliest mistakes of the war.

Whose Holy War is This?

Britain's principal concern in the Middle East was to defend the Suez Canal – as much for its importance as an artery of commerce and military transport as what it would mean to the Muslims of India and Egypt and, most importantly, to British prestige if the Ottoman Army succeeded in capturing it. However, for the British War Council, the primacy of the Western Theatre in Europe was all important and the Middle East was relegated to the backburner for the immediate future. Egypt would get very little in the way of men and manpower while the war in Europe raged.

Germany, on the other hand, was determined to use its alliance with the Ottomans to divert their enemies in any way possible. Accordingly, the Germans urged their new partners to attack the Russians, as well as the British. Berlin especially wanted Turkish forces to strike north into the Balkans and Galicia where the Austrians were under pressure by Serb and Russian advances. At the same time, an assault on the

Suez Canal would disrupt British lines of communication and hopefully lead to an Egyptian uprising against their *kafir* (unbeliever) occupiers.

The Germans had long planned for the moment and urged the Ottoman government to declare not only war, but jihad against its enemies. As early as 1900, Baron Max von Oppenheim had urged the Kaiser to use the power of Islam against Britain and founded a bureau in Berlin to promote jihad to destabilize British and French colonies through disinformation and propaganda.

But the Turks were cautious and delayed. It was only after Admiral Souchon engaged the Russian Black Sea Fleet and brought about the Russian declaration of war, that the Caliph of Islam, Ürgüplü Mustafa Hayri Efendi, proclaimed jihad against the Allies on 14 November 1914. Both German and Turkish leaders were hopeful that not only the Muslims of the empire would rally to their cause, but all Muslims worldwide would answer the call.

Now, committed to the conflict, the Ottoman leadership set out to conduct the war on their own terms, and nearly lost it with their opening gambit. In a moment of grand miscalculation, Enver Pasha decided he would attack east, through the Caucasus Mountains and Afghanistan, all the way to India. There were, however, a few minor details to clean up along the way.

There was no doubt that Enver wanted to conquer the British in India, but his first goal was to regain three Anatolian provinces, territory lost to Russia in 1878. Enver therefore decided his first objective would be the Russian Army at Sarıkamış with its vital railhead and line to Kars.

Buoyed by his army's performance repelling the Russians in November, he envisioned a classic envelopment. He sketched out his plan to the Third Army commander, Hasan Izzet Pasha, who expressed misgivings about attempting an offensive operation in the dead of winter, especially in the difficult terrain they would have to cross. His troops were mostly inexperienced and not equipped for cold-weather operations. The snowbound mountain passes would be treacherous and, moreover, it would be very difficult to execute the precise encirclement Enver wanted. Further, he thought more time was needed to bring up the supplies required for the effort.

Hearing Izzet Pasha's objections, Enver saw only a reluctant, stalling commander and took charge of the army himself. Proclaiming that adequate supplies existed in front of them – the enemy's – he launched his offensive. He instructed the soldiers to carry nothing but their weapons and the bare essentials they would need to surprise the Russians. He also pinned his hopes on a spontaneous uprising of Islamic peoples along the route as his Army pressed forward.

Enver Pasha's forces achieved surprise, but little else.

Some 80,000 Russian soldiers had retired into winter quarters in the region and a number of units had been withdrawn to be employed on other, more active fronts.

Looking from their lofty defensive lines at the rugged terrain and feeling the winter's cold, no one thought an attack would come.

Enver gave the Third Army's 100,000 troops three objectives: XI Corps would attack as a feint to hold the Russians and force them to commit more troops south of the main objective; IX and X corps would conduct encircling movements that would hit Sarıkamış from the west and the north. On 22 December, a major snowstorm hit just as the assault was launched. Lightly clothed, with poor rations, many without shoes, the Turks moved forward.

Enver's plan worked initially, but a cascading series of mishaps including worsening weather and poor coordination led to disaster. The diversion succeeded, but at a great cost. The Russians delivered heavy casualties to XI Corps, but committed more troops, drawing them away from Sarıkamış. IX and X corps advanced deep into the Russian defensive zone, but confusion reigned and the cold killed hundreds as blizzards made an advance through the treacherous mountain passes nearly impossible.

By the time Enver's weary forces were in position to attack Sarıkamış itself, they were too few and too dispersed to hold what they captured. By the end of the month, the Russians had regrouped and, fully aware of Enver's plans, began to systematically encircle and destroy the three Turkish corps. The Turks, or what remained of them, retreated towards friendly lines. By mid-January 1915, only 18,000 of the original 100,000 troops reached safety.

Enver abandoned his devastated army and returned to the capital. As one of the Triumvirate, he was not punished for his failure and the Turks and their German partners kept the débâcle secret. Naturally, the Russians touted it as their first major victory. Those locals that did join the Turkish advance quickly found themselves again under the thumb of the Russians. Far worse, the Christian Armenians of Anatolia, many of whom supported the Russians either in thought or deed, would soon suffer retribution for their perceived disloyalty to the Ottoman Empire.

One month later, the Turks tried another offensive. This time the Suez Canal was the objective and Djemal Pasha would lead the operation across the Sinai. The terrain and weather were different than the Caucasus, but equally as harsh and demanding. Moreover, the enemy – the British and Egyptians – were stronger, with forces of close to 50,000 in position on the far side of the canal. As in the Caucasus, the Ottoman high command hoped the Muslim populace would rise against their British overlords, thus compensating for their own relative weakness.

In contrast to the Caucasus operation, Djemal and his German advisory staff put together an extremely well-organized plan. The main force would cross through the middle of the Sinai to strike the canal in the centre, conduct an assault over the waterway and seize a bridgehead on the opposite side. Despite the fact the defenders outnumbered the Turks by a factor of four, Djemal pinned his hopes on surprise and the people's uprising.

The logistical requirements necessitated the prepositioning of water, food, and fodder, none of which was available along the chosen line of march. Engineer units would bring up the boats and pontoon bridges needed for the crossing after the 12,000 troops were in position on the eastern side of the canal.

Because the Turks conducted the assault through the middle of the Sinai beyond the range of available reconnaissance assets, the British (and French) did not discover the Ottoman advance, although reports had reached them of large-scale movements of forces in Palestine.

On 2 February 1915, the lead division was in place and the boats were brought forward. The Ottoman forces maintained excellent noise and light discipline and remained undiscovered until just before the attack began. When the assault was discovered, the Turkish plan quickly fell apart. British forces and Egyptian artillery brought heavy fire to bear on the Turkish troops, many of whom were untrained in amphibious operations, and many could not swim.

British and French warships on the canal quickly rallied to the site and joined in battle. An artillery duel ensued as Ottoman gunners ashore managed to damage a number of the ships before themselves being knocked out. Within hours, the Turks were forced to withdraw. Several hundred men had made it to the opposite side, but they were quickly surrounded and forced to surrender.

After being repulsed, the Turks fell back. Djemal realized that his small force had no hope of continuing the attack. The desired jihad against the British did not occur and the defenders were still secure in their positions on the far side of the canal. By 4 February, the Ottomans had withdrawn completely, abandoning their equipment and the assault on the canal.

Disaster in the Straits, Death on the Tigris

Now it was the Allies' turn to demonstrate their ability to turn opportunity into disaster.

In early 1915, with a general stalemate on the Western Front and the Russians in serious difficulties after a major defeat at Tannenberg, the Allies decided to launch a peripheral operation to divert attention of the public and the Germans. The thought of taking the Ottoman Empire out of the war with a swift coup de main gained favour within the war cabinet. Although the Russians wanted help in the Caucasus, the British War Council focused on an operation to breach the Dardanelles Straits and threaten Constantinople, in order to topple the Ottoman government.

Despite the fact that both the British Admiralty and the Imperial General Staff had long since concluded that a naval operation alone could not achieve the goal, that is exactly what they decided to do. The Secretary of State for War, Field Marshal Lord Herbert H. Kitchener directed the First Lord of the Admiralty, Winston Churchill, to ask Vice-Admiral Sackville Carden, the Royal Navy's commander in the Aegean, if the straits could be forced through naval action alone. Carden carefully replied that a methodical reduction of the Turkish coastal fortifications by heavy battleship gunfire and mine-sweeping would permit him to accomplish the task.

With that, the operation was approved. A joint British and French fleet launched the attack in late February 1915, destroying the forts at the western end of the straits. They then sailed up the straits and began to slowly advance towards the Turkish capital.[6]

But the Allies' bombardment of the coastal defences the previous November had given the Ottoman-Turk defenders ample warning of what the Allies intended. The Turks and their German advisors had corrected the deficiencies in their defences. Two senior German experts in coastal defence and engineering, along with around 500 specialists, worked with the Turks to reinforce the area with additional artillery, including howitzers that could delivery high-angle fire from behind hills. Additional mines were laid and additional direct-fire artillery was emplaced to engage any ships that made it through the first two obstacles.

On 18 March, the Allied fleet attempted to make a major breakthrough when a French battleship hit and was sunk by a sea mine. In quick succession, a British cruiser and two battleships hit mines. The naval attack was called off.

Kitchener, who had originally opposed the idea of using ground forces, reversed himself and assented to supplying troops for a revised operational plan that would entail amphibious landings on the Gallipoli Peninsula by British forces, as well as on the Asiatic coast of Turkey at Kum Kale by the French. The operation began on 25 April with Allied forces conducting landings at six locations. Although the Allies fought tenaciously to overcome the defenders, the Turks resisted fiercely. At one critical juncture, the Ottoman 19th Division turned back a combined Australian-New Zealand assault on the critical highlands of the peninsula. The 19th Division was led by Lieutenant-Colonel Mustafa Kemal, later known as Atatürk.

By the end of the day, the combined efforts of the defenders had prevented the Allies from reaching any of their objectives and the two enemies settled into a stalemate reminiscent of the Western Front. Attacks and counterattacks dominated the summer months as around 150,000 Allied troops tried to displace the Turks, who had perhaps 120,000 men during the initial phases of the campaign. By the autumn of 1915, the Allies had committed nearly half a million men to Gallipoli, while the Turks employed probably less than 400,000. Both sides suffered casualties that reached nearly half of their total strengths committed to the Gallipoli operation.

By late autumn, the Turks were about to commit even more troops to the fray, when the Allies decided they had had enough. In the only success of the campaign, the British conducted an evacuation on 19/20 December and withdrew the entire

---

[6] Gallipoli was chosen after the French objected to a better plan to land troops at Alexandretta (today's İskenderun) that probably would have succeeded and cut the Ottoman Empire in two.

force without the loss of life. It was a brilliant conclusion to an otherwise humiliating operation. Following the débâcle, Churchill lost his job as First Sea Lord, while the Allied soldiers gained new respect for their Ottoman opponent.

Overreach

To the east, in Mesopotamia, hubris encouraged a drastic bit of overreach by the British Army. To protect the British investment in oil-production facilities at the head of the Persian Gulf that was so important to the Royal Navy, the Government of India (at Simla) began operations to secure the territory. An initial operation to occupy Basra and Abadan Island to safeguard the oil works had gone splendidly, so Simla proposed continuing inland assuming the enemy would be easily swept aside and the roads passable. Many of their conclusions were drawn from prewar intelligence assessments of the Ottoman Army that uniformly criticized its organization and men as poorly led and inadequately trained. Initially, the troops met by the British forces seemed to fulfil that description, but the British did not realize that Mesopotamia was a backwater and most of the Turkish troops were local Arab conscripts, not much better than a militia.

Although the War Office in London was ostensibly in control, the Viceroy, Britain's senior officer in India, controlled operations on the ground through General Sir Beauchamp Duff, the Commander-in-Chief of the Army in India, who answered only to him. General Kitchener and the War Office were forced to communicate through the Viceroy. Completing the coordination nightmare, the Royal Navy in the Persian Gulf took its orders from the Admiralty in London. It was a command relationship unsuitable for a complicated war.

The initial success of India's Expeditionary Force 'D' led by Brigadier-General W. S. Delamain and his successor General Sir A. A. Barrett, encouraged Simla. What the British did not understand was that Mesopotamia was lightly defended by Arab formations of the Ottoman Army who, until October 1914, did not expect the incursion or even that it would be at war with Britain.

Once the objectives at Abadan and Basra were achieved, Sir Percy Cox, the political officer accompanying the Expeditionary Force, advised the Viceroy to permit an advance on Baghdad. Although the Viceroy rejected the idea because of insufficient forces, it would be taken up again when reinforcements arrived.

After the capture of Basra, General Sir John Nixon took command of 18,000 men in a designated II Corps in March 1915 with orders from General Duff to prepare for the conquest of Baghdad. The question of 'what next' that confronted the British was answered with a new objective of questionable strategic necessity.

Beyond the ill-defined reasoning for the offensive, the British were confronted with a more serious problem: how to move and supply the force as it moved north. The increased number of troops with their expanding logistical requirements taxed not only the port of Basra, but the infrastructure of the newly captured territory. Oddly, General Nixon never attempted to correct the deficiency, even as the offensive unfolded. He also believed the Turkish Army – its soldiers and officers – to be inferior to the British and Indian troops he was leading. He was about to discover the fallacy of his racist thinking.

In September 1915, Nixon began operations largely uncoordinated with London. His forces were able to seize Kut al Amara, just 200 miles short of Baghdad. Then, although the War Office recommended no capture of Baghdad be attempted, Prime Minister H. H. Asquith's war council countered and recommended an attack. Had they known of the environmental and logistical problems facing the expeditionary force on the ground, they most likely never would have approved the move.

Thus authorized, Nixon directed one of his division commanders, Major-General Charles V. F. Townsend, to begin operations towards Baghdad by early November. Both Nixon and Townsend were unaware that the enemy had reinforced his position greatly. Alarmed by the British advances and with their victory at Gallipoli freeing troops to fight elsewhere, the Turks had increased both the quantity and quality of their forces. Nixon's intelligence department did not have a clear picture of what opposed them.

With around 14,000 men, Townsend advanced on Ctesiphon, a town 40 miles short of Baghdad. There he met a well-entrenched Turkish force of around 20,000 men, many of them seasoned veterans with much better leadership, training and motivations than those met thus far. Hurling his forces against the Turks, Townsend was able to overcome the first echelon of the defences. He continued to throw his forces at the enemy but was forced to withdraw after incurring 4,200 casualties. With supply lines overextended and harried by the pursuing Turkish soldiers and Arab irregular raiders, he fell back to Kut al Amara and rested.

Here Townsend intended to make a stand with around 11,000 combatant and 3,000 noncombatant troops. Expecting two relief divisions, he thought he could endure a siege. The Turks had other ideas and encircled Townsend's forces with four divisions of 25,000 men and cannon.

A five-month siege ensued. Turkish forces turned back each British attempt to relieve Townsend with costly losses on both sides. By April 1916, Townsend realized his troops could not hold out much longer and began surrender negotiations. At the end of April, the British surrendered Kut and 13,309 men were taken prisoner, the largest British surrender since Yorktown. Over 4,000 died in captivity.[7]

---

[7] Colonel W. H. Beach, Director of IEF Intelligence, along with Lieutenant T. E. Lawrence, who spoke Arabic and was serving with the Intelligence Department in Cairo, and Lieutenant Aubrey Herbert, who spoke Turkish and French, were sent by Lord Kitchener to bribe the Turkish commander, Nurettin Pasha, to release Townsend and his troops. Their arrival on the scene under a flag of truce

The Mesopotamian campaign had cost Britain 40,000 casualties thus far and achieved little. The incompetent General Nixon was relieved and was replaced by General Sir Stanley Maude, who stabilized the British position at Basra but did not commit to any further offensive operations. For the moment, the protagonists in Mesopotamia settled into a relatively quiet stalemate.

Conventional operations by either side had not fared well thus far in the war. With the conflict stagnant on multiple fronts, both sides sought new strategies and tactics to throw their enemies off balance. North Africa and the Hejaz would figure prominently in the coming months and years.

The Red Desert

The vehicles sat under the dark night sky, their engines ticking over quietly. It was 17 March 1916 in North Africa.

There was a last-minute flurry of activity as the men threw all manner of boxes, food, water, and kit aboard the ambulances and the small Ford Model-T patrol cars. It was just after midnight and the air was cool. It would get colder as the night progressed.

In front were ten sinister-looking cars. They were armoured Rolls-Royces. With a long bonnet in front and an open bay in the rear, their most striking feature was a squat crew compartment with a round turret on top that looked like a large tuna fish can. The ugly snout of a Maxim machine gun protruded menacingly out the front. Behind the thirty-odd other vehicles, two more of the beasts brought up the rear of the column for security.

It was cold in the desert and Sam Cottingham 'S. C.' Rolls was wrapped in a woollen greatcoat sitting behind the wheel of his armoured Rolls-Royce.[8] He would soon shed the coat because the driving compartment would heat up as soon as the convoy began rolling. Sam had been with the unit since its beginnings and served in France until static trench warfare invalidated the mobility of the armoured cars. In December 1915, the squadron was ordered off to a new battlefield where their services were required. The unit arrived in Egypt in time for New Year 1916.

His commander, Major Hugh Richard Arthur Grosvenor, 2nd Duke of Westminster, had briefed the unit *in toto* about the mission before they assembled at the start point. And now they waited for the signal to drive off.

The Duke was one of the richest men in England and a veteran of the Boer War. He had volunteered for service again at the beginning of World War I and

---

was far too late to effect a transfer: the die had been cast and the Turks were sure of their position. The scheme failed completely.

[8] S. C. Rolls was not related to Charles S. Rolls, the partner of Henry Royce in the firm of Rolls-Royce.

soon found himself in a position to influence the development of a new type of weapon – the armoured car.[9]

Early in the war, the Duke had taken command of the Royal Navy Armoured Car Division's Number 2 Squadron, which consisted of 12 Rolls-Royce Admiralty 1914 Pattern armoured cars and a number of support vehicles. After a short tour in France, his squadron was sent to Egypt, but now redesignated as an army unit – the Light Armoured Motor Battery (LAMB). Each car was armed with a .303-calibre machine gun in the revolving turret, making them a formidable gun platform. The cars' 7.5-litre straight-six engines made the LAMB a fast-moving assault unit. The Duke even brought his personal Rolls-Royce, an elegant 40/50hp open tourer, to the fray as his command vehicle.

Once the squadron landed in Alexandria, it immediately embarked for the western desert of Egypt to help quell an uprising fostered by the Ottoman Empire. It was a time of trial and error and – moreover – innovation. They had to learn to carry large quantities of water, not just for the men, but for the cars, which burned off about a gallon every hour, as well as for the machine guns that were water-cooled. Petrol was another thing carried in large quantities as the cars consumed one gallon for every four miles travelled. And tyres. The war diaries constantly attest to a shortage of tubes. Rocks and thorns accounted for more punctures than enemy gunfire, although that was also a factor.

After four months of working with the Western Frontier Force, they were finally about to launch their own special mission – a raid to free British prisoners held deep in the desert.

The Senussi

In early 1915, Egypt was a sideshow to the greater war being fought in France. The British War Council concerns for Egypt were only that the Suez Canal be passively defended and that the protectorate remain stable from the threat of jihad. There were no men available for a large offensive against the Turks to the east, but a threat from the west dictated action.

After Djemal Pasha's failure to breach the Nile from the east and Enver Pasha's disaster in the Caucasus, the Ottoman Empire fell back on a strategy previously used with some success against Italy in Libya: an armed uprising to pressure the British in the Western Desert.

As described earlier, Italy invaded North Africa to seize Tripoli and Cyrenaica in 1911, brushing aside the small Ottoman garrison force with an occupying army of over 40,000 men. Despite the Grand Vizier's decision to abandon the territory to Italy, some Turkish officers wanted to make the Italian occupation difficult. In

---

[9] The Duke was rumoured to have purchased the 12 cars that made up his squadron.

late 1911, a small group led by Enver 'unofficially' infiltrated the region to raise an insurgent army to fight the Italians. Once there, they united the local tribesmen, including the Senussi, and then trained and organized them to fight.

Although the Ottoman-led tribesmen were pushed away from the coast, they successfully waged an insurgent campaign against the Italians, keeping them confined to their coastal fortifications. The Italians in Libya were vulnerable; the conflict inflicted high casualties and hit their treasury hard. The only way to win was to force the Ottoman advisors out and to do so the Italians expanded the conflict to the Balkans. Constantinople was forced to sign a peace treaty. That left the Senussi to fight on alone, sandwiched between their enemies: the French to the south and west and the Italians on the coast.

Four years later, Enver saw a way to pressure the British in Egypt. As part of the Ottoman campaign to incite jihad against the Allies, Enver would replicate the earlier guerrilla operation by sending Arabic-speaking Turkish and German officers, money, and logistical support to the Senussi. From their enclave in eastern Libya, they would be able to launch raids on the coastal outposts of western Egypt that were manned by Egyptian troops and coast guard, both officered by the British. They would also strike out from the heart of their kingdom, the desert oases, into Darfur and Sudan alongside their desert allies to the south.

The Senussi were first approached by a German delegation but their leader, Sayyid Ahmed al Sharif, was sceptical of attacking the Egyptians or the British. Egypt had long been a trading partner on whom the Senussi relied and Sayyid had a cordial relationship with the British officers who commanded the Egyptian Coast Guard across the border in Sollum. In February 1915, Enver sent his half-brother, Nuri Bey, to negotiate with Sayyid.[10] Nuri and Ja'far Pasha al-Askari, a multilingual, professional Iraqi soldier, infiltrated Senussi territory by boat from Crete. Nuri Bey was also met with scepticism, but Sayyid Ahmed was eventually induced to participate with promises of military and financial aid. Additionally, the Italian decision to join the Allies and the British setbacks in Gallipoli began to influence his thinking.

The Turks and Germans brought advisors, weapons, ammunition, and other supplies needed to fuel the uprising. This external support was an essential ingredient to the uprising – both to ensure its launch as well as maintain the movement's will, training, and logistics. Their plan was to conduct a classic guerrilla warfare campaign.

The men and equipment were transported by German submarine and landed at remote coastal sites by small boat. Ja'far Pasha and his advisors spent several months training, equipping, and preparing the Senussi for their debut against the British. Ja'far's training consisted of more than just drill: he deployed his troops in action against the Italian occupiers of western Libya as practice, but encountered some of the same problems with his local troops that the British would later face in the

---

[10] Not to be confused with Nuri Said.

Hejaz. In one engagement, the Senussi were more interested in looting a camp they had overrun than pursuing the soldiers they had put to flight. Nonetheless, under Ja'far's tutelage the Senussi coalesced into a relatively formidable fighting force. By the early autumn of 1915, their training was finished. With the arms delivered by the Germans or recovered on the battlefield from the Italians, the Senussi were ready to move against the British.[11]

The German submarine *Unterseeboot 35* (*U35*) was patrolling the Mediterranean off the Libyan coast on 5 November 1915 when it encountered HMS *Tara*, a converted steamer pressed into British service as an armed patrol ship. *U35* fired a single torpedo. The slow-moving *Tara* sank in around ten minutes. The *U35* captain observed the protocols of the time and rescued the crew and then towed them in lifeboats to the shore. Shortly thereafter, *U35* also encountered the transport ship HMT *Moorina*, capturing it and its crew. Both crews, over 100 men, were turned over to the Senussi ashore. This began a curious hostage situation that dovetailed with the uprising the Senussi were about to launch.

On 6 November, German submarines attacked the Egyptian Coast Guard base in the Bay of Sollum on the western border of Egypt with Libya, sinking or damaging two gunboats. At the same time, the Senussi made a series of overland attacks on Egyptian outposts, signalling the beginning of hostilities.

Up to this point, the British were aware of the prospect of conflict, but had hoped it could be held off through negotiations or monetary inducements, known as *baksheesh*. General Sir John Maxwell, commander of forces in Egypt, saw the Senussi as the principal threat to the British position, not the Turkish forces in Palestine. He feared that a successful uprising could cause significant internal disorder. With the November attacks, it was clear that a state of war existed between the Senussi and the British.

The British assessed that the small number of forces it had in western Egypt were vulnerable to attack from land and that the sea lanes needed to support them were endangered by the submarine threat. Maxwell pulled all his British and Egyptian forces from the western frontier and consolidated them at Mersa Matruh, 120 miles to the east of Sollum. He then instructed Major-General A. Wallace to take a new formation, the Western Frontier Force, and eliminate the threat. Maxwell wanted to retake Sollum as soon as possible to reestablish the British presence there, but doing so would require naval support. Although Admiral Sir William Reginald 'Blinker' Hall, Director of Naval Intelligence, thought the loss of Sollum meant the Germans might gain access to a base "too close to Alexandria", the War Office felt the threat was more of a political than strategic issue. Naval support would not be immediately forthcoming.

---

[11] The British assessed that Sayyid Ahmed al Sharif was never fully committed to the jihad and events would prove them correct as he eventually escaped the battlefield, and Libya, leaving the leadership of the Senussi to his cousin Mohamed Idris, who negotiated an end to the uprising.

In mid-December 1915, Wallace began operations, pushing slowly westward overland with around 1,500 men against an estimated 2,500 to 5,000 Senussi. British – more correctly Commonwealth – force numbers were increasing steadily as the evacuation of Gallipoli resulted in many troops being sent to Egypt.[12]

In the first engagements with the Senussi, Wallace and his officers were surprised not only by the tenacity, but the excellent tactics the enemy used against them, a tribute to their Ottoman and German advisors' skills. The wet season also conspired to make the British moves more difficult and slowed the campaign considerably. The battles that followed took place mostly along the coast. The British employed aerial reconnaissance to pinpoint the enemy's camps and then followed up with infantry and cavalry assaults. Each encounter was usually sharp, short, and costly to the Senussi, who retreated into the desert to the west. The 'affairs' at Wadi Senab, Wadi Majid, and Halazin preceded the definitive, if not culminating, engagement at Agagiya.

General Wallace recused himself from command after Halazin due to problems he was having with old war injuries. He was replaced by Major-General W. E. Peyton, who led the 16 February attack on a well-defended Senussi position at Agagiya. Deploying 1,400 men against an enemy force of equal strength, Peyton dispersed the Senussi into the desert with heavy losses of around 500 men. Most significantly, Ja'far Pasha was wounded and captured in the fight. Sollum was reoccupied in early March with little resistance from the Senussi. The fight for the coast was over and, although operations against the Senussi continued in concert with the Italians until early 1917, the threat of destabilizing Egypt had been averted.

After Gallipoli, more British forces were available to Maxwell. With a stable defensive line on the Suez, he was able to concentrate on fighting on a single front to defeat the Senussi. Although the uprising was fully quelled, the Ottoman-sponsored guerrilla war had forced the British to divert its attention and forces with only a minimum of resources and effort on the Turks' part. It was a lesson not lost on Captain G. F. Clayton, the Director of Intelligence in Cairo.

Mobile Warfare in the West

The reoccupation of Sollum did not resolve the HMS *Tara* and HMT *Moorina* hostage issue and the British were still concerned about the welfare of their men. By chance, a letter addressed to the British forces at Sollum by Captain R. S. Gwatkin-Williams, commander of the *Tara*, was found after the town was reoccupied. Gwatkin-Williams was, of course, unaware the British had abandoned the town. The letter was recovered by sheer luck and revealed the location of the prisoners to be at Bir Hakim, an isolated post in the desert west of Sollum. Peyton ordered a

---

[12] The force consisted of British, Indian, New Zealand, Australian, and South African units and troops.

rescue mission. Knowing that speed was essential, he called upon one of his more specialized units, the Duke of Westminster's LAMB to lead the operation.

The Duke's squadron landed at Mersa Matruh in January 1916 and participated in short patrols to test the vehicles and crews and ensure they functioned well as a team. As Peyton advanced westward, the cars supported the infantry and cavalry in a more or less conventional fashion. The vehicles would deploy in overwatch positions to give covering fire to the advancing infantry and cavalry, but often had difficulties negotiating the rocky terrain or deep sand. Route selection had to be carefully considered if the cars were to keep up and have any hope of supporting the main force. Slowly, as the crews became more adept at handling their equipment, the armoured cars proved their worth, delivering firepower not easily provided by ground troops. During the final attack on Sollum, the Duke's cars were 'cut loose' to conduct an encircling movement on a Senussi camp a few miles beyond the town to catch the escaping enemy. On the hard-packed ground, the LAMB was able to pursue the Senussi at high speed. The roar of the cars' unsilenced exhausts and the barking Maxim guns terrified the tribesmen and their beasts of burden, forcing them into a disorderly retreat. The chase covered ten miles and resulted in the capture of many prisoners and much equipment, including the Senussi's three artillery pieces.

To rescue the *Tara* and *Moorina* prisoners, the Duke's LAMB, along with over 30 Red Cross ambulances and support vehicles, would act as an independent flying column to move over a hundred miles across the desert. Employing conventional infantry and cavalry would slow the operation to a crawl, so the mission would use purely mechanical transport.

It had been four months since the ships' crews had been captured. Their condition and location, let alone the place name 'Bir Hakim', were unknowns. A Senussi prisoner revealed under interrogation that he knew the place and was enlisted as a guide for the expedition. After a day of preparation, the Duke of Westminster led his column out of Sollum just after midnight on 17 March.

S. C. Rolls was the driver in the lead armoured car nicknamed 'Blast'. Along with the gunner, a guide and an interpreter, the ride was quite cramped. The first obstacle to be surmounted was the steep escarpment that separated the coast from the desert inland. They followed a path, little more than a donkey trail, to the base and then upwards. The traverse took hours as rocks had to be tossed out of the way and picks and shovels slowly eked out a way forward.

Mile after mile passed until the Duke was certain the guide had no idea where he was. Thus accused, the guide first became angry and then animated, waving his arms and pointing seemingly towards the edge of the world. He swore to all who listened of his sincerity and the convoy continued. Many miles passed, 120, then 150 before the Duke called a halt, intending to return to base after a short rest. The guide continued to stare at the terrain and then yelled out that he could see Bir Hakim.

Still not ready to believe, the Duke's binoculars came out and, several miles away, two mounds could just be seen on the horizon – the ancient Roman wells of Bir Hakim.

Leaving the ambulances and light Fords behind, the armoured Rolls-Royces roared out across the desert towards the wells. As they approached, the Senussi guards ran into the desert attempting to escape. Seeing the emaciated prisoners, several of the cars continued on and caught the Senussi exposed. They opened fire, killing the guards in a blind rage.

The 91 prisoners were somewhat worse for wear, most suffering from acute dysentery and malnutrition, a result of a diet of snails and weeds. But they were alive and most were able to walk. Once the other vehicles arrived, the former prisoners were all loaded and the convoy returned to Sollum with its precious cargo. It was a significant mission – one of the first POW rescues using tactics that would do much to shape future operations with the Arab Revolt in the Hejaz and Syria to the east.

S. C. Rolls and the armoured car squadron continued operations in Libya until the Senussi campaign was finished in early 1917. General Sir Archibald Murray, who had taken command of the Egyptian Expeditionary Force (EEF) from General Maxwell in 1916, wrote in his official dispatches that victory over the Senussi was due largely

> to the excellent work of the armoured cars and light car patrols on the western front. Their mobility, and the skill and energy with which they are handled, have made them an ideal arm for the Western Desert, where the sand is not so heavy as on the east. It is not too much to say that the successful clearance of the western oases, and the satisfactory state of affairs which now exists on the western front, is due more to the dash and enterprise of the armoured car batteries and the light car patrols than to any other cause, and the enemy has found many times to his cost that their range of action is far beyond that of any troops mounted on horses or camels.

S. C. Rolls and other members of the Duke's squadron were ordered back to Alexandria with 'Blast' and another Rolls-Royce armoured car known as 'Bloodhound'. In Alexandria, Blast and Bloodhound were relieved of their armour and converted into utility vehicles known as 'battery cars' or 'tenders'. That modification addressed one of the major deficiencies of the armoured cars – their limited storage space that restricted how much ammunition, fuel, and other supplies they could carry. With the tenders accompanying them on operations there was no need to return to base; the armoured cars' range and mission capabilities were greatly extended. Tenders, stripped of their steel plate, were the beasts of burden supporting their armed companions, but they too were often outfitted with a Vickers for extra firepower, and carried men, explosives, extra machine guns, fuel, food, and water.

Then the two tenders were joined by three other armoured Rolls-Royces to form a new unit. In August 1917, the five cars along with S. C. Rolls and other crewmen embarked on a cargo ship for a new mission.

The Duke's military operations were not the first involving motor vehicles nor even the first that employed armoured cars. But the long-range raid to rescue the *Tara* crewmen was certainly one of the first such 'special' operations.

Another officer whose contributions to combined and special operations yet to come witnessed the operations against the Senussi as well as those of the armoured cars. In November 1915, a young British officer was sent to Sollum with a new communications code for the Western Frontier Force. It was believed the Turks and Germans had cracked the old code and compromised early operations. That man was Second Lieutenant T. E. Lawrence. Employed in the Military Intelligence Department in Cairo where his work entailed mapping and the reporting of intelligence on the enemy, it can be surmised that Lawrence was a keen observer of the rebellion and its particular asymmetric tactics, as well as the operations of the Duke's armoured cars.

CHAPTER ONE

Origins of a Revolt

Grand Sherif Hussein ibn Ali al-Hashimi, Emir of the Holy Cities of Medina and Mecca, Protector of the Hajj, and de facto ruler of the Hejaz, began to contemplate an uprising against his Ottoman-Turk masters as early as 1913. Hussein had grand aspirations. He also had big worries.

He had been appointed to the position by the Ottoman Caliph in 1908. As a Hashemite descendant of the Prophet Muhammad it was his birthright. But he wanted more and the Ottomans in Constantinople knew it. Hussein had long harboured a dream of an independent Arab caliphate and, of course, he wanted to lead it. The Arab dream predated the war and was not exclusively Hussein's, but it began to come into sharper focus with the ascendance of the CUP Triumvirate and the Sublime Porte's abandonment of pan-Islamic policies in favour of a pro-Turkic, secular nationalism. As Hussein later told Lieutenant-Colonel Cyril Wilson, British Representative at Jeddah: "[The CUP] had betrayed and led to ruin the true cause of Islam."

Ottoman rule had never been totally accepted in Arabia and, as its power waned, many of the leaders of the larger tribal groups were pulling away from Constantinople. Among these was Abdul Aziz ibn Saud who had freed his tribal areas further to the east from the Ottomans in 1908.

Hussein, closer to Constantinople and its army, was more circumspect in his resistance. He resented the CUP's efforts to centralize its authority and control over the Hejaz, and opposed the plan to extend the Hejaz railway from Medina to Mecca. Both measures would deprive him of control as well as deprive his people of money they would normally earn from transporting and protecting pilgrims of the Hajj from the railhead to Mecca. The train had already hurt Bedouin incomes further to the north. His opposition to Ottoman control placed him in a precarious position that was exacerbated by the Caliph's call for jihad against the Allies in November 1914. The Ottomans expected Hussein, the senior Muslim Arab in the empire, to support the call. Instead, he made excuses, which created a problem for the Turks as they needed his endorsement and support for the war.

Hussein was born in Constantinople and knew the Ottomans well. His father had been exiled there from the Hejaz and Hussein had later also experienced Ottoman 'hospitality', as sort of a hostage to ensure the peoples of the Hejaz remained docile. He returned to Mecca as Sherif in 1908 and used the authority of the Ottoman government to his advantage, but when a new, hard-line Ottoman administrator was sent to the Hejaz, he understood he was being undermined by Constantinople. He knew he would be eliminated if he refused to back the Ottoman cause and, at the same time, realized that he did not have the military support to successfully rebel. But Hussein had one ace up his sleeve: in early 1914, when he began to contemplate rebellion, he sent his son, Emir Abdullah, to Cairo to gain the support of the British.

The question of support for an Arab movement had been discussed in British circles before the war as a way to counter French aspirations in Syria and again when German influence with the Ottoman Empire became stronger. Field Marshal Lord Kitchener was the Consul-General at the British Agency in Cairo. As one of the more experienced hands in Africa, and Egypt, he knew the importance of western Arabia to British interests but, in early 1914, Britain was still at peace with the Ottoman Empire. He also understood the potential impact of an Arab uprising against the Turks.

Kitchener could not meet with Abdullah privately without raising the ire of the Sublime Porte. According to Kitchener, Abdullah visited his office in February. He spoke of his father's concerns about the increasing centralization of Ottoman power. According to Abdullah's later recollections, he briefly broached the subject of support for a revolt, to which Kitchener replied it would "be an internal matter in which it would not be proper for a foreign power to intervene".

In April 1914, when Abdullah met with Ronald Storrs, Kitchener's Oriental Secretary in Cairo, he asked Storrs "categorically whether Great Britain would present the Grand Sherif with a dozen, or even a half-dozen machine guns" and added that they would be for "defence against attack from the Turks". Storrs, under instructions from Lord Kitchener, told Abdullah that "the Arabs of the Hejaz could expect no encouragement from [Britain] and that our only interest in Arabia was the safety and comfort of Indian pilgrims". It was a disappointing meeting for Abdullah and Hussein, but one that would have immense consequences later.

Despite that, Kitchener was an early advocate of an Arab uprising as a method to counter Ottoman power. He was on home leave when war broke out in August 1914 and was appointed to the cabinet as Secretary of State for War. Sir Arthur Henry McMahon replaced him and became High Commissioner after Egypt was officially declared a protectorate. But Kitchener did not forget Abdullah's offer.

Another important supporter of the uprising was making his opinions known as well: Sir Reginald Wingate, the Governor-General of Sudan at Khartoum, also held the title 'Sirdar', the commander of the Egyptian Army. Wingate had long believed that Britain should improve its position by supporting the Arabs of the Hejaz as an independent nation, both as a means to safeguard Indian Muslims' access to the Hajj and to better protect the Suez Canal and the Red Sea approaches to it. He understood the Hejazi population was dependent on Egypt and the Sudan for much of their food and supplies and did not want to divest themselves of that relationship.

Wingate owed his position as governor-general to Kitchener and supported him wholeheartedly. Kitchener, in turn, listened to and trusted Wingate's views.

A harbinger of the uprising would come at a meeting in Cairo between Captain Gilbert Clayton, the Sudan Agent in Cairo and Director of Intelligence with the Egyptian Army, and Colonel Aziz Bey al-Masri, a Circassian born in Cairo who had been exiled from the Ottoman Empire. A skilled military leader, al-Masri had been a key member of the Ottoman expedition to Libya in 1911 as a senior guerrilla advisor to the Senussi. He had instituted a training programme that incorporated tribal tactics with modern manoeuvre, a methodology that worked well against the Italians. After he returned to Constantinople, he fell out with Enver Pasha and was arrested for his alleged Arab revolutionary activities and eventually banished to Egypt. Ironically, al-Masri's arrest seems to have pushed him further towards Arab nationalism. Shortly thereafter, he founded the secret Arab nationalist group called al-'Ahd or 'The Covenant' in Damascus.

Al-Masri first came to the attention of the British when he visited the British Residency in Cairo in August 1914 and divulged details of al-'Ahd and its plan for a revolution to break the bonds of Ottoman oppression. He also asked the British for arms and money in exchange for an agreement to permit the British to conduct the new Arab nation's foreign affairs.

In September, he met privately with Captain Clayton at the Heliopolis Hotel. Clayton's report detailed al-Masri's ideas about an Arab revolt. Al-Masri outlined how a revolution by a small force from within the empire, supported by funds, weapons and ammunition from Great Britain, could succeed. He stated categorically that no Imperial forces, i.e. Christian, should be landed in Arabia, or the locals would believe their territory was to be annexed. Clayton summarized al-Masri's position: "Great Britain would supply the sinews of war and the Arabs would supply the fighting element." Al-Masri wanted to start in Mesopotamia, which was the Government of India's area of responsibility. Naturally, Simla responded negatively, fearing a rebellion there would complicate matters in India, and the idea was quashed. Al-Masri would reappear later to play a part in the Hejaz.

Militarily, Egypt was considered a sideshow. For the British commander, General J. Maxwell, the protection of the Suez Canal was paramount and he had no more troops available for operations against the Turks. In early 1915, however, with Allied and German forces locked in a stalemate on the Western Front and a plea from Russian Czar Nicholas II to divert the Ottomans from the Caucasus in some way, British leadership in London decided to conduct the Dardanelles and Gallipoli campaigns.

In early September 1914, Wingate wrote to Clayton, his agent in Cairo, advising him of his belief that Britain should throw its "unhesitating support" to the Sherif of Mecca to help defeat the Ottomans. Storrs also told Clayton he felt Britain should ally itself with Arabia against the Ottomans.

Clayton advised Storrs to send a note to that effect to Kitchener. Clayton would also certainly have shared the Sirdar's thoughts with Kitchener. Then, in late September, the first move in what would turn out to be a convoluted negotiation came from Kitchener. He wrote the acting Consul-General, giving instructions to: "Tell Storrs to send secret and carefully chosen messenger from me to Sharif Abdallah to ascertain whether 'should present armed German influence in Constantinople coerce Sultan against his will, and Sublime Porte, to acts of aggression and war against Great Britain, he and his father and Arabs of the Hejaz would be with us or against us'."

Storrs did so and soon received a tentative answer from Hussein himself that was also a request for aid. In late October, on the authority of Kitchener, another letter was sent to Hussein. It contained a promise that would prove difficult for Britain to extricate herself from without consequences and ensured the Middle East would remain embroiled in conflict for years beyond the end of World War I. It said: "If Arab nation assist England in this war, England will guarantee that no intervention takes place in Arabia and will give Arabs every assistance against external foreign aggression."

Trying to ride the fence between the great powers, Hussein stalled and protracted communications ensued. The question of support was not a problem for the British, rather it was Hussein's outlandish demands for eventual control of lands that were neither his to bring under his aegis, nor within Britain's purview to grant. Britain's predicament in Gallipoli – Winston Churchill's brainchild – also made Hussein wonder if he was joining the winning side.

By May of 1915, however, several factors pushed Hussein to break with Constantinople. The first was the Triumvirate's insistence that he join the empire's war by endorsing the call for jihad and supplying men to fight. He knew this would further tie him to Constantinople and essentially hold his troops hostage. The second reason was personal. One of Hussein's retainers had found documents belonging to the new Ottoman administrator of the Hejaz that outlined how Hussein was to be overthrown and killed. Hussein had also recently been contacted by members of several of the Arab nationalist societies in Damascus imploring him to lead a rebellion against the Ottomans.

Hussein then sent his third son, Feisul, to Constantinople, ostensibly to protest the plan to overthrow his rule, but in reality to gauge the level of discontent with his leadership. Feisul found the Triumvirate to be disingenuous in their denials and interpreted their message as that either Hussein should fall in line and support the empire or they would indeed remove him from power. Feisul also discovered that 3,500 Ottoman soldiers were moving south to Medina where 3,000 men of the Hejaz Expeditionary Force (HEF) under the command of Fakhri Pasha were already stationed.

Feisul stopped purposefully in Damascus on his return. While there he sought out the Governor-General to discuss the war. Before his departure, Djemal Pasha presented Feisul with the gift of an Enfield rifle that had been captured from the British at Gallipoli.[1] It was engraved with the words "Part of our booty in the battles

---

[1] Djemal was Governor-General of Ottoman Syria as well as commander of the Ottoman Fourth Army.

for the Dardanelles" and served as a pointed reminder and warning of the power of the Ottoman Army.

Feisul also secretly met with representatives of the shadowy al-Ahd and al-Fatat Arab nationalist movements. On his return trip, the leaders of the societies gave him a document that became known as the Damascus Protocols.

The protocols set out the geographic boundaries of the movements' desired territory, which included all of Mesopotamia, Greater Syria, and Arabia (leaving Aden to Britain) and they agreed to a special relationship with Britain in return for its support of the uprising. Most importantly, they gave their support to Sherif Hussein to negotiate with Britain and promised their support of him as King of Arabia when and if the uprising was successful.

When Feisul returned to Mecca, Hussein called his sons, Emirs Ali, Abdullah, Feisul, and Zeid, together to discuss their options. Ali and Abdullah clamoured for action, while Feisul counselled caution. Hussein would follow Feisul's advice and proceed slowly.

The convoluted and protracted negotiations begun the previous autumn continued. The letters of the so-called 'McMahon–Hussein Correspondence' have been detailed and picked apart since the war, and are beyond the scope of this history. But, along with the Sykes-Picot Treaty, the competing and ill-harmonized opinions and policies of the varied and far-flung offices of His Majesty's Government and those of France would lead to confusion, dismay, and charges of betrayal after the war by the Arabs who believed they had been promised not only independence but a homeland free of occupiers.[2] At the end of 1915 the British promised Hussein the Arabian Peninsula – minus Aden and the Trucial States lining the Gulf, and excepting the territories west of the districts from Damascus to Aleppo. He still did not move.

At the same time, more pressure was put on Hussein by the Ottomans. Djemal Pasha had seized the French consulate in Beirut in 1915, where his intelligence officers had discovered a treasure trove of Deuxième Bureau (military intelligence) documents that compromised many of the leading members of the Arab nationalist organizations with whom the diplomats had been communicating. In early 1915, Djemal used that information to eliminate the opposition he correctly believed to be conspiring against the empire. Djemal's repression effectively beheaded the Arab nationalist movement in the Syrian province and left Hussein with the understanding that he was in danger and on his own. He knew he would have to act soon or risk being eliminated by his Ottoman masters.

---

[2] The many HMG's offices involved included the Foreign Office, War Office, Admiralty, India Office (London), and the Government of India – not to mention the Residency in Cairo. The conflicting policies are well described in Polly Moh's excellent book *Military Intelligence and the Arab Revolt*.

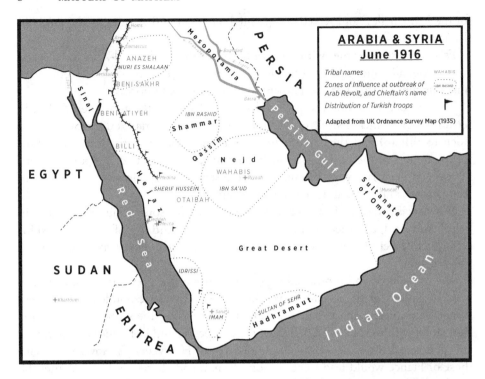

ARABIA & SYRIA
June 1916

Tribal names

Zones of Influence at outbreak of
Arab Revolt, and Chieftain's name

Distribution of Turkish troops

Adapted from UK Ordnance Survey Map (1935)

WAHABIS

IBN RASHID

P E R S I A

Mesopotamia

Persian Gulf

ANAZEH
NURI ES SHALAAN

BENI-SAKHR

Sinai

BENI ATIYEH

IBN RASHID

Shammar

BILLI

Qassim

N e j d

WAHABIS

EGYPT

Hejaz

SHERIF HUSSEIN

OTAIBAH

IBN SA'UD

Riyadh

Sultanate
of Oman

Muscat

Red Sea

Mecca

SUDAN

IDRISSI

Great Desert

Indian Ocean

Khartoum

Sana

IMAM

SULTAN OF SEHR

Hadhramaut

ERITREA

Arab regular army drawn up at foot of hill. (Harry Chase, James A. Cannavino Library, Archives &
Special Collections, Marist College, USA)

By May 1916, the Grand Sherif was convinced Britain would support his claim to a kingdom and was sufficiently alarmed by Ottoman actions to request Storrs travel to the Arabian coast to meet with his son, Emir Abdullah.

On 28 May, Storrs sailed from Suez on HMS *Dufferin* for Jeddah along with Lieutenant-Commander D. G. Hogarth and Captain K. Cornwallis, both from the newly formed Arab Bureau in Cairo. They were carrying £10,000 in gold sovereigns, bullion authorized to be paid to Abdullah. There was a proviso in the Foreign Office instructions for an additional £50,000 to be paid to the Sherif "only in return for definite action and if a reliable rising takes place". Storrs was to make an assessment of the Arab position and convince Hussein to act soon.

On 5 June, and befitting his patrician heritage if not his image as a military officer, Storrs was carried ashore from his launch by two slaves. Still, he was drenched by the sea. He then stood on the beach waiting for the reception he felt his position deserved. It was not Abdullah but Zeid, Hussein's youngest son, who met him. Storrs assessed Zeid to be "soft in his ways and vague in his ideas". When asked about the revolt, Zeid conveyed the news that the uprising had already begun.

Zeid then presented Storrs with a wish-list of things his father Hussein needed. Those included £70,000 in gold, rifles, machine guns, and mountain guns (artillery) with Muslim gunners. The British had already initiated shipments of arms and gold to Hussein earlier that year from Port Sudan under Sirdar Wingate's authority.[3] From December 1915 to that point, £73,000 had been paid to Hussein in British gold sovereigns. Beginning in August, he would receive £125,000 a month.

According to Zeid, Hussein had ordered his sons, Ali and Feisul, to attack Medina that very day. The intent was to demand the Turks in Medina surrender. If they refused, they would be shot. They also planned to destroy the Hejaz railway north of Medina to isolate the territory and prevent further Ottoman reinforcements. Neither operation went quite as planned.

The Ottoman commander in Medina, General Fakhri Pasha, had a reputation for ruthlessness and efficiency, allegedly earned fighting the Armenians in eastern Turkey. His nearly seven-thousand-man force in Medina would be reinforced to over ten thousand in the coming months. For the moment, the troops on hand were sufficient, along with a dozen mountain guns and two heavy cannon, to defend the city. The Arab forces under Ali and Feisul were not prepared to engage well-trained and entrenched troops, let alone artillery.

Ali's troops physically removed long sections of the railway north of Medina, but the line was quickly put back into action by Ottoman repair crews. Feisul's forces also made forays against the Turks on the city's outskirts but did not have the strength to

---

[3] Wingate had broad authority for action in the Hejaz given him by the Foreign Office. First money, rifles, and ammunition were sent, but as the revolt grew, heavier weapons and advisory assistance would also be provided.

overcome Medina's defences. His unseasoned tribesmen were terrified by the Ottoman cannon, which they had never before experienced. Instead, they demanded the Turks surrender and settled in to block any Ottoman move against Mecca to the south.

The coastal ports of Jeddah, Rabegh, and Yenbo were also attacked. Jeddah was the toughest nut to crack. A rebel force consisting of 4,000 Harb tribesmen under Sheikh Muhsin, an ally of Hussein, had been stymied by a smaller force of around 2,500 Turk defenders. Sherif Hussein implored the British to help. He was answered with the arrival of two British Red Sea Patrol ships, HMS *Fox* and HMS *Hardange*, which shelled the city. Several days later, the HMS *Ben-my-Chree* arrived with seaplanes that finished the job by bombing the defensive positions into submission. On 16 June, Jeddah's Turkish commander surrendered.[4]

Grand Sherif Hussein 'officially' launched the revolt when he fired his rifle at the Turkish barracks in Mecca on 10 June. His forces captured much of the city but there were holdouts. The Ottoman fortifications of the city stood in the way of the poorly armed and trained tribesmen who were no match for Turkish firepower and the battle slowed until Wingate's dispatch of Egyptian artillery and gunners shifted the odds. The fortress at Jiyad fell on 4 July, giving Hussein complete control of the city.

His son Abdullah attacked the hilltop town at Ta'if to the south, which served as a summer retreat for the Turks to escape the blistering heat of Mecca. But Ta'if would not surrender until September because Hussein allegedly did not want to harm the many civilians living there. Another possible explanation is that the Ottoman forces were too well entrenched for the Bedouin riflemen to quickly overcome.

Although Hussein's revolt got off to a good start, it would sputter to a stop and nearly collapse in the coming months. The initial enthusiasm of his volunteer soldiers began to drain off after the battles. The tribesmen, feeling no obligation to remain, began to drift away once they finished looting the Ottoman government and military properties. Moreover, the attacks on Medina showed the Arabs they had little hope of overcoming a determined and well-armed defender without having better arms themselves. Hussein needed supplies as well as training for his Bedouin troops and requested such from his new allies: rifles and machine guns with ammunition, artillery with Egyptian crews, over 500 tons of food, and gold. The message was passed to the Arab Bureau in Cairo that had taken over the administration of supplying the revolt.

On the opposite side of the lines, Fakhri Pasha was unfazed. The Hejaz railway had been repaired and the supply line was operating again. Reinforcements arrived by rail and within weeks, the Turkish commander was ready to move out to recapture

---

[4] This was not the first instance of Red Sea Patrol intervention. On 21 March 1916, HMS *Fox* and HMS *Suva* shelled and destroyed Turkish forts at Umlejh and Wejh respectively as part of the blockade emplaced on the Red Sea littoral. The Patrol would continue to make kinetic and logistical contributions to the Arab Revolt until its conclusion.

Mecca and put down the rebellion. The Sublime Porte had chosen a new Grand Sherif, Ali Haidar, to replace Hussein, whom they declared to be "under Christian orders". Haidar was dispatched to Medina and would move to Mecca once the city was returned to Ottoman control. The Turks even had a replica of the Holy Carpet made for the Hajj. It was waiting in Medina and when delivered to Mecca it would completely usurp Hussein's pretensions to rule.

The revolt's critical moment approached and the British were uneasy. Storrs encapsulated his concerns in a diary, "Though it is, I trust you realize, infinitely more than half the battle to have lit this candle, the wick is as yet far from burning with that hard gemlike flame I could have desired."

Lieutenant-Colonel Cyril E. Wilson, Wingate's governor of Port Sudan who visited Jeddah in late June, summed it up a bit more succinctly, "The Grand Sherif appears to have started his revolt without sufficient preparation and somewhat prematurely." He informed his chief that a British officer should be forward based in Jeddah to liaise with Hussein on military matters and to ensure logistics were properly arranged. Wingate agreed and informed Wilson that he would be the lucky one to assume the

Traces of the Hejaz rail line as it descends from the plateau down into the Batn el Ghoul (Belly of the Beast) to the lower desert south of Ma'an, Jordan (Author)

duties. Henceforth, he would be Mister Wilson, 'Pilgrimage Officer', an innocuous title for an extremely important position.

After their failure to take Medina, the Arab armies regrouped as the Turks began to move out of Medina towards the Red Sea port of Rabegh, now in the hands of Hussein's forces. Feisul, with around 4,000 men, moved southwest and sat astride the Medina–Rabegh road at Bir Abbas, while Ali, with 8,000 men, was at Bir al Mashi some 20 kilometres south of Medina on the inland route. Once Rabegh had been captured and occupied, it became the northernmost base for Hussein's revolt. It was also a fixed point that required defence from Fakhri Pasha's forces at Medina. Many Allied officers assessed that Fakhri would attack Rabegh and use the coastal route to attack Mecca. The Rabegh route afforded Fakhri the water wells needed to keep his forces hydrated. Rabegh was the route of choice to Mecca, but it was not the only route.

According to a British report, Fakhri Pasha was moving with nearly 12,000 men, 16 mountain guns, and two larger guns in the direction of Rabegh and Feisul, whose men were scattered in the mountains on either side of the road. Feisul was worried the impending Turkish attack would overwhelm his troops. If Rabegh fell, the coastal road to Mecca would be open to the Turks.

The crisis that ensued at Rabegh in the autumn of 1916 showed the Arab Revolt and its British support to be dangerously unscripted and weak. For the next several months, Rabegh was the focal point of discussions about whether to commit Allied ground forces, either British or French, in large numbers to the Arabian Peninsula in order to preserve the Arab Revolt at its most fragile stage.

CHAPTER TWO

The British are Coming

At the beginning of the war, British intelligence in Cairo consisted of essentially one man, Captain Gilbert Falkington Clayton. Clayton headed the military intelligence department, where he reported to General Sir John Maxwell, General Officer Commanding British and Imperial Forces in Egypt. He also led its civilian equivalent in the Residency, advising the Consul-General (for the moment Milne Cheetham, Kitchener's temporary replacement until Sir Henry McMahon arrived from India to take up the post).[1] Apparently, that was not enough work for him because he also served as the Sudan Agent in Cairo for the Sirdar, Sir Reginald Wingate, the Governor of Sudan.

In these roles, Clayton served three masters and played a big part advising and, some would say, manipulating the British leadership through his control of intelligence information that supported the Arab Revolt. Clayton was joined by a number of experts in late 1914 who would help him guide British aid to the revolt as well as produce intelligence reporting and propaganda for the theatre of operations. The initial people were Lieutenant-Colonel S. F. Newcombe, Royal Engineers; two members of parliament, temporary captains Aubrey Hurbert, MP and Lord George Lloyd, MP; and lieutenants Leonard Woolley, Jay Hay, Harry Pirie-Gordon, and one Thomas E. Lawrence. Newcombe, the only professional military man in the 'wild bunch', had led the Palestine Exploration Fund survey of Palestine in 1913 and 1914 along with Woolley and Lawrence. Their telegraphic name was 'Intrusive'. Lawrence thought it appropriate for their aims.

From early 1915, Clayton and his team, along with Storrs, promoted Hussein and an Arab revolt as a means to subvert the Sublime Porte's call for jihad and to ensure the Ottoman Army in Medina remained there. Clayton rose quickly in rank and

---

[1] Kitchener was on home leave in England when the war began. He was quickly diverted from his post in Cairo to take charge as Secretary of State for War. He died on 5 June 1916 in the sinking of the HMS *Hampshire*. McMahon's title changed from Consul-General to High Commissioner when Egypt was declared a protectorate.

by 1916 had been promoted to brigadier-general and was the Director of Military Intelligence (DMI) at British General Headquarters (GHQ) in Cairo.

In late 1915, Sir Mark Sykes, an agent (advisor) for the Middle East at the War Office in London presented his idea for the creation of a bureau to 'harmonize' the multitude of opinions and reports that were emanating from the many interested offices in the region. A senior-level conference concurred and in early 1916, the Cairo-based Arab Bureau was born. Known as 'Arbur' in official correspondence, the Bureau was intimately involved in not only the collection, analysis, and dissemination of intelligence on the regional situation, but the development of propaganda to support the Arab movement as well. Most contentious was its policy recommendation concerning the Arab question. The Government of India had opposed the idea of the Arab Bureau from the outset and saw its efforts as a blatant attempt to steer British leadership into supporting Hussein's uprising. More importantly, the GOI felt the Arab Bureau would intrude into their sphere of influence: Mesopotamia.

The bureau was placed in HMG's hierarchy as a sub-office of the Foreign Office responsible to the High Commissioner, responsible for the political dimensions of the Arab Revolt, e.g., negotiating with Hussein. Although Sykes wanted the job of director, overall supervision was given to Brigadier-General Clayton.

The bureau set up in the Savoy Hotel in Cairo located adjacent to GHQ's military intelligence offices. Clayton quickly staffed the office with knowledgeable Arabists, including Hogarth, and Captain Kinahan Cornwallis as director and deputy director respectively.

During, and after, the war many felt the Bureau was staffed with amateurs who blindly promoted the pipe-dream of Arab independence with no supervision or control. In actuality, it was a highly professional organization that was hampered in the execution of its mandate by ineffectual coordination and a lack of guidance from London. Under Clayton's leadership, the Bureau attempted to achieve its goals of driving out the Turks and meeting Britain's Imperial interests. Clayton saw a weak patchwork of Arab entities beholden to Britain financially and militarily, that could not challenge the empire. The Government in India did not see that intent and remained sceptical of the Bureau's operations throughout the war.[2]

Propaganda played an important role in the Bureau's work. It sought to neutralize Ottoman–German efforts to start a jihad and its portrayal of Grand Sherif Hussein as a pawn of the British Empire and produced counter-propaganda that dehumanized the Turks as well as the Germans. Major themes were used to demonstrate that Ottomans and its CUF leadership had diminished Islam and the Holy Cities and that the Arab Revolt was neither a new crusade nor was Hussein a pawn of the British.

---

[2] See Bruce Westrate's *The Arab Bureau: British Policy in the Middle East, 1916–1920* for a detailed discussion on this subject.

To promote Hussein as the true protector of Islam, the bureau also helped ensure the annual pilgrimage went off without difficulty. In September 1916, with Hussein's forces guarding the Hajj route from Jeddah to Mecca, ships of the British Red Sea Patrol brought the *Maḥmal* (Holy Carpet) and its transport cart from Cairo. Reaching Jeddah, it was carried in a procession to the Ka'ba in Mecca, demonstrating that Emir Hussein was a capable steward of the Hajj.

One propaganda medium was the newspaper *al-Haqiqa* (The Truth), which portrayed Britain as the friend of Islam, at the same time displaying Britain's military strength. Another newspaper was *al-Kawkab* (The Planet). Both were moderately successful, but as one observer noted after the war, Arabs were suspicious of all newspapers as the Turks had used them to spread their influence.

To prove that the Arab Revolt was a concrete reality and to spread that word, the bureau undertook the design and printing of stamps. According to Storrs, "the best proof that it [the revolt] had taken place would be provided by an issue of Hejaz postage stamps, which would carry the Arab propaganda, self-paying and incontrovertible, to the four corners of the earth."

Propaganda was not a new tool in the warrior's arsenal and both sides sought to capitalize on its advantages. A small cell of Arab Bureau officers was engaged in the propaganda effort until the end of the war. As Lawrence would later state, "The printing press is the greatest weapon in the armoury of the modern commander."

Following the withdrawal from Gallipoli, General Maxwell's Egypt Force was combined with the Mediterranean Expeditionary Force and General Archibald Murray took overall command. Murray moved his headquarters forward to Ismailia, taking the majority of his military intelligence department with him. Left behind were Clayton, who had been replaced as DMI, by Colonel Thomas Holdich, the Arab bureau, and some of the DMI's Middle East experts who now collaborated directly, if unofficially with Hogarth's Bureau. Clayton continued to supervise the bureau while also carrying out his duties as the Sudan Agent and intelligence advisor to the High Commissioner. Lawrence was officially working with GHQ intelligence but hoped to shift over to the Arab Bureau where "all the work of the Sherif's revolt" was being done.

From his vantage point in Sudan, General Wingate not only observed the events in the Hejaz closely, but continued to promote the uprising. From the outset, he had enthusiastically supported the prospect of an Arab uprising and the idea that "the Muslim Holy Places should remain in the hands of an independent Muslim State" after the war. He also wanted to take complete control of the political and military aspects of Britain's support to Hussein.[3]

---

[3] Wingate was appointed Officer Commanding, Hejaz Operations on 9 June 1916 and served in that position until 31 January 1919, according to the *London Gazette* of 24 November 1919, supplement #14290.

General Murray argued for a unified command of the revolt under the High Commissioner in a message sent to General Sir William Robertson, Chief of the Imperial General Staff in London. Robertson did not yet agree. Murray then decided that if he couldn't control the operations he would at least ensure his intelligence officers had nothing to do with an uprising that appeared to have no control. He allowed that he would continue to supply the revolt in so far as he could, but forbade DMI officers from working with the Arab Bureau. Many men working in the bureau believed Murray was piqued because he was jealous and wanted to "make the spectacle of the High Commission [McMahon] running a private war look ridiculous". McMahon would be out of a job by the end of 1916, a victim of Murray's wrath, and the hostility of the former Viceroy of India, Lord Hardinge, who was now in London.

CHAPTER THREE

A Hopeful but Inauspicious Beginning

On 16 October 1916, the HMS *Lama*, one of the ships of the Royal Navy's Red Sea Patrol, rocked gently in the calm waters of Jeddah harbour. On board, a group of Englishmen were greeted by a searingly hot blast of wind off the mainland. Storrs and T. E. Lawrence, now a captain, were there to meet Abdullah and assess the situation for the High Commissioner. Lawrence had another job as well; he wanted to meet with Hussein's sons in order to write personality notes for the Arab Bureau. Essentially he was evaluating them as leaders, a typical intelligence officer's task. Clayton, who sent Lawrence on the trip, felt his opinions and observations would be useful. Lawrence had succeeded in annoying his superiors at GHQ so well that they were happy to grant his leave request to cover the travel. Holdich had no idea that Clayton had sent Lawrence on the mission, nor did he know why.

Storrs and Lawrence were met by one of Lieutenant-Colonel Wilson's deputies, John Young, who escorted them to the British Consulate where they found Wilson complaining about his rather unclear chain of command. Soon, Abdullah and his chief of staff Abdul Aziz al-Masri arrived at the consulate.

Before he decided to support Hussein's revolt, al-Masri had originally been selected by the British for a proposed venture to raise the Arab tribes against the Turks in Mesopotamia. Cairo thought the British expeditionary force at Basra would be aided in its advance by a guerrilla movement and suggested that to London and Simla. The Viceroy in India and all his subordinates, however, thought the idea was an abomination and quickly quashed it. They had no wish to manage a revolt nor did they wish to encourage a Muslim uprising against the Turks; the parallels to their own situation in India were more than they wished to entertain. Stopped from taking on that job, al-Masri was instead recruited and sent to help Hussein to train a ragtag group of volunteers into what was hoped would become a disciplined, regular army to fight alongside the camel-mounted Bedouins.[1] Al-Masri travelled to Rabegh in September with his deputy, Nuri as Said, also a former Ottoman soldier. Once there

---

[1] Al-Masri's 'bands' were drawn mostly from Arabs captured while serving with the Ottoman Army.

they began work to prepare what Wingate called "Arab Trained Bands" – 5,000 men for the defence of Rabegh and operations thereafter.

For the next several hours, Storrs and Wilson were occupied with fending off Abdullah's complaints about the lack of support for the precarious situation at Rabegh. Abdullah had lobbied for aircraft and a brigade of troops to protect the port and to hold off an expected Turkish attack. Now Storrs had to explain why the troops and planes weren't coming.

Since June, there had been considerable debate between Cairo, Khartoum, and London on the pros and cons of deploying British troops, whether Christian or Muslim, to Rabegh. Although Wingate, and Wilson and, at one point, Lawrence supported the idea, McMahon and several members of the Arab Bureau did not. Wingate and Wilson were the most vocal proponents of sending troops to Rabegh. Clayton and Mark Sykes thought landing foreign troops so close to the Holy Cities would endanger Hussein's reputation as their protector and lead to disaffection of many of his supporters.

One argument that drew some support was to send Muslim colonial troops, either from British Sudan or French Algeria, to avoid the religious implications of Europeans occupying the town. Hussein himself vacillated on the issue, at times opposing it violently, at others – especially when he heard rumours of a Turkish advance – pleading for reinforcements.

Although everyone agreed that supporting the Grand Sherif was a moral obligation, how to do it was a question to which there was no good answer. A landing at Akaba was discussed and dismissed – due to an unfavourable assessment of the situation done by T. E. Lawrence at General Murray's request, among other factors.

The British War Council and Chief of the Imperial General Staff, Sir William Robertson opposed sending forces, less on religious grounds than the fact that it would take much needed resources away from the main effort in France. Additionally, it was believed that the introduction of Christian troops would be propagandized to signal a new crusade – a colonial land-grab that would delegitimize Hussein's revolt. The issue of Rabegh continued to be contentious through the summer and early autumn, when officers on the ground including Colonel Parker reported the Arabs were short on everything needed to fight the Turks. Reports of Turkish reinforcements arriving at Medina exacerbated the alarm and led some to recommend the landing of 5,000 troops. In late October, it was believed the Turks were only three days' march from Rabegh and little was in their way to stop them.

As the revolt progressed into the autumn of 1916, the surrender of Ta'if and Feisul's success in slowing the Turkish advances towards Rabegh, did much to elevate Arab morale. Ali moved his troops to Rabegh and Feisul continued to hold the hills straddling the Medina–Rabegh road. This served to relieve some of the pressure to send foreign forces to the Hejaz.

That was the situation just before Storrs and Lawrence arrived. Following their meeting with Abdullah, Lawrence and Storrs along with Colonel al-Masri went to Rabegh to better assess the situation. Lawrence had decided he needed to meet all of Hussein's sons in order to choose the one best suited to lead military operations. But to meet Feisul, he would have to go upcountry, something no foreigner had been permitted to do. It took Storrs's persuasive skills to convince Abdullah and then Hussein that the trip was necessary for a full accounting of the situation and what was needed.

Before they departed for Rabegh, Storrs and Lawrence met the head of the French Military Mission, Colonel Édouard Brémond, and listened to his reasoning on why the Arabs should be discouraged from capturing Medina. Brémond wanted to keep Hussein from taking his uprising to the north, into Syria, which the French planned to occupy. Brémond also supported sending French Muslim troops to Rabegh, but only if British support, i.e. artillery, was sent to protect them. He knew support for Hussein would be undermined and that it would also hamstring Murray by taking forces he needed to advance into Palestine. Lawrence, who did not trust the French before, had even more cause to remain wary now. Brémond would eventually lord over 400 North African troops who would actively assist the revolt's military objectives, but his overriding concern was always for France's eventual occupation of Syria.

Landing at Rabegh, the delegation was met by Ali and treated to a long diatribe about the difficulties the Arabs were facing being provided with numerous wish-lists. Lawrence was not impressed with Ali's qualifications to be a leader, nor was Storrs. After three days, Lawrence set off to see Feisul, while Storrs, not being a field man, returned to Cairo. Before the meeting, Lawrence decided that Abdullah would be the one if Feisul did not measure up.

Reaching Feisul's camp, Lawrence spent several days talking with Feisul and assessing the local situation. He was impressed with Feisul and took in his preparations for the defence of Rabegh. He also looked in on the Egyptian artillery detachment which he pronounced to be equipped with unserviceable weapons and ammunition and to be poorly trained in manoeuvre warfare.

Returning to the coast at Yenbo, the port for Medina until the Hejaz railway rendered it useless, Lawrence wrote several reports while he was waiting for his Red Sea Patrol ride home. One entitled 'Feisul's Operation' is noteworthy for its precision and readability. In discussing what he learned, as well as his insights, the document reflects Lawrence's knowledge of both the Ottomans and the Arabs. He weaves together an operational and sociological assessment of the situation that faces the revolt as well as his view of how the Ottoman counterinsurgency may unfold.[2]

---

[2] The term 'counterinsurgency' did not exist at that time, Lawrence merely calling it an "offensive" of which there were several "courses" the Turks could take.

In the writings of his meetings with and appraisal of Feisul, Lawrence showed he was impressed with the sheikh's qualities from the outset. Feisul's strengths, according to Lawrence, were his political acumen, energy, personal magnetism, and cleverness. His weaknesses were his hot-temper and impatience. Overall, Lawrence felt Feisul was a far better candidate than the other brothers, to meld and wield the various tribes of the region against the Turks. Lawrence's recommendation was the second that supported Feisul's role. The first was that of Captain Norman Bray of the Indian Army, with whom Lawrence would later have several disagreements. In this instance, however, both recognized Feisul as a leader.[3]

Feisul gave Lawrence a long rendition of his operations in the revolt, of how they failed to overcome the Turks at Medina due to a lack of arms and ammunition as well as the perfidy of one of the allied tribes, and of how, since that time, he had placed his forces on the Sultani Road to defend Rabegh and prevent a Turkish approach. Wingate had sent Egyptian mountain guns and crews to reinforce the Arabs which buoyed morale, but that advantage was lost because their crews had not been well trained to handle the guns and were useless at long range. Feisul then had fallen back on Hamra, placing covering forces in the hills. He described his future plan for a number of dispersed attacks, which Lawrence felt was ambitious but would probably not work due to the lack of inter-tribal communications.

Lawrence began to modify his opinion of the importance of Rabegh and thought the Turks incapable of forcing the road to the port because of the danger Feisul's troops in the hills would present them: "Two or three hundred determined men knowing the ranges should hold any section of them." He graphically described the terrain as valleys that were often narrow and turned into "chasms and gorges for miles ... full of turns and twists, without cover, and flanked on each side by pitiless hills". In short, perfect ground for guerrillas to harass an advancing army. He assessed that the Turks would have to increase their numbers to achieve their goal, but believed a number of factors would keep them from it, including the approaching rainy season (November to January).

Lawrence went on to suggest the wisest course for the Turks would be to pacify the Hejaz from north to south, ensuring they had the loyalty (paid for, most likely) of all the tribes astride the all-important Hejaz railway – the strategic link to Damascus. He also mentioned some of the equipment that would be needed to support the revolt, including wireless radio sets, light machine guns, aircraft for reconnaissance, and armoured cars to secure Rabegh. He closed the report with an interesting reflection, an observation that would later play an influential role in his thoughts on how the revolt should proceed:

> A thing which has struck me rather forcibly while in the Hejaz is the bigness of the revolt. We
> have here a well-peopled province ... more than a fortnight [14 nights'] long in camel journeys,

---

[3] Bray's assessment was written on 18 October, Lawrence's was completed at the end of the same month.

whose whole nomad and semi-nomad population have been suddenly changed from casual pilferers to deadly enemies of the Turks.

HMS *Suva* picked Lawrence up on 31 October at Yenbo. On board, Lawrence met Colonel Alfred Chevallier Parker, a nephew of Lord Kitchener and a military intelligence officer. Parker, the former governor-general of the Sinai, had been called to join the General Staff in Cairo and was working with Clayton before being tapped to take over intelligence duties in Jeddah. He worked with Wilson but reported to Wingate in Khartoum and Clayton in Cairo. Parker, like Wilson, was very much caught up in the intrigue of working with the Arabs and the back and forth of the British leadership on whether or not to send troops to Rabegh. Parker was inclined to believe it would be a good idea and downplayed the possible negative propaganda that might ensue. He felt the presence of the Egyptian artillery section was a case in point, although there was still a great deal of animus between them and the Hejazi Arabs.

Both Lawrence and Parker had extended conversations with Aziz al-Masri about his plans for the formation and operations of a regular force. To Parker, al-Masri put in requests for the material to bring his planned 5,000-man element into existence. Al-Masri discussed his strategy for operations against the Hejaz railway with Lawrence, something Clayton had asked Lawrence to fathom with the Circassian officer. He discovered that al-Masri was much more intent on the rails north of el-Ula, the northern border of the Hejaz, and that he wanted in the longer term (after capturing

'Native' Lewis Gun section with unknown British officer. (Gilman Family Collection)

Medina) to conduct operations in Syria, far north of where the revolt was currently concentrated. Al-Masri's thinking seems to have influenced Lawrence greatly. He also discouraged the landing of British troops at Rabegh, but encouraged advisors, a thought Lawrence would incorporate into his later reporting. Not everything with al-Masri was good, however. He voiced discontent over the difficulty of working with the Arabs, especially Sherif Hussein, and mentioned the possibility of his resignation.

Parker sailed with the *Suva* specifically to hear what Lawrence had learned from his visit with Feisul. After hearing what Lawrence had to say, he instructed him to travel to Khartoum to brief Wingate, who by this time had been designated as the overall chief of operations in the Hejaz. Wingate would soon nose McMahon out of the High Commissioner post as well and move to Cairo.

The voyage had not started well. Lawrence's inimitable style and complete disregard for army, or in this case, naval, protocol had led to his first conflict with the Royal Navy. Lawrence strolled aboard with his hands in his pockets and announced to the ship's commander, Captain William 'Ginger' Boyle, that he was "going over to Port Sudan on this ship". Boyle quickly straightened Lawrence out and told him to report himself properly to the deck officer. Lawrence later admitted that they didn't have a "good first meeting". In due course, the two would come to better appreciate each other.

The *Suva* now sailed to Jeddah where Lawrence transhipped to the HMS *Euryalus*, the flagship of the Red Sea Patrol, commanded by Admiral Rosslyn Wemyss. One assumes Lawrence had since learned the proper etiquette for reporting himself on board, but Wemyss reported that he too was not initially impressed with Lawrence.

On the African side of the Red Sea at Port Sudan, Lawrence and Wemyss disembarked to travel overland to Khartoum. At the docks they met two British officers, Major Pierce Joyce of the Connaught Rangers, and Captain William A. 'Wady' Davenport of the West Yorkshire Regiment, both of whom were then serving with the Egyptian Army. Wingate had selected them as advisors to the Arab forces. They were heading east towards Rabegh where they joined another, Major Herbert Garland, better known by his Egyptian Army rank 'Bimbashi'. Garland, who was fluent in Arabic, had been at Yenbo since 27 October, one of the first British advisors sent to the Hejaz. He was a large bear of a man with a temper and little patience for dealing with the Arabs, but he enjoyed demolitions. The big bangs he made and his teaching methods drew the Arabs to him. Lawrence thought his methods were rather unique in that he handled explosives with a certain disregard for safety that would have frightened the normal Royal Engineer officer.

Wemyss was another influential officer who appreciated the possibilities of the Arab Revolt from the outset and placed all his naval assets at its disposal. Before arriving in Egypt, he had capably organized the withdrawal of forces from Gallipoli once the campaign was abandoned and supported operations in the Persian Gulf, before taking charge of the Red Sea Patrol. In that position, he became an ardent supporter of Hussein, provided the firepower to cover the Arabs' conquest of the littoral ports, and contributed the logistical link for the uprising. His patrol consisted of at least 15 elderly navy and converted civilian ships, which would prove vital to the revolt's success.[4]

He and Lawrence travelled overland to Khartoum, located 600 miles inland. Wingate's Palace Residence sat on the edge of the Blue Nile, not far from where it joins the White Nile. Lawrence provided Wingate his assessment of the situation and argued against the landing of a British brigade at Rabegh, stating his conviction that Feisul's irregulars would be able hold back the Turks. Instead, he argued that material support would be more beneficial.

Wingate had by that time received word from the War Office that no British troops were available for Rabegh. Despite that, he continued to hope for troops (either British or French North African Muslims) to be sent as a contingency force. Wingate accepted Lawrence's other recommendations for increased support, including rifles, machine guns, aircraft flown by British crews (a limited presence of foreigners was acceptable as long they remained on the coast). It was also agreed that the main goal for the Arabs would be to take Medina, but that they would first have to be trained, organized, and provided with better communications. Additionally, better intelligence on the Turks – as well as on the Arab forces themselves – was needed from the Hejaz as the information provided by the Arabs was often erroneous or purposefully inaccurate.

The discussions then turned to advisors. Wingate had been talking about the need for additional advisors with Clayton for several weeks. The organization would be known as the British Military Mission (BMM) to the Hejaz and was intended to bring a sense of order to what had been a rather disorganized effort.

Clayton recommended bringing S. F. Newcombe into the advisory group. Wingate initially intended that Newcombe would be responsible for operations at Yenbo and north, liaise with Feisul and Abdullah, and train the Arab regular army. In short, he would relieve Wilson of the workload that prevented him from doing much beyond trying to advise Sherif Hussein and 'regulate' his ever-changing moods and requests. Wilson, Clayton observed, was out of touch with military operations there.

A small group had already been dispatched: the first were Garland to teach the esoteric art of demolitions and Joyce to command the small contingent of Egyptians and improve the Arab forces' organization at Rabegh with Davenport to assist.[5] Newcombe had experience in Gallipoli and Flanders, as well as prewar experience

---

[4] Among them were the cruisers HMS *Fox, Minerva,* and *Dufferin*; RIM ships *Northbrooke, Hardinge,* and *Minto*; armed boarding steamers *Lunka, Lama, Perth, River Fisher, Suva, Scotia,* and *Enterprise*; the monitor *M.31*; and the seaplane carriers HMS *Ben-my-Chree* and *Raven*.
[5] Joyce's first title was 'Officer Commanding Troops & Advisor to Feisul'.

in the region. Clayton also suggested bringing in an artillery and machine-gun officer and a doctor.

In the actual implementation of Wingate's plan, Wilson did not give up any of his policy-making responsibilities. Both Newcombe and Vickery recommended he remain in charge and Wingate concurred with the suggestion that the mission be under the supervision of Wilson and that it move to Feisul's headquarters. Keeping Wilson in full control thus ensured that he would prevent individual advisors from presenting and putting into action "divergent views and opinions" concerning operations and retain "unity of command". With the creation of the BMM, support that had been both circumspect and circumscribed by the restrictive demands of the Grand Sherif, began to grow.

When Lawrence returned to Cairo, Clayton asked him to write a memorandum on the situation at Rabegh. With respect to sending British troops to Rabegh, the decision-making process was still in flux with Wingate and the French on one side and Cairo on the other. Lawrence repeated his argument for why the landing was unnecessary and possibly destructive to the revolt, but maintained that British logistical support was still required. For one, if Fakhri chose to use the inland route to attack Mecca, a brigade at Rabegh, whether Muslim or Christian, would be of little consequence in preventing its capture. He was followed by Wemyss who telegraphed the Admiralty with his own, similar conclusions. The War Office once again stepped in and refused to permit the brigade to be landed.

Lawrence had expected to return to a new job in the Arab Bureau having burned his bridges with DMI. Instead it seemed he had made himself invaluable to the cause and would be returned to Yenbo temporarily to set up an intelligence network. Clayton had also decided that Yenbo would be a better training base than Rabegh and proposed to move the BMM advisors there. This was because he felt it provided a better platform from which to launch operations towards the railway. Additionally, Aziz al-Masri felt his bands should be subordinate to Feisul because Ali was hindering his efforts to raise and train the force at Rabegh. He also thought this would enable better communication between himself and the British.

By December 1916, the Rabegh 'crisis' had grown to panic proportions. Hussein continued to waver between wanting reinforcements and rejecting them, while the British government argued at the highest levels about sending troops and who would be to blame for the failure of the revolt should the Turks reach Mecca. Lawrence's visit and Clayton's vision had done much to prevent the landing of Allied forces, but the topic was still very much on the table. Much indecision and vacillation played a role in the confused decision-making process.[6]

---

[6] See John Fischer's 'The Rabegh Crisis, 1916–17: "A Comparatively Trivial Question" or "A Self-Willed Disaster"', *Middle Eastern Studies*, Vol. 38, No. 3 (July 2002), pp. 73–92, Taylor & Francis, Ltd., for a detailed discussion of the issue.

The British presence at Rabegh now included six Royal Flying Corps (RFC) BE2c aircraft of 'C' Flight, 14th Squadron under the command of Major A. J. Ross – in addition to the Egyptian artillery and infantry. Major Joyce took over as the senior officer and base commander. Colonel Parker returned to Cairo.

Hussein's forces held the key towns and ports of Mecca, Jeddah, Rabegh, Yenbo, Kunfida and were blocking an Ottoman force on the Sultani Road. The Arabs were conducting raids to the east of Medina and against the railway to prevent the Turkish garrison from being resupplied.

The Turks again threatened. Ali's forces had retreated to Rabegh after a rumour had sent them packing. On 8 December, Fakhri's forces attacked the Arab blocking positions inland at Nakhl Mubarak. Panicked, Feisul's troops either evaporated into the desert or fell back on Yenbo. The enemy was now at the gates, only ten miles away.

Lawrence asked for British reinforcements and contacted Captain Boyle for assistance, while Bimbashi Garland set about organizing Yenbo's defences.[7] Boyle would order the monitor *M.31*, the HMS *Hardinge*, and the seaplane carrier HMS *Raven* to anchor off the coast. Lawrence then went to Rabegh to arrange for aerial reconnaissance with Major Ross, the commander of 'C' Flight. The intelligence the aircraft could supply would be crucial for the defenders.

On the night of 12 December, the Ottoman forces approached Yenbo to attack. When they reached the plain before the city they were met with an ominous sight. Ships' searchlights were sweeping the town and the flat ground in front of them. Confronted with the realization that they would have to cross the open terrain in full view of the defenders and the ships' guns, the Turks called off the attack. Lawrence would later write that "they turned back: and that night, I believe, the Turks lost their war". The Rabegh crisis was over and the revolt had been saved, but only just.

In general, thinking about the Arab Revolt in Cairo and Khartoum was centred on four primary areas: improving the provision and distribution of material support, obtaining better intelligence, providing advisory assistance, and the limited tactical objectives of disrupting the Hejaz railway and capturing Medina. But one tiny crack in the strategy appeared when Clayton wrote: "The Hejaz railway is the key to the whole problem. The Turkish force at Medina can stay there as long as it likes, provided it is rendered incapable of a serious offensive …"

A new year was about to begin.

---

[7] Garland was awarded the Military Cross for his actions during this engagement.

CHAPTER FOUR

Advisors, Dromedaries and Guerrilla Warfare

The Hejaz show is a quaint one, the like of which has hardly been on earth before …

LAWRENCE TO COLONEL C. E. WILSON, 9 FEBRUARY 1917

Despite the unexpected reprieve from the Ottoman advance, the revolt was still on shaky ground. Grand Sherif Hussein interfered with operations by issuing contradictory orders and requests, while the Arab troops themselves were undisciplined and poorly led. Supplying them was poorly managed and the equipment was often obsolete or faulty. Further, Aziz al-Masri's attempts to train a 'conventional' force were in difficulty. He was not trusted by Hussein and Ali interfered constantly with his activities.

The setbacks suffered as a result of the Turkish thrust towards Rabegh and Yenbo had demoralized the Bedouin and many had returned to their villages. It was only Feisul's force of personality that held the remainder at Yenbo. That and British gold.

A success was needed and Feisul, always thinking of Syria, looked north towards the seaport of Wejh. With Abdullah located at Khaibar to the northeast of Medina, however, Feisul hesitated to move, fearing a Turkish attack. After discussing the need to move forward, Feisul and Lawrence (who was back with Feisul as his principal liaison officer) agreed that Abdullah should move to Wadi Ais on the western side of the Hejaz railway. There he would be in better position to threaten the rail line and block any Turkish move towards the coast. Still, it required the personal guarantee of Colonel Wilson that the Royal Navy would help defend Emir Ali's forces at Rabegh before Feisul would move.

An Arab reconnaissance patrol was sent out to determine the Ottoman forces' location and strength on 2 January 1917. It was Lawrence's first foray out on an armed patrol. The reconnaissance proved the Turks had moved back towards Medina. Feisul was able to start north but, even then, the move was complicated by a lack of transport animals. A plan was made to transport much of Feisul's supplies and over 500 troops by ship to Wejh while Feisul's 10,000-man force moved overland.

Feisul was to attack the town from the south while the Arab troops from the HMS *Hardinge* and several other ships would be landed as a blocking force to the north.

Lawrence was joined by a new officer, Major Charles Vickery, at Um Lejh, the halfway point where the transshipment of troops and supplies took place. Vickery was to be part of the British Military Mission along with Newcombe, who arrived on 18 January and had just caught up with Feisul as his force broke camp to begin their march north. Lawrence had been told that his liaison duties would be turned over to Newcombe and fully expected to leave Feisul and return to Cairo. Newcombe, however, invited Lawrence to stay on until Wejh, a week's journey away. Lawrence was in no hurry to leave the Hejaz and was happy to ride north with the force.

En route a messenger from Abdullah reached Feisul and informed him that his brother had defeated a Turkish column and captured an important Turkish officer, Eshref Bey, along with valuable supplies including 20,000 Turkish lira in gold.[1] This naturally required a celebration and delayed Feisul for two days. When the *Hardinge* reached its rendezvous point, Feisul's main force was nowhere to be seen. Admiral Wemyss, in command of the flotilla, was concerned with the Arab troops and the worsening sanitary conditions aboard the ships. He ordered Major Vickery and another officer, Captain Norman Bray, not to wait and landed the Arab troops along with a Royal Navy contingent. They captured the town by themselves after a hard-fought battle.

Both Bray and Vickery criticized Lawrence, who made excuses for the delay but did not mention the true cause: the celebration and his interrogation of Eshref Bey. For his part, Lawrence was upset the attack had gone off without Feisul as he thought the Turks would have surrendered without a fight. In the event, the Arabs lost around 20 men. Lawrence's opinion of Bray, an intelligence officer with Wilson in Jeddah, and Vickery fell that day. He wrote of the incident: "Vickery's impatience was justified, perhaps, in cold blood." His hostility was reciprocated by Bray and Vickery.

Regardless of who was right, the capture of Wejh dramatically changed the Arabs' fortunes. It was the propaganda generated by this success that brought the fence-sitters over to Feisul's side. Lawrence noted in his diary that the victory also led to a flood of tribal envoys who wished to present their compliments and swear their allegiance. Gathering the disparate and often hostile tribes together, he swore the sheikhs on the Koran "to wait while he waited, march when he marched, to show mercy to no Turk, but to everyone who spoke Arab, whether Baghdadi or Aleppine or Syrian, and to put the needs of the Arab Independence above their own lives, their goods, or their families".

---

[1] The money was believed to be intended to cultivate two of Hussein's rivals, ibn Saud and ibn Rashid, as well as leaders in Yemen further south.

Feisul would make use of the distant tribes in their traditional role: "[O]nce we determine the day of our attack on the Railway, word will be sent up and down the line. The Howeitat tribe said they would stop every trolley, cut the wires, besiege every station and arrest every patrol – for which Feisul would send them his new ally: dynamite and men to use it to interrupt the line as far as possible N[orth] and S[outh] in as many places as possible."

Feisul was heartened by the victory, but had no desire to lose Lawrence. He wrote a strong letter to Clayton requesting Lawrence remain with him as an advisor. Clearly, the empathy earned from much time with the Bedouin had served Lawrence well. He would remain as Feisul's personal liaison. Feisul embodied Lawrence's vision of a leader of the revolt. Abdullah was sincere but not a military commander – he was more of a dreamer and also a better politician. Abdullah's force, with prompting, would continue to harass Turkish outposts and sabotage the railway immediately north of Medina, fixing the Turks there. Feisul would begin to raid north of el-Ula, some 200 miles from Medina.

At Clayton's urging Wingate appointed Newcombe to lead the British Military Mission. Newcombe would report directly to Colonel Wilson in Jeddah. His instructions from Wilson read:

> You will be my representative in all Military and Political matters with the Emirs Abdulla and Feisul. The field of operations with which you will deal will, for the present, be from Yanbo North …
>
> Majors Vickery and Cox and Captain Lawrence are directly under your orders …
>
> Garland (Egyptian Army) has been employed in training Arabs in demolition work. He is also directly under your orders.
>
> Major Joyce is in charge at Rabegh and reports directly to me.

With that Newcombe assumed command of northern operations, while Wilson provided general guidance on strategic objectives from Jeddah. The success at Wejh also ended the question of landing regular British formations at Rabegh. Hussein, no longer concerned with a Turkish advance on Mecca, made up his mind definitively that the troops were not needed and the British War Office was happy to comply.

The British strategy remained the same. Having recently witnessed Arab tactics, Major Vickery wrote that coordinated, combined operations of Hussein's sons (Feisul, Abdullah, Ali and Zeid) to capture Medina were the only method to ensure success. He also noted the value of Hussein's armies was nil if they were directed on the wrong tasks and they should best be confined to guerrilla operations. Vickery estimated that the Sherifial forces disposed the following numbers: Emir Ali at Rabegh with 3,000 men, Emir Abdullah with 5,000 men at Wadi Ais, and Emir Feisul at Wejh with a claimed 15,000 men (only 7,500 observed). The Ottoman forces in Medina numbered around 12,000.

Still, in Vickery's mind – and that of most other British officers – Medina remained the primary objective for the Arab Armies.

Newcombe was aggressive and immediately urged Feisul to begin raiding the railway. His aim was "to destroy the Hejaz railway as permanently as possible". One of Newcombe's subordinates, Bimbashi Garland, would be the first Briton to go upcountry. He did not have an entirely happy experience as evidenced by his after-action report on the operation. Garland rode out of Wejh on 12 February 1917 with a party of 53 men, mostly of the Gehenna Anazah and Ageyl tribes. He quickly found out how challenging working with the Arabs could be. Their nominal leader, Abdul Kaim Bedewi, a Gehenna whom Feisul had charged with the task of guiding the party, changed their route of travel and managed not to inform Garland who was frustrated with the poor discipline of the Gehenna and the bad guides who kept losing their way. After many stops to allow Abdul Karim the chance to socialize with the villagers on the route, eight days' travel brought them to the railway. At that point, Garland was convinced that the Gehenna had no intention of attacking the railway or endangering themselves. Although Garland was already disinclined to work closely with the Bedu, his assessment proved correct.

The Ageyl, however, had no reservations of the sort and worked well with Garland. His plan was to destroy 500 yards of rail and to emplace two mechanically fired mines at either end of the broken rails. One of the mines would be set off by the first locomotive to arrive. It would likely carry repair crews and approach the demolition site from the nearest station. It was dark when Garland carefully moved to the rail with his assistants. They found a small, two-culvert bridge in front of them and he showed the Ageyl how to properly place 40 pounds of gelignite to destroy it. He then moved south along the line with some guards to place his first mine.

Herbert Garland was a chemist and a metallurgist at Cairo's Citadel before the war. He was commissioned into the Egyptian Army after he invented a simple trench mortar and grenade that was used extensively in the Gallipoli campaign. Through his work, he had learned of a simple firing mechanism employed by Boer guerrillas against British rail traffic in the South African War.[2] It was a cut-down Martini-Henry rifle action placed upside down with its exposed trigger placed under the rails. The downward pressure of a train would fire a cartridge and ignite the detonator and explosives buried with it. He planned to test the firing mechanism and wanted to personally observe it to see if it actually worked. Garland would get a very close view of its effectiveness as the guides had actually brought the party close – too close – to the Toweira railway blockhouse.

The party waited for the cover of night to advance on the railway tracks. Garland chose a suitable location and began to dig a hole for his mine when one of the Arabs came running up to tell him that a train was approaching. Having been

---

[2] Also known as the Second Anglo-Boer War, it was fought between Britain and the Boer republics of the South African Republic (the Transvaal) and the Orange Free State between October 1899 and May 1902.

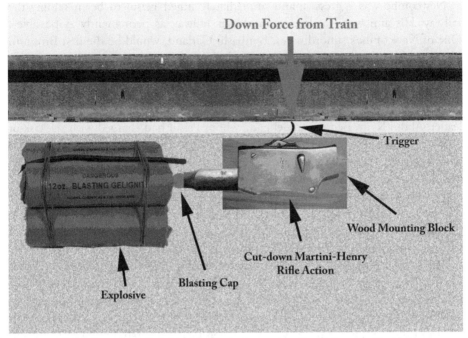

Down Force from Train

Trigger

Wood Mounting Block

Cut-down Martini-Henry Rifle Action

Blasting Cap

Explosive

Garland trigger, copied from similar version used by Boer saboteurs. (Author)

informed by intelligence reports that said the Turks did not run trains at night, and hearing nothing, he ignored the report and continued to dig unconcernedly. Then he heard the whistle and steam of a train departing the station and was startled by the realization that he should have heeded the warning.

He had only been in position for five minutes but decided he would continue with the emplacement. Filling the hole with 15 pounds of explosives, Garland looked up to see a locomotive 200 yards away approaching at a fast clip. He told the guards to run and finished laying the charge. But having taken his boots off to prevent tell-tale tracks in the sand, he painfully hobbled over the rock-strewn ground to escape. He was only 50 yards from the tracks when the train hit the mine. Garland turned just in time to see the blast and the train roll off the track. At around 7,000 feet per second, the blast wave knocked him to the ground. He counted himself fortunate to have witnessed the event and not to have been injured by the flying debris. It was the first train derailed during the revolt.

After the locomotive came to a crashing halt, the Ageyl ran unbidden back to the bridge and managed to fire their charges successfully before they withdrew from the area. Garland was quite pleased with their behaviour and later told Feisul that he would take a hundred Ageyl on the next expedition but never again a Gehenna. He returned to Wejh on 26 February to write up his reports.

Ottoman blockhouse on Hejaz railway at approximately Km 518. (Author)

Although he had never seen the line before, Garland benefitted from the intelligence reporting that had been received and was able to note that changes in the Turkish defences appeared to have taken place. He saw that the Turks had built blockhouses every mile (each manned by 20 to 30 soldiers), and he learned from locals that the Turks employed mounted patrols after an attack. A detachment would be sent out from each blockhouse in a triangular pattern on both sides of the track to trap the raiders. The security forces also used hand trollies each morning to travel up and down their assigned length of rail looking for mines.

At Feisul's request Garland also looked at the feasibility of employing cars from Wejh to move raiding parties quickly to the railway and back again. Colonel Parker had previously mentioned the possible deployment of armoured cars at Rabegh to secure the aircraft, but they hadn't arrived. Feisul had asked for four armoured vehicles to be deployed to Wejh.

Garland was sceptical that vehicles could be used successfully. First, the wadi trails were bad and would require extensive preparation to permit the cars to traverse them. Only then, the cars could reach the railway but still "it would be a feat suitable only for description in a Car Journal". He also thought route choice was limited to two narrow valleys, which left the cars vulnerable to ambush from the heights of the surrounding hills. He depreciated the cars' utility and the hardships the crews would have to endure, imagining them to be part of a visionary scheme that was "quite unnecessary". Essentially, Garland believed that camels were the only form of transport suitable in the Hejaz and camels with Maxim machine guns were even better. Time, practice, and experimentation would prove him wrong.

Garland closed his report with a comment that his attack had taken place in Abdullah's area while Abdullah had been sitting near the line with explosives and trained men but had done nothing for two months. Garland hoped his attack would somehow spur Abdullah to action.

By February there were a number of British officers who joined the mission to assist the Arabs at Wejh including Captain Davenport, Lieutenant Henry Hornby of the Royal Engineers, and a number of French officers, including Captain Sidi Raho of the Algerian 2nd Spahis.

Newcombe soon got his chance to strike at the railway. On 21 February, he and Sherif Nasir left Wejh on his first combat patrol in the Hejaz. Lawrence would later say, "Newcombe was like fire, burning both his friends and enemies." The Arabs for one were not used to foreigners in their midst. Early in the campaign, Nasir reacted to criticism with the comment, "Don't forget that until a month ago we never had a European in this country; if we had, we should have shot him. You must give us time to get used to it."

Nevertheless, Nasir and his new English companion went off together towards the Hejaz railway. They mined the lines, and attacked the station at Dar el Nashra, tearing up 2,500 metres of track. They managed to take a number of prisoners before a troop train arrived and recaptured the station. Confronted by a large number of Ottoman troops, the Arabs retired from the scene. Two Turks were killed with no friendly losses. The news reached Wejh on 7 March and Lawrence recorded that no celebratory shots were fired – a new rule prohibited it, much to the satisfaction of the Europeans who dreaded being hit by the falling, spent bullets.

Royal Navy ships arrived at Wejh in early March with a new cargo: a dozen men of other ranks and two officers disembarked from the HMS *Lama*. They were followed by a Talbot truck, a Triumph motorcycle, a Ford Model-T, and two Rolls-Royce 1914 Admiralty Pattern armoured cars. A wireless van was also offloaded, assembled and rigged to provide communications among the different stations at Jeddah, Cairo, and Suez. The motor vehicles were by far the most exciting things yet seen by the locals. They called the motorbike a "devil horse" and every time it backfired they would run away. The two Rolls-Royces had been sent by General Murray at the urging of Clayton. The cars had most recently seen action in East Africa against the German guerrilla leader Colonel Paul von Lettow-Vorbeck. The askari soldiers had called them the "rhinos that spit lead". Unfortunately, the red clay soil of *Deutsch-Ostafrika* limited the heavy cars' mobility against the Germans in the rainy season and they were sent to Egypt.

Lieutenant Gilman and men of the Hejaz Armoured Car Section in Egypt. 1) Bond, 2) James Brown, 3) Tommy Lowe (KIA), 4) Gilman, 5) Jackson. (Edward Metcalf Collection, The Huntington Library, San Marino, California)

The new section was commanded by Lieutenant Leofric Hale Gilman and was made up of enlisted drivers from the Army Service Corps (ASC) and gunners from the Machine Gun Corps (MGC). The austere and remote areas they operated in required the drivers to be fully trained mechanics, while the gunners knew their weapons as well as an armourer. Each had been schooled in their craft in England and some had served from the beginning of the war either in France or Africa. Gilman's first military experience was in Hong Kong, where he was working for his family's business. During the 1911 Xinhai Revolution, he led a rickshaw-mounted, mobile machine-gun team when the city was turned into a British fortress. In 1914, he enlisted with the Honourable Artillery Company and served in France where he earned the Mons Star. He was commissioned in the field before being gassed at the Somme and experienced the horrors of Passchendaele, which would continue to haunt him.[3] Recovering in England, he was offered command of the Hejaz Armoured Car Section. He accepted the job but, like his men, he had little idea what awaited

---

[3] Also known as the Third Battle of Ypres, there were over half a million casualties in the three-month-long battle.

HACB men relaxing. OC Gilman with pipe. (Gilman Family Collection)

him at Wejh when they stepped off the ship. Despite that, 'Leof' never lost his sense of humour, which may have been one of the reasons his men valued his leadership.

The cars had been contemplated for employment in the Hejaz since the occupation of Rabegh, primarily to be used in defence. Lawrence, like Clayton, had ideas of his own. He had seen how useful the cars were against the Senussi in the Western Desert as a mobile gun platform supporting conventional forces and a raiding force. He hoped the vehicles would be a powerful tool to strike the railway and Ottoman positions.

The Rolls-Royces were exceptionally durable. To begin with, the factory in England had over-engineered the cars. They required little modification other than several extra spring leaves front and rear to carry the extra 2,000 pounds of steel-plate armour, a Maxim machine gun (later replaced with the improved Vickers-Maxim), plus a three-man crew and supplies. The cars came from the factory with specially made dual rear wheels. After preliminary testing, Gilman decided they should be added to the front as well both to help negotiate sand and to give redundancy in case one tyre had a blowout. Running on hard terrain, the cars could reach a top speed of over 60mph. None of the other vehicles – Fords, Crossleys, or Talbots – could keep up with them.

After an initial sorting out of the cars in Egypt, they were shipped to Wejh where duties in the first few months were typically military – hurry up and wait. Their orders were simple: find a way to get to the railway overland. The best part of the duty was that there were no schedules. The crew would load up the armoured cars with food, fuel and rations and explore the myriad of routes each wadi offered, attempting to penetrate the forbidding terrain. Rocks, soft sand, and heavy brush slowed each foray to a crawl. Camelthorn trees with three-inch, spike-like thorns were a menace to man and tyres alike. Next to fuel and water, tyre tubes were the most precious commodities in the desert.

Repairing tyres in the field. (Gilman Family Collection)

Three armoured cars standing by. Vickers tripods on the ground. (Gilman Family Collection)

The cars penetrated forty to fifty miles inland but never reached the railway, which was around fifty miles further inland over treacherous terrain. Occasionally, the cars would be used to conduct reconnaissance for advanced landing grounds for 'C' Flight's BE2c aircraft, which were based at Rabegh to the south. The landing grounds were stockpiled with fuel delivered by camels or the cars and enabled the aircraft to extend their range inland.

One man of the section, James Brown, a gunner, described duty in Wejh as a never-ending battle with millions of flies. Eating required a lot of finesse to avoid swallowing the pests along with the food. The threat of sand fly fever, dysentery, and malaria was ever present. Sick Allied soldiers were usually evacuated to hospitals in Egypt because proper long-term care wasn't available in the Hejaz. Brown was the section's motorcycle dispatch rider and was responsible for rendering Lawrence's handwritten notes into reports for the Arab Bureau. Lawrence's habit of spelling Arabic places and names differently throughout his reports often puzzled Brown during his transcriptions. He would spell out the word as he read it to which Lawrence would respond, "That will be alright as long as no one knows what is meant."

After the capture of Wejh, Lawrence made a quick journey to Cairo, where he again met Brémond, whose tactics remained much the same albeit with a new destination. Instead of Rabegh, which had been surpassed by the conquest of Wejh, he now argued for an Anglo-French landing at Akaba, a key port to the north that lay at the base of the Sinai where it joined the Arabian Peninsula. His goal remained to fix the Arab forces in the Hejaz and to keep them from moving north and spreading the revolt into Syria, which he wanted to protect at all costs for future French occupation. Lawrence told him the plan would not work, that Akaba could be seized but the push inland through the Wadi Itm valley would be resisted quite ably by the Ottoman defenders. Despite Lawrence's admonition, Brémond intended to present the idea to Feisul. Lawrence returned to Wejh ahead of him and warned Feisul of the Frenchman's intentions.

Brémond arrived several days after Lawrence. Despite his 'gift' of six Hotchkiss machine guns, a wary Feisul addressed Brémond, using the tactical argument given him by Lawrence and his tribal logic to refuse Brémond's proposal outright. Lawrence began to formulate his own plan, one that would shift the Arab intent away from Medina and to the north. But he dared not tell his own superiors about it, knowing they would disapprove.

Soon after he returned to Wejh, an urgent message arrived by ship from Clayton in Cairo. It was an intercepted set of orders sent to Fakhri Pasha telling him to evacuate Medina for Ma'an. General Murray was very concerned as his push to the east was in its opening phases and he did not want nearly 20,000 Ottoman troops to suddenly appear on his right flank. Clayton gave the order for the BMM officers to push Abdullah and Feisul to increase the tempo of operations against Medina and the line to preclude any move north by the Turks. Destroying Fakhri at Medina was out of the question, so three of Feisul's sheikhs would move against the length of the line from Tebuk to el-Ula. Abdullah would need to move on the line below that. With Newcombe out on camel raids against the railway, Lawrence left Feisul at Wejh and travelled by camel to Abdullah, whose camp was to the southeast at El Ain in Wadi Ais.

En route, Lawrence killed his first man. One of their party, a Moroccan called Hamed had killed an Ageyl in a feud. To prevent the conflict from widening, Lawrence took it upon himself to execute the man. He knew if he, an outsider, killed Hamed, the feud would end there. After a formal trial, Lawrence took the man out of the camp to an isolated ravine. Lawrence needed three shots to carry out the sentence and, after Hamed was buried, they quickly moved on. He had to be away from that place. His description of the incident in *Seven Pillars of Wisdom* is sparse, as if it affected him deeply. It may well have been the most difficult thing he ever had to do.

At El Ain, Lawrence was to give letters from Feisul urging Abdullah to action, but when he arrived he was only able to make perfunctory greetings before being confined to his tent. Sick with a malarial fever and suffering from boils, Lawrence lay for days in a semi-conscious state between wakefulness and dreaming. It was during these spells that he said he came up with his strategy to carry the revolt forward, which he later described in 'Evolution of a Revolt'. The most relevant section is quoted here:

> These reasonings showed me that the idea of assaulting Medina, or even of starving it quickly into surrender was not in accord with our best strategy. We wanted the enemy to stay in Medina, and in every other harmless place, in the largest numbers. The factor of food would eventually confine him to the railways, but he was welcome to the Hejaz railway, and the Trans-Jordan railway, and the Palestine and Damascus and Aleppo railways for the duration of the war, so long as he gave us the other nine hundred and ninety-nine thousandths of the Arab world. If he showed a disposition to evacuate too soon, as a step to concentrating in the small area which his numbers could dominate effectively, then we would have to try and restore his confidence, not harshly, but by reducing our enterprises against him. Our ideal was to keep his railway just working, but only just, with the maximum of loss and discomfort to him.

Lawrence, amateur tactician that he was, had studied enough theory and had enough experience with his charges to understand the strengths and weaknesses of the Arabs. He colourfully wrote about his revelation saying the Arab army should be "an idea, a thing invulnerable, intangible, without front or back, drifting about like a gas". The Ottomans would be forced to defend a huge area never knowing where an attack would materialize. Its army was tied to its bases at Medina and Ma'an, as well as the blockhouses strung like pearls on a necklace along the vital lifeline of the Hejaz railway that connected them. If the necklace is broken, the pearls fall, one by one.

Rather than attack fixed, defended points like Medina, which he knew the Arabs incapable of overcoming, they would attack those places least defended to destroy supplies and material along their lines of communication. The Arabs excelled at raids and they could not afford to lose men. Lawrence's strategy would capitalize on their

Three armoured cars and RFA Talbots in camp. (Gilman Family Collection)

strengths. He would not risk fighting the Turks directly on their terms, but would seek to wear them down. Not all battles are won through destruction of the enemy, they can be won by failing to lose and slowly crippling the enemy's ability to fight.

Additionally, the Arabs also possessed the 'unassailable' bases at Jeddah, Rabegh, Yenbo, and Wejh that were secure from attack because the Red Sea Patrol's firepower protected them. That guarantee, plus Allied logistical support, would prove crucial to the success of the uprising.

Nothing in Lawrence's thinking was original – 'tip and run' raids had been the way of Bedouin warfare for centuries – but he knew the capture of Medina would be meaningless, especially if any of the troops stationed there escaped north. Better was its continued existence as a Turkish albatross strangling at the end of a rope. It would keep Fakhri's forces at bay and take some pressure off the British Army to the north. Clayton had thought taking Medina might be unnecessary, but his orders had not been changed and he insisted that the Arabs keep attacking the railway in the Hejaz and harassing Fakhri Pashas's positions at Medina. Guerrilla warfare had also been spoken of, but no clear strategy had been voiced. Lawrence had a strategy and would do his best to sway Feisul to his thinking.

In late March, he set out from Abdullah's camp with the sherifs Fauzan el Harith and Suleima, along with the Algerian Captain Raho and 30 men towards the line to conduct a reconnaissance of the station at Abu el Naam, guided by Mohammed el Kadhi who, unlike Garland's guide, actually wanted to get to the destination. Lawrence was impressed with the leadership of the group. Sheikh Shakir, Abdullah's second-in-command, was an enthusiastic leader and Fauzan was the man who had captured Eshref the month before.

The force reached the rail line several days later and a preliminary reconnaissance was done. There were two double-storey buildings, a water tower, and surrounding tents which housed about 300 Turkish soldiers. A large 20-arch bridge, which had been previously attacked and damaged by Dakhilallah, another of Abdullah's leaders, lay to the north of the station. That night, the Arabs sheltered in the hills, having left a few riflemen close to the station to harass the approximately 400 Turks posted there. The Bedu riflemen kept the Turks awake and expectant of an attack.

Sheikh Shakir arrived with the main force the next evening. At the rendezvous point, his force turned out to be only 300 men rather than the 900 promised, so it was decided that a full-scale assault on the station could not be carried out. But Shakir did have two machine guns, a mountain gun, and a small howitzer. An alternative idea was hatched. The next morning a demolition party would be sent north to cut the rails and drop the telegraph wire just before the attack began.

That night, a small party with Lawrence and Raho descended on the line to the south to plant a mine. The party returned to the main group which was now in position with the artillery several hundred yards west of the station. Just as they arrived, the guns opened up on the station buildings and continued firing, expending around 50 rounds of shrapnel and 250 rounds of machine-gun ammunition until the upper storeys collapsed into the ground floors. A train that was sitting in the station was set on fire; its apparently inflammable stores burned fiercely. The locomotive, shielded behind a building and thus spared being hit by the artillery, cut itself loose

A blown multi-arch bridge. The drain of one arch was used for the explosives. (Edward Metcalf Collection, The Huntington Library, San Marino, California)

from its burning cargo and headed south in reverse, only to set off the explosives buried under the rail, knocking it off track.

Half the garrison deserted the station, but the troops in the southern building kept up their fire to defend the building. The Arabs, with Lawrence and Raho in tow, managed to capture around 20 Turks and some camels before they withdrew.

After returning to Abdullah's camp, Lawrence went out on another raid with Dakhilallah el-Gadhi and a smaller group of around 45 men with the express purpose of trying out the 'Garland' mine – which was what Lawrence named the cut-down rifle action. After experiencing a 1,500-feet-tall *haboob* (dust storm), the group found the railway at Kilometre 1121 and prepared the mine.[4] Lawrence buried rail-cutting charges 15 yards north and south of the trigger which was then buried and camouflaged to prevent detection.

Dakhilallah withdrew his men to a hilltop vantage point, set sentries to cover all the approaches to the position and then waited. It wasn't long before a trolley passed by and then a work party to repair poles knocked down by the storm. They were followed by a Turkish patrol which was closely inspecting the line looking for evidence of tampering. The soldiers found footprints at Kilometre 1121 and began to search, but after 20 minutes found nothing. Then the sound of a train was heard and Dakhilallah's men held their breath as it chugged north from Medina. They watched it roll over the mine but nothing happened. At first they were disappointed, but they then saw it was packed with the families – the wives and children – of the Turkish garrison. Perhaps it was providence, but the attackers were relieved; no one wanted the lives of innocents on their conscience.

Knowing he had to fix the failed mine, Lawrence went back to the site. To cover his work, Dakhilallah led his men down to the railway. A pious man with a bit of humour, he dismounted and led evening prayers in the middle of the tracks. As darkness set in, Lawrence went about the "most uninsurable business" of digging up the trigger and resetting it while surrounded on two sides with live explosives. When he was finished the men tore down the telegraph wire and blew up some rails to the north. Then the raiding party retired from the scene.

The next morning, a train with a work party and around 300 soldiers came to repair the rails damaged the evening before and hit the mine. Unfortunately, the two men left to watch had departed the scene quickly after seeing all the soldiers and could not say what damage had resulted. Lawrence heard the blast at their camp miles away.

Lawrence returned to Abdullah and thence to Feisul to carry on with his mission. Newcombe, in the meantime, had returned from his first attack to be told of the imminent Turkish withdrawal from Medina and the need to ensure the line was disrupted. He too went back to his attacks on the rail. Despite the usual difficulties

---

[4] A spot on the railway that measured 1,121 kilometres south from Damascus.

every Englishman – with the possible exception of Lawrence – railed about, Newcombe reported that his operations were generally successful. He complained about the lack of transport, a poor logistical situation, and the Turks' ability to repair damage quickly. He was assured by Feisul that things would improve. What he and other officers could not get out of their mind was the Arabs' unwillingness to move without being paid more than they could get from the Turks. At one point, a British officer asked a tribal leader if the men he was observing were fighting for Feisul, to which the Sheikh responded that they were there for the gold.

Newcombe's response to the news of the imminent Turkish withdrawal was to alter his tactics. He now planned to set upon the rail line in a determined fashion. His force would camp in dispersed groups close to the line, be resupplied regularly with convoys from the coast, and continually strike the line and any Turkish train or military formation.

Newcombe's report from early April outlines his accomplishments and his frustrations with the Arabs, especially their lack of discipline. Newcombe was very concerned with his inability to control the Arabs, thinking he was their commander rather than only an advisor.[5] After returning from his first foray against the line and reading Clayton's order to keep the line broken, Newcombe set out again with Mirzuk Tikheimi, a "clever" camel merchant from Mecca, along with 120 men, two machine guns, and a mountain gun. Ten of the men were trained in demolitions, but despite the fact that he was well supplied with explosives, Newcombe had to first dissuade Mirzuk from his intent to capture stations (to loot) and Turks (for reward). After enlisting Feisul to make sure that Mirzuk knew the primary mission was to stop the trains from running, the operation began.

Moving upcountry, Newcombe reported that he met many tribal parties going in the opposite direction to meet Feisul and opined that they would have been welcomed to assist his task. But they hadn't signed up for the revolt yet, and needed to first pay homage to Feisul. His next disappointment was arriving at an agreed forward resupply point to find the food that was supposed to be waiting for them had been taken by another sheikh, thus limiting the number of days he could remain in the field. Nevertheless, Mirzuk and Newcombe continued their work, striking the rail line, destroying 100 to 150 lengths of track with the explosives, cutting telegraph lines and harassing stations at several locations. In one instance, Mirzuk's men attacked the line, blowing a number of tracks and pulling down wire, after which they sat down on the rails to sing songs before they withdrew. The Turkish soldiers in a nearby station locked the doors and did not venture out to see what was happening. Newcombe's attempts to mine the railway were not as successful

---

[5] It was an issue that Lawrence would allude to in his 'Twenty-seven Articles' and that led to Newcombe's reassignment in early 1918.

because the Turks discovered most of the devices. It was admittedly difficult to erase all the tell-tale signs when the mines were emplaced at night.

At one point, Newcombe requested resupply because his stocks had been depleted. He would need more supplies or he would have to return to Wejh. On 1 April, Joyce dispatched the materials on two cars, a Rolls-Royce and a Ford, to meet Newcombe inland. He noted the mission would be a good test of the vehicles' capabilities. The experiment worked in so far as the cars made the journey inland and returned safely but Newcombe failed to meet them at the rendezvous. Intent on destruction of the railway, Newcombe's report ended with several observations that led him to suggest a long-term camp near the line, because the efficiency of the Turkish repair crews necessitated an attack every other day. He also advocated for a better supply system so the trained men could remain in action longer and not be required to shuttle supplies to and from the coast.

Newcombe's plan was a formula that might disrupt the Turkish withdrawal from Medina, but would expose Feisul's force to a Turkish response. His set-piece tactics were in sharp contrast to Lawrence's hit-and-run raids and would lead to a personal disagreement.

Overall though, it was clear the revolt had taken a turn for the better. Clayton summarized the situation in several reports from the Arab Bureau to London that emphasized the Ottoman position in Medina was strained. Using information from wireless intercepts, BMM officers, and field agents, Clayton detailed the Turkish order of battle in the Hejaz along with the Arab forces of Hussein that stood in opposition.[6] The Turks on the other hand had very little information on their enemy.

Another sign of the revolt's endurance was evidenced when Sherif Ali Haidar, the man the Ottoman-Turks wanted to replace Hussein in Mecca, returned to Syria because his mission was impossible to carry out. The Turks did not want him to be captured. Withdrawals of non-essential personnel from Medina continued and civilians were being forced out of the city because the food and fuel situation was becoming strained. Fakhri also increased his security on the rail line itself in an effort to prevent Arab guerrilla forces from disrupting it further. The Turkish counter-guerrilla tactics were simplistic, however, and limited to a linear defence of the line with little or no effort made to separate the fish from the sea that supported them.

Emir Feisul was attempting to accomplish the tactical goal of crippling the Hejaz railway while also consolidating the many tribes of the region onto his side. He was wary of moving too fast as he did not want any wavering or hostile groups operating behind him as he moved north. He brought the northern nomadic Bedouin into the revolt – the Howeitat, Beni Sakhr, Rualla, Anzeh and others – but told the

---

[6] For a detailed Order of Battle, see Appendix 1.

semi-nomadic tribes to remain quiet and await orders. He knew the Turks would be apt to seek reprisals on those who possessed land.

Further south, Hussein's forces under Abdullah, Ali, and Zeid were engaged in a desultory campaign of harassing the Ottoman forces around Medina and the railway itself. They were not in a position to take the city as they lacked most things needed to do so: manpower, firepower, training, and the will necessary to overcome the occupier's defences. They did prove a deterrent to Fakhri, who had settled back into a defensive posture and was unlikely to venture out. To do so would have subjected the Ottoman forces to harassing raids and an even more uncertain logistical lifeline if operations extended much beyond the city limits. The Turks also chose to conduct a static defence of the 1,300-kilometre-long railway, employing several armoured trains and increasing the troops at the blockhouses along the line. The security forces did not venture far from their hardened shelters and only concerned themselves with the railway, not the surrounding territory that hid the guerrillas. Given the limited number of troops and their poor mobility, aggressive counter-guerrilla operations would have been a nearly impossible task.

Aziz al-Masri had begun to make some progress with his training of a conventional force but he was still frustrated with Sherif Hussein and Emir Ali. His troops were made up mostly of Meccans (city-dwellers), along with Syrians and Yemenis who had been taken prisoner and had volunteered to fight for the cause. By February, his force had reached 1,500 men. But in early March, al-Masri decided he could no longer work for Hussein and quit his post to return to his home. He was replaced by another former Ottoman officer, Ja'far Pasha al-Askari, the same Ja'far who had been captured by the British during the Senussi uprising and had been languishing in prison in Cairo. Upon hearing that many of his Arab compatriots had been hanged by Djemal Pasha in Damascus, he foreswore his previous allegiance and offered his services to Hussein. He would have better luck than al-Masri in the position. Ja'far would become Feisul's chief of staff.

The Arabs, maturing as a military force, were starting to come into their own. From an inauspicious beginning, they had reached a point where they were about to become more than a distraction for the Ottoman forces. They were turning into an auxiliary – a surrogate – force able to protect and to some extent secure General Murray's Egyptian Expeditionary Force's right flank through hit-and-run guerrilla raids.

CHAPTER FIVE

Akaba

When Lawrence returned to Wejh in February he warned Feisul of Brémond's intentions. Specifically, he told Feisul that Brémond wanted Allied troops to land at Akaba to restrict Hussein to operations in the Hejaz. Beyond informing him of Brémond's duplicity, Lawrence also decided to tell Feisul about the Sykes-Picot Treaty, which had been concluded in May 1916. Its provisions included a description of how the Middle East would be carved up into spheres of influence to be shared among Britain, France, and Russia after the war. The Arabs were only to be told that the Allies would help them create an independent state, not that the area had been divided up.

Lawrence knew enough of the still-secret treaty to understand that Hussein's claims to Syria were in danger and that the Allied governments did not intend to honour their previous commitments. He shared the information because he felt the Allied governments of France and the United Kingdom were duplicitous, promising the Arabs an independent homeland while planning to occupy and oversee parts of the promised territory at war's end. He knew also that if the secret was revealed elsewhere (as it would be) and he had not told Feisul, their relationship would be damaged. Lawrence was not alone in this. Newcombe, Joyce, and Wilson also objected and protested the policy in messages to Cairo.

Another factor played to Lawrence's decision: under the terms of the treaty, for the provision on Arab independence to be effective, they had to capture Damascus, Homs, Hama, and Aleppo. Lawrence reasoned that trusting Feisul with the secret would give him further impetus to move north and abandon the limited campaign of isolating Medina. If they captured those cities ahead of the Allies, the Arabs would have grounds to dispute the treaty.

Feisul had two choices: reveal his knowledge of the treaty to his father, which would probably enrage the Grand Sherif and endanger further Allied support (as well as getting Lawrence cashiered) or keep the secret to himself and drive his army north towards Damascus with British help. Feisul struck a devil's bargain with Lawrence and went for the golden ring that was Damascus.

Lawrence's revelations led Feisul to reconsider his options for the revolt. Unlike his brothers who spoke of the revolt in abstract terms and with little in the way of

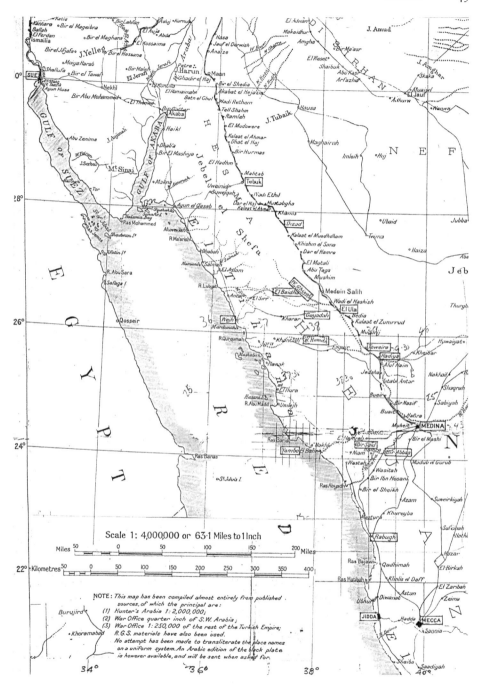

Scale 1: 4,000,000 or 63·1 Miles to 1 Inch

Miles
Kilometres

NOTE: This map has been compiled almost entirely from published
sources, of which the principal are:
(1) Hunter's Arabia 1: 2,000,000;
(2) War Office quarter inch of S.W. Arabia;
(3) War Office 1: 250,000 of the rest of the Turkish Empire;
R.G.S. materials have also been used.
No attempt has been made to transliterate the place names
on a uniform system. An Arabic edition of the black plate
is however available, and will be sent when asked for.

military tactics except in the near term, Feisul thought of the strategic end goal and how best to achieve it. For the moment, he was preoccupied with tribal negotiations, but all the while he was contemplating his next move. He knew his brothers, Abdullah, Ali, and Zeid, were fully capable of investing and possibly capturing Medina. His help was not needed there.

As Feisul explained it to Newcombe, he had two options. His first was to move along the railway, clearing the Turkish posts north to capture Ma'an; then, using Akaba as a base, he would move north towards Damascus. His second option was to proceed to the Druse Mountains (Jebel Druse) and descend on the railway between Damascus and Ma'an and Dera'a and Afuleh. Newcombe tried to steer Feisul towards the second option opining that it would be more economical and quicker than the first. It was clear that Feisul wanted to be finished with operations in the Wejh area and move north as soon as possible to bring the revolt to Syria. Feisul's immediate plan was to advance north, leapfrogging several small towns along the coast. Feisul also shared his plan to capture Akaba by sea with Vickery who thought it feasible but counselled that while taking Akaba might be easy, holding it would be difficult.

Clayton's response to Feisul's plans was that the "business at hand" – to defeat the Turks at Medina – needed to be finished first. He clarified his position in an internal letter to Wingate, which stated "the occupation of Akaba by Arab troops might well result in the Arabs claiming that place hereafter, and it is by no means improbable that after the war Akaba may be of considerable importance to the future defence scheme of Egypt. It is thus essential that Akaba should remain in British hands after the war". Despite his support for the Arab Revolt, Clayton was not altruistic; he was as mindful of 'Empire' as the most ardent imperialist. Wingate Pasha also said as much in a 18 June 1917 letter written to Sir William Robertson, CIGS, specifically that "the local needs of the moment, as I see them, are to secure a permanent British predominance on the Eastern Red Sea Littoral".

Lawrence, on the other hand, was not an imperialist. He knew that Feisul had to move north to eventually capture Damascus to satisfy the terms of Sykes-Picot as he understood them and Akaba was key to those operations. He also understood that Akaba could not be captured from the sea, as Feisul envisioned. A landing at Akaba would require his forces to advance up Wadi Itm, which would be impossible if the Turks had time to prepare defences.

Lawrence was well acquainted with the idea of capturing Akaba from the sea. General Murray had asked the Arab Bureau to study the idea and Lawrence did much of the analysis. In short, the long, narrow defile of Wadi Itm would permit the Turks to easily defend against a landing from the sea. Having seen the aerial reconnaissance reports, he knew the only way to success was to capture Akaba from the landward side. Feisul, as well as Newcombe and Brémond, failed to see or understand that tactical detail. Second, he knew the attack had to be done secretly so as not to alert the Turks. If the Turks became aware of an Arab plan, they would defend Akaba as well as the eastern approaches down Wadi Itm and close off that avenue for the duration of the war. For the moment, Lawrence tried to dissuade Feisul from any operations to the north and counselled patience. The time was not yet ripe.

Lawrence did not tell anyone he had revealed the existence of Sykes-Picot to Feisul, nor did he mention his thoughts on taking Akaba. In the first place, the treaty was still secret and he would be risking treason charges and, second, Brémond would object to any plan to take Akaba. Clayton would likely forbid the operation in any event.

Through February and March, operations against the railway continued. Feisul seemed to accept Lawrence's counsel to go slowly, but he was still itching to head north, Lawrence's information about Sykes-Picot had upset him greatly and rumours that the French were about to land 60,000 troops in Syria added to his worries. If that happened, he told Joyce, he would fight the Turks first and then the French. Joyce was beginning to understand that Feisul's ambitions were more than local.

When Lawrence returned from Wadi Ais, he met a greatly distraught Feisul. He now saw that it was time to advance the plan for Akaba. He had argued against Newcombe's plan of concentrating near the rail line or occupying stations, insisting that Newcombe's column would be an easy target for a Turkish countermove. To divert the Turks, he advocated for a small force conducting raids near Ma'an as a good way to occupy the Turkish forces. The other British officers were dismissive as they were focused on "rail smashing" operations in the areas closer to Medina.

Colonel Joyce looking comfortable on a camel at Akaba. (Gilman Family Collection)

Lieutenant Gilman in Akaba by W. F. Stirling. (Gilman Family Collection)

Newcombe and Hornby were convinced they could disable the Turkish supply line indefinitely, but were oft frustrated by their Arab charges. First, Ramadan intruded and none of the Bedu would fight during the Holy month. Additionally, the Turkish security patrols were extremely effective at discovering the demolition charges laid at night – it was difficult to hide tracks in the dark. Garland did not believe they could destroy enough rail as supplies of repair material seemed inexhaustible.

Two tenders, LC341 and LC1105, on the 'road'. (Gilman Family Collection)

Armoured car LC0809 in the field. (Gilman Family Collection)

Another factor that entered into Lawrence's calculations was a decision that divided the command responsibilities for the Arab Revolt. Sir Reginald Wingate, one of the revolt's original enthusiastic supporters, was given control of operations only in the Hejaz, south of the Ma'an–Akaba line, while General Murray was given responsibility to the north. Lawrence knew that Murray needed to be convinced of the revolt's worth once it moved north of the Ma'an–Akaba line or the support previously provided by Wingate would dry up. That said, Wingate had supported the idea of operations to disrupt the Turkish lines of communication carried out from the vicinity of Jebel Druse.

Lawrence saw that the Egyptian Expeditionary Force's advance would leave its right flank open and vulnerable to a Turkish attack. If Akaba was taken and the EEF's flank thereby protected, Murray might see the Arab Revolt in a better light. And if coordinated operations between Murray's conventional and Feisul's unconventional forces took place, Lawrence felt that British support for the Northern Army would continue unabated.

After enduring several Turkish incursions against the British lines, the EEF had begun to move east to start its own offensive operations in December 1916. Murray had prepared the route thoroughly by placing forward supply dumps, building rail lines and laying water pipelines to sustain the force in their march across the Sinai and into Palestine. Although the British succeeded in advancing to Rafa, the first attempt at taking Gaza failed in March 1917.

Several weeks later, Murray prepared a second attempt. The British War Council had given him the new objective of Jerusalem. Once again, with the Turks forewarned and a dearth of British artillery support, the offensive failed. The Egyptian front fell again into stasis. Beside the capture of Wejh, the only good news from the region was the fall of Baghdad to the British led by General Maude on 11 April.

Never one to toe the line, Lawrence secretly decided to go ahead with his plan for Akaba before his superiors figured out what he was doing. Lawrence and Auda abu Tayi, an eastern Howeitat chieftain, planned an approach from the landward side. It would not be an easy mission. And, although some Arab leaders had previously contemplated capturing Akaba, it would not have been possible without the cooperation of many tribes working together or of others permitting the raiders to pass through their territory – their unity was a result of the trust Lawrence had earned with Feisul and the gold he brought to the revolt.

Lawrence's concept of operations was simple, but simple did not equate to easy. He had discussed the plan with Feisul and Auda, one of Feisul's fiercest allies. Auda was ready and willing to fight with Feisul and Lawrence saw his involvement would be crucial to the mission's success. Auda would enlist the support of his people and local leaders from the territory around Ma'an to permit the transit of the raiding force through their lands and to recruit more men as they moved.

Unlike Feisul, whom Lawrence considered politically ambitious but not well versed in military affairs, Auda was a warrior who claimed he had killed over 70 men in

Auda abu Tayi (centre) and two brothers. (Harry Chase, James A. Cannavino Library, Archives & Special Collections, Marist College, USA)

single combat (he didn't count Turks). Auda was a brigand experienced in *ghrazzus*, the traditional raids that were a hallmark of Bedu life in the desert. He seemed to be a man with a violent disposition towards the Ottoman Empire. After all, he was a wanted man, branded an outlaw by the Turks for killing some of their tax collectors.

The plan to take Akaba was ambitious. It would involve an over 300-mile camel trek through the desert. The route would take Auda and Lawrence cross-country, east over the Hejaz railway then northeast to Wadi al Sirhan on the edge of the great Nefud Desert and into Auda's home territory east of Ma'an. Once their recruiting drive was complete, they would turn west, cross the railway again and head down Wadi Itm to Akaba.

In Lawrence's mind, the raid was a purely Arab affair and he carried nothing that could be construed as British support. The men, the arms, explosives, and £22,000 in gold were Feisul's alone. Lawrence told his British colleagues and superiors that Feisul intended to strike the rail lines between Ma'an and Damascus to divert the Turks and keep them from moving south against Newcombe's and Garland's operations near el-Ula. This manoeuvre would mask his true intention (and Feisul's) of taking Akaba, which would be 'incidental'. For the first time, he would be truly on his own as a guerrilla advisor deep behind enemy lines.

Moreover, Lawrence was putting his head on the block to advance his agenda. First, he wanted Feisul to move north, counter to the desires of the French. Second, he wanted to take and hold Akaba as a secure logistical base to support his northern operations, and last, he wanted to abandon the goal of capturing Medina as he knew that remaining in the Hejaz, would undermine the revolt's true purpose of uniting all Arabs, especially those in the north. Taking Akaba would give Feisul the initiative over his brothers, preeminence in the revolt, and would serve to fulfil the conditions of the Sykes-Picot Treaty, which filled Lawrence with guilt and a sense of duplicity.

Lawrence was the only outsider to witness the mission that followed. It would be difficult to improve on his description in *Seven Pillars of Wisdom*; what follows is a summary of the mission. The capture of Akaba ranks as one of the most audacious and daring undertakings of the Great War and which to date has rarely been equalled.

It was classic irregular warfare and, by definition, a special operation. As the only British guerrilla advisor to the small band, Lawrence was in his element. He had learned how to balance the spontaneous nature of the Arab with the high strictures of the British military profession. He had learned how to influence Arab leaders to act, but at their own speed and how they knew best. That said, he avoided Arab leaders, like Abdullah, who did not respond to his methods.

Led by Sherif Nasir ibn Ali ibn Radha, one of Feisul's most able lieutenants, the small group departed Wejh on 9 May 1917. Not more than 40 men, it included Lawrence and Nesib al-Bekri, a Syrian nationalist who had been imploring Feisul to bring the uprising to his lands. Auda would be met at Nebk on 2 June.

They faced a formidable adversary: the desert. It was a place that could not be overcome, it could only be survived. This expedition would prove this as they travelled from the relatively easy plains, wadis, and hills of the coast into a hellish place called *al Houl* – The Terror.

They prepared their camel loads in anticipation of a long, hard journey. The Arab quartermaster packed flour instead of rice because it was lighter and, therefore, they could carry more. Feisul's gold was distributed among all the riders so that if calamity befell one or two men, or a small group of the party all would not be lost. Explosives were packed securely on the camels and each man carried several water skins. Water would be the key to survival and each segment of travel was planned with that in mind. Knowing the location of functioning wells and how to reach them would be the only way the expedition could survive the crossing.

To those remaining behind, it appeared the party's destination was Jefer to begin establishing forward supply points for the anticipated operations in Syria.

The first stage was easy but the expected trials awaiting them counselled slow movement so as not to affect the camels' endurance. The path was busy. After several days' travel inland, the party encountered Lieutenant Hornby returning from a railway-wrecking expedition with another of Feisul's demolitions teams. Hornby reported his success and that Newcombe had already headed back to Wejh to discuss new operations with Feisul. (One of Lawrence's more memorable descriptions of a fellow officer was of Hornby, whom he described as a wild engineer who would worry the steel rails with his teeth if he ran low on explosives.)

Soon they reached the railway. After carefully reconnoitring the area they began to wreak a bit of destruction by blasting a few lengths of track. They cut the telegraph wires and tied them to the saddles of six camels that were driven into the wadi on the eastern side. Twanging wires and snapping poles were music to the raiders' ears as they rode on until the camels could pull no more. Once freed of the tangled burden, the group continued onward, deeper into the desert with Auda singing poetically about the power of the explosives he had witnessed for the first time.

On the far side of the tracks the party entered the hot desolate plain called *al Houl*. Progress was 50 miles a day through the arid waste with the sun burning them from above, its reflection off the glittering sand searing their eyes. Lawrence foolishly asked Auda to enter the Great Nefud, perhaps for no other reason than several British explorers had done so before. The Nefud desert was an even more treacherous belt of sand dunes, traversed – as Auda counselled – only of necessity and on healthy camels, which they did not have. And so, they moved further north, across the sun's anvil, hopping from well to well, towards Wadi al Sirhan and the hopes of finding the friendly tribes with whom they could ally.

The desert was unkind, as one of Lawrence's servants discovered when he fell off his camel. Luckily he was found delirious hours later by Lawrence who had ridden back to save him. Unkind too were the other tribes who rode in the desert and sniped at them in the darkness of night. They could not risk discovery of their identity or their mission by anyone who might be supportive of or paid by the Turks.

At the end of May, Auda located his fellow Howeitat tribesmen who were on the move with their flocks searching for water and fodder. A great celebration ensued and days of feasting were the order. Auda departed to the north seeking allies and met with the Rualla chief, Nuri Shaalan, who was supportive of Feisul's revolt but not willing to rise up at the moment, exposed as he was to the Turks. Auda gave Nuri £6,000 to suffer the raiders' presence in the Wadi which was his tribe's territory.

Recruitment of other tribes was bringing the raiders' numbers up in their new camp at Nebk. But there was also disaffection from within as Nesib al-Bekri felt that the intermediate goal of taking Akaba was unnecessary. He wanted to take his gold and raise the Syrian tribes to achieve greater things but he had unrealistic goals. He wanted to attack Dera'a and Damascus, not accepting Lawrence's argument that to take those places prematurely would invite retribution from the Ottomans and be an unsustainable objective. Nesib was reluctantly released from his obligations to Feisul and his departure brought the question of Akaba to the fore, some leaders questioning whether or not Nesib should be followed north. Lawrence explained to them that raising the Syrians to revolt early was premature. Feisul's forces were not yet in a position to support or protect the Syrian tribes. Lawrence decided to prove his assessment and rode north with two companions to gauge the level of Syrian support for Hussein's revolt. It was to be another daring feat within the one he was already undertaking.

On this leg of the journey, Lawrence took on a classic task as a special operator and intelligence operative: along with seeking intelligence on Turkish dispositions, he was also trying to determine the intentions and leanings of the tribal chieftains in Syria. This information would be crucial to choosing future courses of action and identifying which tribes were capable of assisting the revolt and in what manner. He observed not only the chiefs' attitudes, but the strengths and weaknesses of the tribes, as well as their location and vulnerability to the enemy. Although, Lawrence had an agenda, specifically to ensure the plan for Akaba was undertaken, the information he gathered on this trip would be valuable to future operations as well.

During the trip he demonstrated demolitions to the Anazeh Shiekh Dhami by blowing up a small steel bridge at Ras Baalbek on 10 June. He met with leaders, including Sherif Nuri Shalaan, a powerful chief who would be very important to Feisul when his campaign finally reached Syria nearly a year later. After being convinced that none of the chiefs was willing or actually in a position to actively support the revolt at that moment, he decided to exploit Nesib's departure with a deception plan that would convince the Turks that the Arabs were in fact moving further north and not towards Ma'an and Akaba. This included spreading rumours that they planned to man a base at the old castle at Azrak and taking credit for two raids carried out 140 miles north of Ma'an that blew sections of rail and damaged a repair locomotive.

Lawrence's deception may have been inadvertently aided by Newcombe who, during a skirmish with a Turkish force, lost his pack that contained maps and notes that discussed plans for attacking Dera'a and Damascus. The documents seemed to convince the enemy that the threat existed as a 400-man force was sent out to find the Arabs. A Turkish garrison at Tadmor to the northeast of Dera'a was instructed to remain in that location in anticipation of rebel activity.

The ruse also served to confuse Lawrence's superiors who learned from signals intercepts and other intelligence, including a report on the destruction of the Ras Baalbek bridge, that something was afoot.

He then returned to camp to find Auda eager to launch the attack on Akaba. The first step was to recross the rail line, while further diversionary attacks took place northwest of Ma'an and the main attack at their crossing point of Ghadir el Hajj at Kilometre 479 south of Ma'an. The hope was to keep the Turks occupied away from Wadi Itm, the valley that descended towards Akaba, the raiders' first objective.

The Turks, however, had already reacted to a small attack on Fuweilah southwest of Ma'an by sending a 550-man battalion to relieve the post, then occupying Aba el Lissan – directly on the route Auda intended to take.

Lawrence dryly described the battle that followed in his formal report with militarily important facts such as unit designations, numbers killed and wounded, prisoners captured, road conditions and supply levels. In *Seven Pillars*, the narrative is charged with the emotion of the battle.

After being told of the Turkish battalion's arrival, Auda, Nasir, and Lawrence knew they needed to move quickly or their long trip would be wasted. The Ottoman battalion blocked their way forward. Marching immediately, the raiders reached Aba el Lissan on 2 July. They found the Turkish forces poorly positioned and camped in a valley near a well. The troops had just arrived in the area and appeared to be inexperienced, based on how poorly they were tending to their own security.

The Arabs moved into position above the enemy on the high ground that surrounded the valley and began to shoot down upon the Turks. Through the day, the air and ground on which they lay grew hot as the sun rose. Their rifle barrels, hotter still, blistered their hands and many suffered so greatly from the heat they had to be withdrawn from the line and placed in the shade to recover.

The Turks responded with ineffective rifle and howitzer fire, but their sights couldn't identify targets and the cannon fire simply went over the hills into the void beyond, hurting no one.

In the afternoon, Lawrence too was overcome and lay down in the shade trying to drink water from a small hollow in the hills.

This is where Auda found and challenged him, saying, "How is it with the Howeitat?

"All talk and no work!" Lawrence cheekily answered. "They shoot a lot and hit little."

This prompted an enraged Auda to rally his men and charge down the hill directly into the midst of the frightened Turks. At Nasir's urging, Lawrence jumped on his camel to follow and plunged down the hill with the howling mob.

The first indication that something was awry was when his camel went tumbling heels over head down the long slope of the hill. Lawrence flew over the animal's head and hit the ground hard, knocking him unconscious for moments. Seconds or minutes later he awoke to find himself in the middle of a gun battle. Turkish soldiers were firing their Mausers at screaming Bedouin rebels while the Arabs replied with their Enfields. Swords flashed as Turkish officers tried to defend themselves from the onslaught. The Turkish enlisted men turned and ran or died fighting. Lawrence thought he would be impaled on a Turkish bayonet as the fight swirled about him. He was defenceless at the moment; all his personal weapons had been lost when he was dismounted.

Then a shadow passed over him and Lawrence turned to see Auda grinning at him from his mount. His cloak had been pierced by numerous bullets, his binoculars destroyed, and his sword scabbard bent where it was struck by another. The battle was over.

Lawrence glanced across the field and saw many Turks dead or dying while others were being pursued over the next ridge line. They too would soon fall. He would have preferred more prisoners, but there was little he could do at that point.

He looked at his camel. She had been a splendid animal, but he was even more dismayed when he discovered the wound that felled her was in the back of her head. In the fever of the charge, he had accidentally shot his own mount. Lawrence would mourn only briefly as there was still much work to be done.

He quickly interrogated several prisoners who revealed that their expedition was in little danger from the Turks at Ma'an as only two companies remained there. Then, despite the urge to capture Ma'an (which could not be long held), the raiders rode on, down Wadi Itm valley towards Akaba, leaving several parties behind to harass and capture small outposts on the road to Ma'an to frighten its garrison.

The closing engagement at Akaba was an anti-climax compared to the battle at Aba el Lissan. Most of the Turks had withdrawn from their posts to the mouth of the valley at Khadra four miles from the sea. The Arab force had grown to over 1,000 men as local tribes got word of Auda's presence. To their front, around 300 Turks waited securely in their fortified bunkers and trenches, which protected them from an attack from the sea, not from the valley behind them. After two days of negotiations the Turks, who had plenty of water and ammunition, surrendered believing the Arabs had sufficient provisions when they actually had none.

Once past Khadra, the Arab Army raced the final few miles to Akaba and met no opposition. They celebrated by splashing into the waters of the gulf. But Lawrence knew that he had only a little time before the army ran out of food and the Turks put together a force to retake the port, which the Arabs would be unable to stop without heavy weapons and reinforcement. At this critical moment, the Arabs needed naval backup and resupply – but first he needed to tell Cairo of the 'incidental' victory.

The next day, Lawrence set out on camel with a small escort to cross the Sinai Desert heading for the Suez Canal 150 miles away. It was 7 July 1917 and everything had changed.

CHAPTER SIX

Rearrangement[1]

On 9 July, after a 50-hour ride across the desert, Lawrence crossed the Suez by boat and arrived at a rail station to catch a train to Cairo. There he learned that General Archibald Murray was gone, relieved of command after the failure of the Second Battle of Gaza and replaced by General Edmund Allenby on 28 June. Lawrence was worried that the efforts made by the Arab Bureau to win Murray over to supporting the revolt would be for naught. He felt the task of winning the new commander over to the cause would have to be repeated. En route at Ismailia station, he met one of Admiral Wemyss' Red Sea Patrol officers and was able to arrange for supplies to be sent straight away to Akaba on the HMS *Dufferin*.

In Cairo, Lawrence first went to the Savoy Hotel and met with his boss, General Clayton, who had just finished a report to London stating that nothing significant had happened in the past week. He quickly revised the report as he excitedly questioned Lawrence about his trials and ordeals. Clayton's hesitation over Arab possession of Akaba was replaced by the realization that the revolt had suddenly jumped 250 miles north and significantly changed the strategic calculus in the region.

Lawrence was then taken to meet Allenby, who wanted to congratulate him, but who also wanted to talk about his ideas for Feisul's northern operations.

Lawrence had sketched out his ideas for Clayton with a map that proposed using Akaba as a base to support operations in the Syrian desert northward towards Damascus and Aleppo. His plan laid out seven locations where an anticipated force of up to 8,000 Arab rebels could interdict Turkish rail lines and bridges and disrupt traffic. That, along with local uprisings, would serve to assist Allenby's advance.

He put down two conditions for the plan to go forward: the first was material and financial support for the Arabs, the second for Allenby to move forward and engage the Turkish forces in Palestine. Without that support, a general uprising in Syria would fail.

Allenby must have been intrigued as well as amused by Lawrence who had come to the meeting still in Arab mufti, much to the shock of many of the staid British officers on the staff. On top of that, he'd dared to propose a major operation and

---

[1] The title of Lawrence's chapter 61 in *Seven Pillars*.

General Edmund Allenby, side view, close-up. (Harry Chase, James A. Cannavino Library, Archives & Special Collections, Marist College, USA)

essentially told Allenby to commit his forces to the offensive. It was Allenby's intent to do so in any event, but Lawrence didn't know that and it required extreme confidence for a mere captain to engage a superior so boldly.

At the end of the interview, Allenby was convinced and said, "I will do for you what I can."

Allenby and Clayton believed that not all of Lawrence's plan would or could be carried out, and Lawrence later admitted to inflating the Arabs' capability, but he was the only person in the headquarters who could judge. Allenby sent a telegram to General Robertson at the War Office in London recommending Lawrence's plan be adopted. He received the approval the following day. The news of Akaba's capture and Lawrence's solo ride through Syria quickly spread. And, for his audacity, he was promoted to major.

To the south, emirs Abdulla and Feisul continued unabated with the railway-breaking operations from el-Ula towards Toweira. Feisul's camp had been moved inland to a location near Jeidah where the other officers of the BMM – Newcombe, Garland, Davenport and Hornby – were striking out against multiple targets. Sherif Ali's and Zeid's efforts from Bir el Mashi to Medina had yielded some benefits including cutting up a relief force sent by Hussein's rival, ibn Rashid, that resulted in around 80 Turks killed and 250 captured, along with four mountain guns, 200 rifles, and a large number of camels and sheep. Fakhri Pasha had pulled many of his outposts closer to Medina as a result of the engagements. As Clayton wrote in a 11 July 1917 report to the Chief of the Imperial General Staff (CIGS) at the War Office in London, "the number of Turks thus shown to be immobilized by the Arab Rebellion, and the extra strain imposed on the rolling stock of the Syrian and Arabia Railway System is ample justification from the military point of view for the expense involved". He also opined that the revolt must be the cause of "grave anxiety and embarrassment".[2]

The antiquated BE2c aircraft of 'C' Flight were also put to good use as aerial reconnaissance platforms and to bomb and strafe Turkish positions along the railway including the railyard at el-Ula. The detailed photographs the pilots took and sketch maps they made proved invaluable in preparation for operations.

Because of the Arab pressure, Fakhri reinforced his defensive positions along the railway in the view of a possible, eventual withdrawal north. But, his plan did not include aggressive counter-guerrilla patrolling that would have threatened the Arab rebels. Instead, the Hejaz railway became a linear defence structure of fortified stations, hilltop camps, and blockhouses along the length of the line. With railway and security and construction companies based at Ma'an, el-Ula, and Medain Saleh, destruction of the rail line became more difficult and breaks were repaired quicker.

Adding to their difficulties, Newcombe and other officers were disappointed by the martial qualities of the Bedu tribesmen and bitterly complained in their reports about the difficulty of working with them. Garland especially advocated using the "trained Arabs" under Ja'far Pasha al-Askari rather than the unpredictable and hard-to-control Bedouin.[3]

Ja'far Pasha al-Askari's Arab Army Regulars at Akaba. (Gilman Family Collection)

---

[2] It was at this point in his report that Lawrence came into Clayton's office to give him the "marvellous" news of Akaba.

[3] Garland would be withdrawn from the Hejaz because of his health prior to the end of the war.

Pierce Joyce, now a brevet lieutenant-colonel, who had mostly been attending to operational support of the Arabs at Wejh, was directed by Wilson to undertake his own railway-breaking mission. Launching from Wejh on 26 June with 30 Egyptian troops (and possibly Lieutenant Gilman), he was met by 300 of Abdullah's men led by Sherif Fanean.[4] They moved at night to a location close to the line at Wegir, set up flank security and descended on the line in the early morning. They set and fired over 800 charges and pulled down telegraph wires while being shelled and shot at from a Turkish position nearby. The Arabs had set out security on Joyce's flanks and they kept the Turks from attacking while the demolitions were completed. Joyce then took his force south towards Toweira and repeated the attack with 1,600 pounds of guncotton and an additional 300 Arabs. There they laid over 1,400 charges and destroyed a six-kilometre length of track. After he got back to his base at Wejh, Joyce had no negative comments to report about the Arabs other than they were useless for laying charges, a task that he and his Egyptians undertook.

Perhaps as a result of increased Turkish activity on the line or his desire to put it out of action completely, Newcombe began to drive himself and his charges harder. One operation nearly cost him and Captain Davenport dearly. Along with Ja'far Pasha al-Askari and 400 regulars mounted on horse and camel, he departed Wejh to attack the line. The force also carried two mountain guns and two machine guns. Reaching the line, a reconnaissance was conducted and a decision was made to destroy the rails near the station at Sahl al-Matran. On 26 July, Newcombe and his sappers set charges and destroyed a small number of rails.[5] As the charges went off, the attackers realized the Turks were moving in to intercept them and a firefight broke out. After a sharp skirmish, Newcombe and Ja'far escaped with their men.

They hoped to set up a temporary base in an old castle at Qala'at el Zumrud (Zumurrud), which lay west of the station on the rail line. Before they reached the castle, the Turks engaged them and another firefight ensued. A flanking attack by a mounted unit left the Turkish troops exposed and Ja'far was able to press forward and capture the station. Newcombe was now free to set out his charges, after which the force withdrew to the castle to camp. The next morning Ja'far and his force returned to Feisul's camp, leaving Newcombe behind with his small force of sappers. Newcombe was intent on destroying the line and moved back to the railway to attack it again at a nearby location, but was unaware that the Turks had sent out a trainload of reinforcements in response to the first raid. Newcombe's element was surprised and quickly engaged with the Turks in an intense battle. He and his men

---

[4] Major John Bassett, Colonel Wilson's deputy and a close confident of General Wingate, stood in for Joyce at Wejh during his absence.

[5] The damage was insignificant and repaired in several days.

barely escaped capture, but he mislaid his rucksack filled with sketch maps and notes he had made on the campaign. It was picked up by the Turks.[6]

It was early August 1917 and nearly a month had passed since Akaba had fallen to the Arabs. The British Military Mission was still intent on investing Medina to hold Fakhri Pasha's army in place and to disrupt the Turkish line of communication – the Hejaz railway – between Ma'an and Medina.

As he listened to Lawrence's plan, Allenby immediately understood the significance of Akaba and how the Arab forces could underpin and secure his right flank beyond the River Jordan. Like Lawrence, Allenby grasped that taking Medina was of secondary importance. What Feisul's forces could do in his area of responsibility was more significant. Lawrence suggested and Allenby agreed that Feisul's Northern Army should be placed under his command. Lawrence remained a principal advisor to Feisul. Lawrence understood that just as Feisul had built a coalition of supportive tribes to arrive at Wejh, he would now need to do the same with the Syrian Arabs of the Hauran region south of Damascus. But first, Akaba needed to be readied for its role as the newest 'unassailable' base. Troops had to be shifted and defences set up to prevent the Turks from recapturing the port. Although Medina would

The men and weapons of the Hejaz Armoured Car Battery. (Gilman Family Collection)

[6] Whether the bag was either dropped on purpose or not is unknown; Lawrence suggested it was a deliberate ruse to deceive the Turks.

The HACB. Lawrence of Arabia standing at front of second car from left in Arab headgear with inset enlargement of TEL. (Gilman Family Collection)

remain invested by the Southern Army until the end of the war, the move north was about to begin.

To ensure the security of the port, Lawrence prevailed upon the commander of the Red Sea Patrol once again. Admiral Wemyss quickly agreed to support Akaba with his flagship, the four-funnel HMS *Euryalus*, after having already sent the *Dufferin* with supplies. *Euryalus* with its 29 guns would stand guard at the port from 27 July to 4 August to ward off the enemy before being replaced by the nine-gun monitor HMS *Humber*.

CHAPTER SEVEN

Northern Operations

Lawrence's first task was to obtain Grand Sherif Hussein's permission for Feisul to be placed under Allenby. General Wingate, as the Resident, would retain control of operations in the Hejaz, but readily agreed that the Arab Northern Army should take its direction from the EEF Headquarters in Cairo as its greater use would be with Allenby.

Lawrence left Cairo for Jeddah on 17 July to meet with Colonel Wilson and to brief Hussein and convince him that Feisul should be "cut over" to Allenby. Wilson and he anticipated a hard sell as Hussein had proven to be obstinate and suspicious, as well as wily. Luckily, the ground work done by Wilson eliminated any difficulties and Hussein agreed to Feisul's assignment with Allenby as 'Supreme Commander' of the Arab forces operating out of Akaba.

Lawrence first travelled to Wejh where Captain F. W. Stent, the new commander of 'C' Flight, flew him to Feisul's advance base 100 miles inland at Jeida. There, along with Newcombe and Joyce, he first told Feisul the story of how they captured Akaba and then worked out the details of transferring the army to Akaba. The following morning, he returned to the waiting *Dufferin* and proceeded on to Jeddah where the task of convincing Hussein had been made easier by Wilson's preparation. Wilson's political and diplomatic skills would be tried intensely in the months to come as Hussein often tried to interfere with or became suspicious of his son's activities.

The move north to Akaba would require a realignment of personnel. Wilson discussed the makeup of the BMM with Lawrence in late July 1917. Clayton had also talked about it in Cairo and one of the key changes was to Newcombe's position: his service would no longer be required. Even before the capture of Akaba, Newcombe had been frustrated with the failure to break the line completely and was close to being burned out. He wanted some time away and would later return to the Palestinian Front and take part in the Beersheba operation.[1] Clayton and

---

[1] Newcombe conducted a diversionary raid with less than 100 men near Hebron that succeeded in diverting six battalions and helped ensure Allenby's victory. Unfortunately, he and his men were captured and spent the remainder of the war as POWs.

NORTHERN OPERATIONS

+++++ *Hejaz Railway*

✈ *Advance Landing Ground*

0 10 20 30 40 50 miles

Beirut
Baalbek
Damascus
Kiswe
Hauran
Jebel Druse
Lake Tiberius
Tell el Shehab
Haifa
Afuleh
Dera'a
Umtaiye
Minifir
Mediterranean Sea
Jerusalem
Salt
Amman
Azrak
Gaza
Dead Sea
el Mezraa
Beersheba
Kerak
Wadi al-Sirhan
Hishe Forest
Tafileh
Jurf el Derwish
Nebk
EGYPT
Bair
Wadi Musa
Petra
Tahuna
Jerdun
Fuweila
Ma'an
Jefer
Aba el Lissan
Kuntilla
Wadi Itm
Guweira
Batn al Ghoul
Wadi Rum
Aqaba
Wadi Rutm
Sinai Desert
Decie
Tell Shahm
Gulf of Aqaba
Abu Suwana
Ramleh
Mudowarra
Great Nefud
Km 587 →

Wilson agreed that Joyce would take over as base commandant, while continuing to supervise the armoured cars, the RFC flight, the Egyptian and the Indian machine-gun detachments, as well as all the trainers working with Ja'far Pasha's regular Arab force. He would have his hands full! He would be joined by Captain W. E. Marshall as medical officer, Major T. H. Scott and Captain R. Goslett as supply officers, and

NORTHERN OPERATIONS • 63

Captain Hornby as the engineer (sapper/demolitions) officer.[2] Both Wilson and Clayton sent out messages outlining the changes and immediately began making arrangements for the shift of operations northward.

Leaving Jeddah, Lawrence returned to Cairo by way of ship after a brief stop in Guweira to discuss loyalty with Auda and his immediate entourage.[3] After bringing Auda back into the fold, Lawrence returned to Cairo for a week's leave. Among other distractions, he was asked to write a treatise on his experiences with the Arabs, which he penned as a 'series of commandments' called the 'Twenty-seven Articles' that appeared in the August issue of the *Arab Bulletin*.[4]

As usual with a working vacation, Lawrence spent much time with Clayton and Wilson discussing the revolt. The Arab Bureau would be the focal point between Allenby's headquarters and the BMM (and all things associated with the revolt), although it appeared that Clayton would be moving to the position of the Chief Political Officer for Palestine to replace Mark Sykes.

He also spoke with the head of the EEF's air arm, General W. Geoffrey H. Salmond, who promised to assist with bombing Ma'an while the RFC's 'C' Flight was en route from Wejh to Akaba. The RFC needed an airbase closer to the front to do so, however, and Lawrence arranged for a location to be set up at Kuntilla in the Sinai, 50 miles north of Akaba. The fuel and bombs for the aircraft were caravanned by camel from Akaba to the landing strip while the planes were flown from their base at el Arish in the north.

Several thousand Turkish troops reinforced Ma'an following the loss of Akaba and reinforcements were moved forward to Fuweilah and seemed prepared to launch a counterstroke down Wadi Itm. Measures were taken to divert and dissuade them from pressing onward.

On the beach, Goslett orchestrated the arrival of troops, equipment, and supplies as Akaba grew. Ja'far Pasha's trained troops moved north in early August and commenced training again. They would act as the defence force for the post, as well as being the 'regular' troops of Feisul's command. Over several days, Ja'far's men arrived from Wejh until his force reached about 2,000 troops. Ja'far pushed a force of 1,000 men forward to Guweira, while local tribes began to strike out with pinpricks against the Turks further north. A key goal for these small raids was to capture enemy mounts – mules – that Feisul's forces badly needed.

---

[2] Recently promoted from lieutenant.

[3] Auda, angry at his lack of remuneration from Feisul, considered going over to the Turks. Lawrence convinced him of the great rewards to come if he stayed. British wireless intercepts gave rise to Auda's near treachery.

[4] Lawrence indicated the articles applied only to working with the Bedouin but, despite that admonition, it has become a guiding theology for military advisors in counterinsurgency operations.

LC336 being offloaded at Akaba, November 1917. (Gilman Family Collection)

The RFC launched their first raids from Kuntilla in late August, against Ma'an, Fuweila, and Aba el Lissan dropping over 100 bombs. The bombardment seemed to dampen the Turks' desire to progress further.

Wilson directed that Gilman's two armoured cars be shipped from Wejh to Suez where they were refitted and prepared for their new base. They would be joined by several more Rolls-Royce armoured cars and tenders released from the Duke of Westminster's old squadron.

Lawrence was in his element once again, pondering next moves. The geography, people, and politics of the Hauran (Syria) were different and more varied than the Hejaz. Feisul would have to deal with many diverse and sometimes internally divisive factors to bring the revolt north, but he and Lawrence thought that, as an outsider, Feisul could serve as the rallying point to focus that diversity on victory. It would require building what Lawrence called a "ladder of tribes" to reach into the new and strategically important areas and to build bases at isolated places like Azrak. In *Seven Pillars,* he repeated his mantra of 'tip and run', simplicity, and economy of force, to never hold territory, and to deny the enemy targets, self-contained fighting force without a front or rear that fought as singular men, not an organized, disciplined force. He was more optimistic about the qualities of the Bedu than his colleagues, perhaps no more so than when he stated that "irregular warfare was far more intellectual than a bayonet charge". Ja'far's regular troops were the means to secure their gains (like Akaba) and they needed to be made fit for that role. Likewise, he and Joyce began to contemplate an expanded role for the armoured cars beyond that of the static defence task they did at Wejh. They were weapons of "attack and pursuit". Although their employment with the "unarmoured camels" in joint fighting was not favoured, the cars could be used to strengthen raids or act by themselves in decisive fire and movement. Both elements, the camel raiders and their vehicular colleagues, would come into their own in the northern campaign.

With the Turks occupied in areas well away from his new intended targets, Feisul's lieutenants began a series of raids similar to those run out of Wejh, but from Ramleh to Tebuk, south of Ma'an. Lawrence decided he should also lead his own raid and settled on mining a train. On this occasion, he thought a surer, instantaneous method was called for and, with the help of Captain Arthur L. Snagge, who was in command of the *Humber*, he learned how to use an electric blasting machine that had been sent down from Egypt.[5] It would be the campaign's first use of electricity to detonate a mine.

His chosen target was the area around Mudowarra, an important water station on the Hejaz railway. Because Mudowarra was on the border between the territories of the Howeitat and the Beni Atiyeh, he put together a force comprised of both tribes. He added some men from the Hauran to show them how Feisul was operating.

In making up his force, Lawrence decided to add firepower to ensure success and brought two weapons that the Arab regulars were being trained to use, the Lewis light machine gun and the Stokes mortar. Both were lightweight and simple, easy to carry and easy to use. When two of the instructors learned of Lawrence's operation, they clamoured to join in. Both were from the Imperial School of Instruction at Zeitun, Egypt and neither spoke Arabic. They had been at Akaba for about a month conducting the training and were due to soon return to their base, but Lawrence agreed to their participation and sent a note to the Arab Bureau asking that they remain a while longer. Besides, he thought, once they moved into the interior, their headquarters wouldn't know where to find them.

They were nicknamed 'Stokes' and 'Lewis' for their "jealously loved tools". Lance-Corporal Walter Herbert Brooke of the 25th Battalion, Royal Welsh Fusiliers was 'Stokes' and Sergeant Charles R. Yells, an Australian of the 9th Light Horse Regiment, was 'Lewis'. Even after Lawrence tried to dissuade them by explaining the hardships of cross-country camel travel with the Bedu, they remained convinced that they wanted to see action.

They set out from Akaba on 7 September. The trip required several extra days as Lawrence had difficulties negotiating intertribal disputes that required intercession from Akaba. With ibn Zaal at their head, they set out again towards Wadi Rum, moving through the valleys towards Mudowarra. On 17 September, the party made camp several miles west and conducted a night reconnaissance of the station, its buildings and the surrounding hills. They found it well fortified with trenches and

---

[5] A gift from General H. B. H. Wright, the EEF's chief engineer.

Hallat Amar. Looking south from railway ambush point towards hill where Lawrence, Stokes, Lewis, and Arabs were positioned. (Author)

rock sangars[6] and manned by at least 300 Turkish troops, which eliminated it from consideration for attack as Lawrence only had 116 men. Backing off the target, they moved south to the low hills above Hallat Amar, a smaller train station.[7]

On the 18th, they situated themselves on the northern side of a hill in a spot shielded from the station. The railway ran along the base of the hill and then curved off to the north. A culvert (Kilometre 587) was about 300 yards away to their front. Lawrence placed the Stokes and two Lewis guns on the hill to rake the length of a train on the track. The Arabs were hiding along the face of the hill where they too could fire on the train.

Lawrence laid an electric mine at the culvert and ran electrical cable 100 yards back to a firing position hidden at the base of the hill. They then retired to sleep through the night, but their presence had been noticed by a Turkish outpost. The next morning about 40 men came out from Hallat Amar station to attack them.

---

[6] Sangars are temporary fighting positions constructed of stones. Temporary or not, the fortifications at Mudowarra remain today.

[7] In his after-action report, Lawrence noted that Mudowarra would be a candidate for future operations given its water and importance to the railway.

Zaal detached 30 men to stop their advance. Several hours later about 100 men came slowly down the line from Mudowarra to the north and it seemed like the Arabs were going to be caught in a pincer. In the early afternoon, the tension ratcheted up when a train consisting of two engines and 12 box cars came up the track from the south. As it travelled along the length of the hill, soldiers began to fire at the Arabs from loopholes in the boxcars and sandbagged gun positions on the carriage roofs. Lawrence fired the mine under the first engine, destroying it and the culvert. The shock of the explosion forced the raiders to keep their heads down to avoid being hit by the steel rain of pistons, wheels, and boiler plates that came down on them. When the smoke and debris stopped falling, they could see that the ruined locomotive lay steaming beside the track. 'Lewis', manning one of the two machine guns, opened fire, along with his Arab partner on the other, to clear the remaining soldiers from the roof of the train. Lewis had set up his position well. He slowly traversed the gun from side to side, directing its deadly .303 calibre projectiles as easily as a fireman directs the stream from his hose.

The Arabs, intent on loot, charged from their protected positions to within 20 yards of the train and began to fire at the unarmoured cars. With wood splinters flying, the Turks poured out of the train and sought cover on the far side of the embankment, firing back between the carriage bogies and stopping the Arab charge but, unfortunately for them, Stokes had their range and dropped a couple of bombs among the cowering enemy. With the benefit of the mortar's high angle of fire, the exploding shells first bracketed the Turks, then, with a deft adjustment, Stokes found his target and the shells tore into their ranks. The Turks panicked and ran into the open desert trying to escape as Lewis once again poured fire into them. When the smoke cleared, 70 soldiers lay dead. Another 30 were wounded while the Arabs had lost one man. Around 90 Turks were captured.

In the ensuing chaos of Arabs looting the train, Lawrence managed to further damage the second locomotive with an explosive charge, but confessed in his report that it had been difficult because the train was carrying many Turkish families trying to get to Damascus and they were hanging onto his robes pleading for mercy. Typically for the Bedouin, all sense of discipline was lost in the riot and most disappeared as soon as they had grabbed their spoils of war. Only a few Arabs remained, ibn Zaal among them, as the Turks closed in from the north and south, the covering forces having abandoned their positions to get their share of the booty. After destroying excess mortar rounds and small-arms ammunition, Lawrence, Brooke, and Yells escaped with Zaal's small party. They camped for a night before making it back to Wadi Rum on 20 September.

The official report Lawrence wrote differs from the literary version in *Seven Pillars* and letters he wrote home. In the latter, he described the battle and the aftermath viscerally. He wrote of opening a wrecked train car to find typhus victims, of fending off the survivors, and mentioning that he himself came away with a nice Baluchi carpet (that he would later call a gift from a grateful old lady from the train). His report specifically noted the contributions of

> the two gun-instructors, Sergeant Yells A. I. F. and Corporal Brooke 25/R. W. F. who came with me on this trip. Neither spoke a word of Arabic, and they went into action with only Bedouin support, against superior numbers. They accounted for about half the Turkish casualties and behaved well on the march as in action. I do not think the Arabs could possibly have carried the train before Turkish relief came had they not been present.

For their actions both awarded the Distinguished Conduct Medal.

The fort at Mudowarra was the most important stop between Medina and Ma'an but it could not yet be attacked with the forces available to the Arabs. It would have to wait. Returning to Akaba, Lawrence and Joyce continued their discussions on operations.[8] Through Clayton, Lawrence tried to communicate his displeasure to Sykes over the agreement to partition Arabia after the war. He penned an extremely negative letter on the politics and deception he was required to undertake with Feisul and the movement. Clayton chose not to forward the letter and counselled Lawrence to drop his disagreement with the issue for the time being. It was an indicator of the burden Lawrence and a number of the politically attuned officers of the Mission had to silently deal with while advising the Arabs.

More French advisors had joined the operation at Akaba, including Captain Rosario Pisani, a French Algerian officer who commanded around 200 colonial troops. They also brought four Schneider quick-firing mountain guns to the fight, which would later prove valuable. Pisani was not as politically attuned or demonstrative as Brémond, but he did know that France intended to occupy Syria at war's end and was determined that he and his men should not accompany any of Feisul's expeditions into that territory.

At the end of September, Lawrence departed on another mission while Joyce was left to deal with the supply conundrum at the port. The Arabs were becoming restless because the Arab Bureau could not compute their numbers and how short they were of supplies.

Lawrence took Pisani on this raid to introduce him to the Bedouin way of war, tempting him with the mention of the possible award of a British Military Cross in the future.[9] After Hallat Amar, there was no shortage of volunteers and many had to be denied participation. Only 150 men would go out on the trip. That said, a huge caravan of camels was brought along in anticipation of much loot. They looked at one possible raid site but found it too heavily guarded by newly constructed

---

[8] It was during negotiations with Feisul that Joyce came to understand that Lawrence's contribution to the revolt was invaluable.

[9] Captain Raho had already been awarded the MC for his railway sabotage operations with Emir Abdullah.

blockhouses and backed off to search for another location. Finding a more suitable spot with over two miles between guard posts, they laid a new type of automatic mine and then retired up a valley to wait. It seemed like an interminable amount of time for a train to pass. While waiting, hidden in the bushes, Lawrence was stung by a scorpion. He was dealing with the pain when a water train passed but the mine did not fire. The Arabs were thankful as water was not good loot.

The second time was more successful. They reburied the mine with an electric mine on top of it and changed the plan to include placing the detonator operator in a hidden location. Another train soon approached slowly up a long grade. This time the charge exploded, the train lay dismembered and the Arabs along with Pisani and his men charged. A gunfight broke out during which Lawrence could only gape as the rear half of the train began to slowly roll backwards from the uncoupled, destroyed front. A few shots were exchanged with the military passengers as the cars rolled away; one round grazed Lawrence's hip before the back half of the train disappeared down the hill. The cargo from the front half, foodstuffs, was looted and carted off. Lawrence facetiously left a receipt for the owner.

He was satisfied. The Arabs had been pupils and done the work well enough themselves. It was, after all, their revolt. Pisani had proven himself to be concerned more about the fight than the politics surrounding the revolt. Over the next months, the raids would continue in intensity and frequency. By the end of the year, 17 locomotives had been destroyed. The attacks also served as a propaganda tool for the revolt. The populace of cities like Damascus became afraid to ride the railway; a simple leaflet announcing an attack would cause employees to strike. Moreover, they put a strain on the Turkish supply system. The shortage of locomotives began to tell on railway operations between Ma'an and Medina, but more importantly in the Palestinian sector that served the Ottoman forces facing Allenby's army in the west.

Reading Lawrence's reports, one can sense a subtle shift in his choice of targets. Like Newcombe in the early days of the revolt, he had encouraged destruction of the entire railway. After Akaba, he began to move towards targeting critical aspects of the system, specifically locomotives and water points. As long as supplies held out, tracks could be replaced and culverts could be repaired; engines and wells were more precious and more difficult to replace.[10] That would change again in the final phase of the war, as the Turks began to employ armoured trains protected by heavy artillery. Facing a hard target, the Arabs would return to blowing up bridges and tracks.

Allenby in the meantime was preparing for his next move and called Lawrence to his headquarters. Since Akaba, Feisul's force had become a direct part of the EEF's

---

[10] Target analysis is the objective assessment of factors including criticality, accessibility, recuperability, vulnerability, effect, and recognizability to determine the most effective way to cripple or defend an 'object', be it an enemy's power, transport, communications network, or its leadership.

planning rather than a distant factor of consideration. The War Office in London instructed Allenby to quickly force the Ottoman Empire out of the war, a rather optimistic goal but the Allies needed a victory and Allenby would do his best to provide one. Lawrence went to Allenby's headquarters near el Arish to meet with him, Clayton, Hogarth and the EEF staff.

Allenby had profited from Murray's preparation of the battlefield, whose extension of rail and water lines across the Sinai had alleviated many of the difficulties entailed in supplying the EEF's advance. Allenby was in the final stages of training the EEF and planning for the Third Battle of Gaza. He wanted to know what Feisul could do to help the assault, but first he wanted assurances that the train-bashing raids were worthwhile and not just a useless bit of brigandry. Lawrence explained his theory about Medina being an albatross around the Turks' neck and the value of keeping the railway minimally operational to pin Fakhri down. That would keep him from reinforcing Djemal Pasha's army in Palestine. He also advised that the Northern Arab Army was not yet ready to take on the well-protected station at Mudowarra or the railhead at Ma'an.

General Allenby shared Arab Bureau intelligence indicating that Turkish forces from Ma'an were preparing to retake Akaba and wanted to know if Feisul was prepared. Lawrence outlined how the Arabs had created a diversion to lure the Turkish commander to Wadi Musa, instead of the vulnerable Arab camp at Guweira. By attacking the Turkish supply depot in Shobek and interfering with the harvesting of wood in the Hishe Forest, the Arabs had consciously given the Turks a target to go after and,

Feisul's Northern Arab Army on the move. (Gilman Family Collection)

sure enough, the Turks were massing their troops for an attack.[11] But the Turks had as imperfect intelligence on the Arabs as the Arabs had precise information on them.

On 21 October, when the Turkish attack on Wadi Musa came, the enemy force was drawn in and ambushed in the impassable canyons and cliffs of the Moab Mountains. The shattered army fell back and their failure left Akaba secure. At this point, the Turks didn't understand the guerrilla army in front of them to fight it effectively.

When Lawrence returned to Akaba, he understood that Feisul was to complement Allenby's upcoming attack. But, unsure of Allenby and less so of the EEF after Murray, Lawrence was hesitant to commit to large measures and settled on half. He decided that destroying a major bridge on the railway branch line from Dera'a across the River Jordan to Haifa was the ticket. It would cut a major supply line into Palestine and the Turkish line of retreat. The attempt that followed would be a significant disappointment.

Along with Lawrence's ambush of the train at Hallat Amar, the attempted destruction of a bridge in the Yarmouk Valley is one of the most quoted of Lawrence's field adventures. One a success, one a failure, both are germane to the discussion of special operations.

In late October while Allenby's staff planned for the assault on Gaza, Lawrence left Akaba with his close friend Captain Sir George A. Lloyd, and the Indian Machine Gun detachment, carrying two Lewis and two Vickers machine guns. Because the bridge demolition needed to be precise – it would be one of 13 50-metre steel girder bridges in the valley, he brought Lieutenant C. E. Wood, the base engineer, to direct the effort. The party went north and were joined by two groups of Arab raiders and continued on to Azrak, but not before Captain Lloyd returned to Akaba (his august presence was needed at Versailles).

They were slowed en route by two things: first, the Indian detachment rode badly because they had little camel experience and second, it was difficult to recruit Bedu who were willing to participate in a raid that had no loot to offer other than the satisfaction of seeing a bridge (albeit a rather large one) blown up. A third issue cropped up later when one of the party, Abd el Kader, deserted at Azrak and took with him the knowledge of their intended target. Lawrence had been warned of his untrustworthiness by Auda abu Tayi and when trusted with information that would be useful to his Turkish masters, he proved Auda correct and disappeared.

Shaken by the revelation of the treachery, Lawrence and his Arab partners believed they had to move quickly to reach the valley before the Turks were alerted. That narrowed their choice to one bridge. They reduced the size of their party for speed and rode hard for Tell el-Shehab and reached the deep valley late on 7 November,

---

[11] Wood fuel was crucial for Turkish train and railway operations, making it a critical – and accessible – target for the Arabs.

already behind schedule. It was dismal weather but Lawrence and the party moved in on foot. The Indian machine-gunners were moving into position high above the bridge while Lawrence and Wood approached it directly. The men carrying the explosives were walking behind him when one of them slipped on the rock scree and dropped his rifle on the stones. The Turkish guards heard the commotion and poured out of their tents. In the light of the rising moon they could see the Indians on the hillside and began to fire at them. Bedlam ensued. The men carrying the explosives panicked, thinking the explosives would go off if hit by a bullet, and tossed their satchels into the deep valley below. Recovery was impossible. Lawrence abandoned the raid and the men retreated into the night. In the distance, they could hear the incessant thunder of Allenby's guns. The British offensive had begun.

The raiders would head back to Azrak where their reserves were stored, but not before attempting a consolation attack on the railway. Although the raiders were exhausted from a 22-hour, 90-mile ride over the previous two nights, they wanted to do something, anything, to make up for the failure, so they decided to mine a train. Lacking food, Lieutenant Wood led the Indians back to Azrak, while the Arabs descended on the rail line at Minifir (Kilometre 172). They had been there before.

With only about 30 pounds of explosives left and a short length of blasting wire, the Arabs' task was more than a bit complicated. Additionally, the machine guns had gone with the Indians, there being no one else to man them. That meant they would not have the security of covering fire. Nevertheless, a suitable spot was found at a culvert that had been blown the previous spring and rebuilt by the Turks. Before they had completed the set-up for the ambush, one train then another passed them by at high speed. Once they finished and were ready, they had to wait in a cold, wind-whipped rain. After what seemed to be an eternity, a train was heard approaching. Hooking up the blasting machine, Lawrence sat next to a small bush as the locomotive approached slowly pulling a long line of cars. As it came abreast of him, he plunged the handle down. Nothing. He plunged it down again. Nothing.

There was nothing he could do, so in full view of a completely loaded troop train, Lawrence just sat and smiled. Once the train passed, he grabbed the machine and ran, but not before he hid the wires. He then scrambled up over the hill and disappeared. Luckily so, because the train stopped and sent back a search party to poke around the bush but found nothing. The blasting machine was repaired and they again waited in the cold.

Nearly a complete day would pass before another train approached. Moving into position, Lawrence hooked the machine and fired the mine just as the engine passed over it. As he feared, he was too close. All he could do was make himself small as the air was filled with a thousand flying deadly pieces of metal, one of which destroyed the blasting machine he was holding.

Almost immediately, the area became a firestorm of bullets as Turk soldiers on board rapidly regrouped following the blast. The too-few Arabs tried to hold off the too-many soldiers but the first locomotive had been destroyed and the second lay in the culvert. The front passenger cars had concertinaed in on top of them. The remaining cars were a beehive of troops. It was the train of the 8th Army Corps commander Mehmed Djemal Pasha[12] who was travelling to help defend Jerusalem from Allenby's attack. With bullets flying in both directions and outnumbered, the Arabs decided that discretion was truly the better part of valour. They withdrew, but not without the loss of seven killed and several wounded. The Turks had fared worse. Jemal Pasha's second-in-command had been killed, as had many of the soldiers who tried to assault the Arab position on the hill. More were lost in the blast.

Breaking free of the Turks, the raiders ran back to their camels, mounted up and moved out. They picked up their trail back to the safety of Azrak where they would rest easy, knowing they had achieved at least some measure of success.

The operation ended on a high note, but just. It was a close-run thing with many mistakes: the operation was rushed, the Indian detachment had no experience with camels, a preraid target reconnaissance was not done, the wrong person was trusted with information, and then there was the weather and, of course, chance – all contributed to the failures they had encountered and weighed heavily on Lawrence as the leader.

The weather continued to be bad. Further west, Allenby's advance slogged on, his troops taking Beersheba and then Gaza. The Turks then abandoned Jerusalem and on 11 December 1917 Allenby accepted its surrender from the local officials left behind. After Lawrence returned to Azrak, he travelled to Allenby's field headquarters to report on his failure. In the euphoria of Allenby's success, however, Lawrence was invited to enter Jerusalem with the commander's party. Unlike Wilhelm II, Allenby showed the city due respect and entered on foot. In contemporary photos, Lawrence can be seen walking behind Allenby in a borrowed uniform.

The Turks would attempt a counterattack against Allenby, but it failed. Then winter weather decided things and movement on the Palestinian front ceased. The Allied front line was secure, and quiet, which was opportune as Allenby's lines of communications and logistics needed to catch up. It was a time for consolidation.

To the east and south behind the Turkish front lines, the Arab Revolt strengthened as the build-up in Akaba continued. Men came ashore and supplies piled up on the beach. Wireless radio sheds and antennas popped up, and vehicles were winched off the ships onto lighters that carried them ashore. Much as they had at Wejh, the appearance of armoured cars and trucks amazed the Arab contingent.

---

[12] Mehmed Djemal Pasha 'Küçük' – the Lesser, not to be confused with the Fourth Army Commander Ahmet Djemal Pasha 'Buyük' – the Greater.

Lieutenant Wade of the HACB. (Gilman Family Collection)

On 21 November, the two armoured cars from Wejh, refurbished and ready for action, arrived in Akaba. They were joined by three additional Rolls-Royce armoured cars, two Rolls-Royce tenders, and a number of other support cars, mostly Ford Model-Ts and a lone Wolseley. They were again under the command of Gilman – now a temporary captain – and lieutenants Dowsett, Grisenthwaite, Wade, and Greenhill, who were accompanied by a larger contingent of other ranks, or enlisted men – drivers, gunners, and mechanics – and a number of other junior officers. The unit was named the Hejaz Armoured Car Section (HACS).[13] Clayton informed Joyce that the unit would be assigned to him in October. In a note, Clayton wrote:

---

[13] There were around 75 other ranks in the unit. It would be later redesignated as a battery in 1918.

Lieutenant Stanley Dowsett of the HACB
(Gilman Family Collection)

I think you will find the Armoured Cars a useful unit. It would have been unsound to send them until they were complete and ready for service. If they are to be any good they must be absolutely of the best and now I think they are that. Five Rolls Royces should be able to go almost anywhere and we are lucky to have got hold of them as we were actually able to take a complete patrol out of the Western Desert and bring it here for service in Akaba.

A sixth car would join them in early December, a civilian 1909 Rolls-Royce that Lawrence commandeered from a British diplomat in Cairo. Its formal body was removed and the car was converted into a tender. It was called 'Blue Mist', the name given to it by a previous owner.

On 25 November, they were joined by another unit: the Royal Field Artillery 10-pounder Motor Section. Lieutenant Samuel H. Brodie was the unit commander, and Lieutenant George C. Pascoe, as Brodie's deputy, arrived with ten more men in March 1918. Clayton had seen their work in Egypt and decided they would also be a good addition to Joyce's force.

Brodie was commissioned in the Royal Field Artillery in December 1916 and had been ordered to organize the unit and test it in the Western Desert of Egypt. It was made up of two obsolete breech-loading 10-pounder mountain guns and six Talbot SY trucks. Two trucks were used to carry the guns and four carried supplies or served as spares. Usually the guns would be offloaded and put into action, but they could also be fired from the truckbed, making them one of the first mobile gun platforms. The cannons had come from Indian Army stock and like many antiquated weapons, they were sent off to the 'sideshow' in Egypt. After testing the equipment

'Blue Mist', 1909 Rolls-Royce tender LC1298, the oldest car in the HACB. (Gilman Family Collection)

and finding it "capable of doing what was required", Brodie and the first group of 26 men shipped out to Akaba on 21 November 1917.

Initially the trucks and cars conducted limited reconnaissance forays up Wadi Itm, determining the best routes to the Guweira plain and beyond, testing the endurance of the cars and the men who often had to push the vehicles through the deep sand. The Rolls-Royce had been equipped at the factory with dual rear wheel assemblies to carry their extra weight. That arrangement helped in the sand, so Gilman decided to mount dual wheels on the front as well. That made steering more difficult, but helped float the car over soft ground. The drivers' arms began to resemble those of boxers from the constant physical effort of steering in the sand.

But before they could deploy operationally, the camel track out of Akaba had to be improved to accommodate the vehicles. One of the machine-gunners, Sergeant T. W. Beaumont, described how the men were tasked to improve the road to Wadi Itm and then onward to Guweira. First, rocks had to be cleared by blasting and removing the rubble. Then they laid wire netting over the sand and staked it down to hold it in place. It was a hard job the men would have to repeat many times as the heavy Rolls-Royces and Talbots periodically tore up the netting. The occasional Arab also complicated matters by pulling up the wooden stakes for their campfires. When Feisul moved his headquarters to Aba el Lissan later in the campaign, there was the long steep pass off the Guweira plain up the Negab Pass. It was one of the most difficult tracks the cars had to negotiate and invariably the heavily laden cars,

Lieutenant Samuel Brodie, Officer Commanding, RFA 10-pounder Motor Section. (John Pascoe & John Winterburn)

whether light Fords or heavy Rolls-Royces, had to be pushed up the hill by their crew and passengers.

By late December, both the armoured cars and the 10-pounder section were encamped above Wadi Itm at Guweira. This location would serve as their main base for most of the campaign. When supplies or repairs were needed, the tenders would shuttle back and forth between the camp and Akaba to the main depot there.

Lieutenant George Pascoe, Deputy OC of the RFA 10-pounder Motor Section. (John Pascoe & John Winterburn)

Lieutenant-Colonel Joyce and Major Lawrence had plans for the mobile weapon platforms, what would today be called 'technicals' – civilian vehicles adapted to military purposes. In late December a raid was organized to test their theories. It would be launched against the large railway station at Mudowarra, a target Joyce had wanted to attack in November but couldn't risk because of the Turkish threat near Wadi Musa and a lack of forward-based forage for the animals. With vehicles, he could now launch a raid without impacting the Arab defences.

Men of the HACB work to make the Wadi Itm road passable. (Gilman Family Collection)

Joyce's after-action report, written in typical 'militarese', summarized the operation:

> On 30 December a force of three Rolls-Royce armoured cars with two tenders, and three Talbot trucks carrying one 10-pounder mountain gun departed Guweira for operations against the railway line south of Ma'an. The object of the operation was as follows:
>
> 1) to ascertain the extent Motor vehicles could operate against the railway line.
> 2) if possible, to lay a mine and destroy a certain train reported to be leaving Damascus on 29 December.
> 3) by operating against the rail line south of Ma'an, to force the Turks to withdraw troops from the Ma'an sector and Aba el Lissan and thereby reduce opposition likely to be encountered by Arab forces operating in that area.

The cars departed the base early in the morning on the 30th and arrived at a point about 12 miles west of Mudowarra station at sundown. A tender went out on a reconnaissance the next morning and discovered a route that led directly to Ramleh station. A second foot reconnaissance showed the railway line was defended by several small entrenched guard posts. It was decided to abandon the idea of laying a mine because the area was too well defended. A less ambitious plan was made to attack a single post near a large culvert on the railway between Wadi Rutm and Tell Shahm stations.

Early on 1 January, the column approached the post. Joyce, who was in charge, and Lawrence took up an observation position on a hilltop 2,000 yards to the west, a location from which they could observe the entire battle with binoculars. The cars nosed around the post at a distance. The Turks, who had never seen anything like them, were curious, at least until Brodie put his 10-pounder guns into action and fired several high-explosive (HE) rounds at them. But, because of the rough ground and a mirage, he had mistakenly positioned the gun too close at around 1,500 yards. After only firing several rounds, intense Turkish rifle fire forced Brodie and his crews to withdraw under the protective fire of the armoured cars that approached the post to within several hundred yards and poured several belts of .303 ammo into it. The Turks fired back but it was like "shooting at a rhino with bird shot", and the cars were unharmed.

The force withdrew after making a nuisance of itself and proceeded south to Tell Shahm station where the 10-pounder gun fired about 30 HE rounds at the station buildings, destroying several train cars sitting at the siding. The armoured cars followed suit, closing in and firing into the building, forcing the Turkish soldiers to withdraw into the hills to the east. But, with only two men in each car, they were unable to dismount to capture the station. In the future, additional troops would be brought for that task. After the battle, the force withdrew west to Abu Sawana where an advanced staging base had been set up. It would later be used as an advanced landing ground (ALG) for the aircraft of 'X' Flight, the formation that had replaced 'C' Flight in October 1917.

Joyce wrote that the cars' appearance on the railway had undoubtedly surprised the Turks. This was the first time the cars had got within range of the line and the outcome was generally good: he called it a victory of sorts, but stopped short of saying it was a complete success as the objectives were not completely neutralized. They knew now that the railway was a day's easy march from Guweira and Joyce and Lawrence were satisfied with the results, but they made several notes for future operations. The armoured cars needed to work in pairs and at least one car was required as a tender, as it was the only method that would permit cars a chance to escape in the event of breakdown. Joyce stated that this first operation proved that armoured cars could be utilized against the Hejaz railway, with the Rolls-Royce proving to be the most efficient type to negotiate the sand. He also mentioned that he opted not to take Ja'fer Pasha's regulars because they weren't ready. They would not be ready for a while to come. Next time he would take the Bedouin.

Lawrence's reaction was later set down in *Seven Pillars* when he said "armoured car work is fighting deluxe". Joyce and he had just created a new paradigm for mobile warfare in the desert.

A second mobile operation took place two weeks later. This time Joyce chose to employ a larger force that included the 10-pounder Motor Section, three armoured cars of the HACS and their tenders, a group of the trained Arabs with three artillery pieces, a French detachment with two mountain guns, and around 1,000 Bedouin tribesmen. The force move out of their assembly area at Abu Sawana on 21 January and headed for Mudowarra about 25 miles away.

The attack began when two 'X' Flight Martinsyde G.102 aircraft bombed the station at Mudowarra and the fortified hills that guarded it. They had flown from Akaba, landed and refuelled at Abu Sawana and then made the ten-minute flight to the station as the Arab attack commenced.

On the morning of 22 January, Lieutenant Brodie employed his two cannon to open the ground assault, firing at the hill from around 2,300 yards. The explosive rounds breached some of the rock sangar walls. Joyce then ordered Brodie to fire on the station. Accompanied by the armoured cars, the unit deployed forward and began firing again. Brodie observed dryly that the Arabs did not attack and after receiving a second signal, he moved back to the original firing position and resumed firing on the fort. Again, the Arabs did not attack. By late afternoon, it was apparent the Arabs were content just to watch the fireworks and Joyce ordered a general withdrawal. The unit returned to Guweira on 24 January. The miscarriage of the raid highlighted the difficulties of cooperation between regular and irregular troops, a flaw that would reoccur often in the upcoming months. The Arab forces, unless suitably motivated, wanted the guns and armoured cars to do the hard work, which led the advisors to separate the two groups and their objectives whenever possible.

Lawrence was elsewhere occupied during Joyce's thwarted attack on Mudowarra and did not participate. He was on one of his visits to Allenby's headquarters, where he was told the British offensive would not resume until mid-February. In the meantime, Feisul could assist by beginning operations towards the Dead Sea. It was an area Feisul wanted to bring under his control anyway. In mid-January, the Arabs attacked and captured the villages of Shobek and Tafileh. Another raid was carried out on Jurf el Derwish station and a parked train yielded a lucrative bounty for the Bedu. Canned goods and tobacco for the Turks at Medina were carried off by a huge caravan of camels with minimal risk to the Arabs. The capture of the goods hurt the morale of the Turks, while the Arabs were greatly enriched financially and psychologically.

The Turks wanted revenge and, on 23 January, a Turkish regiment of around 1,000 men with two Austrian Škoda mountain guns and over 20 machine guns left Kerak and advanced on Tafileh to recapture the town. The Turks made contact with Arab pickets to the east of town and quickly pushed them back to Tafileh. The main Arab force under Emir Zeid left the town to set up a blocking force on a ridge east of the town facing the Turkish advance. Zeid had been sent north by his elder brother Feisul and brought with him a company of Ja'far Pasha's trained men and machine guns. One of Zeid's lieutenants, Abdulla Effendi, was sent forward with two machine guns to reinforce the next crest line which spurred a short-lived counterattack. That, in turn, drove the Turks to concentrate their machine-gun and artillery fire on the hill. Abdulla and most of the Arabs fell back on their main line and a duel developed between the two sides. As the battle developed, two Arab fighting groups with machine guns were sent out to flank the Turks while Lawrence and Zeid's forces engaged the enemy with an old howitzer and machine guns. Because Lawrence had already paced out the range between the ridges, the Arab strikes were accurate, while the Turks were struggling to adjust their fire.

When both Arab flanking parties were in position, the main force attacked forward. The Turks were caught by intense machine-gun fire from three directions, two of

Turkish Škoda M.16 10cm Howitzer. (Public Domain)

which poured bullets down the length of their line. The Turkish line collapsed and the soldiers retreated but not before many men and weapons were lost. The two Škoda guns, machine guns, 200 horses and mules, supplies and 200 men were captured. As many as 1,000 Turks were estimated to have been killed in the battle and the ensuing pursuit. The Arabs lost 25 killed and 40 wounded. Once again, this was far more than Lawrence wanted or thought the Arabs should have endured. Lawrence's leadership in the attack was crucial and he sometimes wielded his guerrillas as if they were a conventional force, a fact that gave him pride, but his narrative in *Seven Pillars* he tells of his regret at the Arab losses. His official report outlines the facts dispassionately, but also with flippant parody. Lawrence was rewarded once again, this time with the Distinguished Service Order.

With Tafileh safe for the moment, Lawrence urged Sherif Abdullah ibn Hamza in late January to carry out a small raid to eliminate the Turkish supply route across the Dead Sea. Allenby's intelligence department had determined the Turks were using small motor launches and lighters to ferry food and other supplies across the inland sea. He saw it as a threat to his right flank and asked that it be eliminated. A swarm of 70 Bedu horseman under the headman Ibrahim abu Irgeig set out through the Moab Mountains and descended upon the lake's eastern shore at el Mezraa where the Turks harboured their boats.

The Turks, all members of the Turkish Navy, had no inkling of what was about to happen. In the grey morning of 28 January, the Arab cavalry charged out of the mist into the Turkish camp. Within minutes the engagement was settled. The Turks

T. E. Lawrence, D. G. Hogarth, Alan Dawnay, close-up. (Harry Chase, James A. Cannavino Library, Archives & Special Collections, Marist College, USA)

were completely surprised and surrendered without a fight. Ibrahim's men destroyed the boats and took 60 prisoners with no casualties to either side. Allenby's request was met and, although he was not physically present, Lawrence fancied it to be one of his best expeditions yet.

During the previous December, Clayton had reorganized the Arab Bureau in an attempt to improve its functioning. The bureau's main tasks of policy, intelligence, and propaganda were being overwhelmed by its other requirement to support and supply the Arab Revolt's operations. To alleviate the burden, a new staff within the bureau was created. Called the Hejaz Operations Staff (HOS), its telegraphic codename was 'Hedgehog'[14] and Lieutenant-Colonel Alan Dawnay was appointed as its chief. Born Alan Geoffrey Charles Dawnay in 1888, he was commissioned into the Coldstream Guards in 1909. His upper-class background was quite evident in his dress and manner. Lawrence described him as "Eton and Magdalen, Oxford, and the Guards: and is everything that is absolutely right: and the best of it is that

---

[14] An alternative spelling, 'Hedghog' is used in some cables. BMM officers often called their unit 'Hedgehog'.

Two Admiralty Pattern Rolls-Royce armoured cars on patrol. Colonel Dawney stands by the front wing. (Gilman Family Collection)

he looks like it". But he was also one of the best planners on Allenby's staff as well as being the brother to Brigadier-General Guy Payan Dawnay, the man who crafted the successful plan to take Beersheba. Alan Dawnay was a professional soldier and, although Lawrence worried that he had no experience in guerrilla warfare and spoke no Arabic, he later said Dawnay "married war and rebellion in himself".

Hedgehog was responsible for coordinating military operations between the EEF and the Arab forces and Dawnay was its senior advisor. As expected, Clayton was promoted to be Allenby's chief political officer in February 1918, while Cornwallis became Arbur's director.

Dawnay needed a first-hand look at the situation, so he travelled to Akaba to meet with Feisul and, after a fortnight's visit, reported his findings and thoughts on the direction of the revolt. It was the clearest enunciation of the Arab Revolt's strategy yet put to paper. The document is important to understand not only his concepts for the mission and the capabilities of the Arab forces, but also how he thought the British Military Mission and its specialized units (the 10-pounder Motor and Armoured Car sections) would fit into the operation. His report to Allenby's Chief of the General Staff, Major-General L. J. Bols, was accompanied by an amplifying (and less formal letter) to his brother, Guy, whom he had apparently nicknamed 'Gazeka'.[15]

---

[15] Probably after the name of a character in the P. G. Wodehouse novel *Mike* who looked like a 'Gazeka' a Papuan Devil-Pig from Papua, New Guinea.

With the title of Brigadier-General, General Staff (BGGS), Guy Dawnay was Bols's deputy and was in a good position to help explain his brother's plan for the revolt.

Writing from the Savoy Hotel in Cairo, Dawnay set out his concept of future operations which revealed his organizational ability as well as his skill in assessing the material with which he would be working: the Arab army. The objectives he set out were to extend the tribal revolt north to occupy the food-producing region around Kerak, an objective that Lawrence had already set out for Zeid and second, to destroy the enemy's 1st Composite Force and capture the critical railhead at Ma'an, which would permanently isolate all Turkish forces to the south. The first task would be carried out in its entirety by Feisul's tribal forces, the second and main objective would be achieved by Ja'far Pasha's Arab regular force.

In both cases, British units – the RFA and the HACS – would be operating far away to remove any opportunity for the Arabs to let their partners to do the job while they watched from the sidelines as had happened at Mudowarra.

Dawnay knew a direct attack of the fortifications of Ma'an would fail and outlined how the Arabs operating from an advance base should attack the rail line north of the city to isolate it and draw out a response. Another attack further north by Arab tribal forces and by British units far to the south at Mudowarra or Fasoa would delay and hold off Turkish reinforcements. He outlined the support required in some detail including the animals, the forage, and ammunition needed. Dawnay estimated that Ja'far would be able to field 30 companies totalling 3,000 men with 20 machine guns, two 18-pounder guns, two 2.95-inch and two 10-pounder mountain guns. The operation would require three stages of transport: Akaba to Guweira, followed by Guweira to Ain Basta, the advance base, and then from Ain Basta to the front line, around 110 miles overall. A final consideration would be to improve communications with the provision of wireless radios, as the current methods – camel and telephone – required anywhere from one to three days, each way, to send a message.

Dawnay recognized the plan was the only practical way for the Arabs to demonstrate they could successfully bring the revolt to a conclusion on their own. The major weakness he saw was the Arab army, who had yet to prove themselves capable. Dawnay noted that his proposal had been reviewed and accepted by Feisul and Ja'far, who along with Joyce and Lawrence, thought it feasible for the Arab force to carry out. He pointed out in his letter to 'Gazeka' that

> if it fails, the only alternative will then be to do the job for them, which probably would not be very difficult, but in the circumstances in view of the political advantage of the Arabs working out their own salvation, and of the vast amount of trouble and money already spent to bring this about, I feel that we ought to give them at least one fair run, with all the help we can give them to bring it off, if they are men enough to do so.

Dawnay's operational concept integrated many elements of combined and special operations in a three-pronged approach: a tribal force conducting guerrilla or irregular operations with Lawrence as its advisor; a surrogate 'regular army' conducting a conventional attack with Joyce advising; and British specialized units conducting unilateral raids against hard targets. It would be an ambitious programme, and no plan ever survives first contact.[16]

In addition to acting as the base commandant and supervisor of all things British at Akaba, Joyce had become the de facto commander for the Arabs while Ja'far was its nominal commander. Joyce was much more active in the overall operations while Lawrence was often with various tribal chiefs running raids and spent little time with Feisul. His superiors often had no idea where he was other than 'presumably' off on operations with the Arabs. He had been a spectator during the recent engagement with the armoured cars, an operation that needed Joyce's hand as a more experienced organizer.

Dawnay rectified arrangements so that Feisul would be well taken care of by Joyce while Lawrence continued his forays with Feisul's lieutenants. Joyce thereupon relinquished his base duties to Major Scott and was classified as Special Service Officer Grade 1. He would take over as the director of field operations and liaison to Arab regular operations, while retaining command of the British technical and specialized forces. Lawrence would be promoted to lieutenant-colonel and charged with liaison with the Bedouins.[17]

Although Dawnay's plan was to go hand in hand with Allenby's push to the east, Lawrence encountered a setback that would cause a personal crisis and shake his trust and support for the Arabs. After Tafileh and the 'naval' mission, Lawrence returned to Guweira to discuss operations with Joyce and Dawnay, who was at the end of his fortnight visit to the area. He also needed to pick up £30,000 in gold to fund the Arab push north around the Dead Sea. He rode back through the Moab Mountains to Zeid's camp at Tafileh where he turned over the gold. Lawrence then left on a reconnaissance of the Jordan River Valley to familiarize himself with the area before the campaign. Returning to Tafileh after several days, he was confronted by Zeid who had spent all the gold. Lawrence knew he would not be able to execute Dawnay's plan and became despondent. Lawrence's authority had been challenged by Zeid, something he had not experienced before: Zeid had placed his personal requirements – rational or not – over those of the mission. This phenomenon is not unusual when dealing in large amounts of money with leaders, especially those who have never seen £1,000 in gold sovereigns, let alone £30,000. Under pressure from greedy and dishonest peers and, with little or no accountability, Zeid spent the money paying off debts and obligations that should have waited. He may have expected that Lawrence could easily obtain more as he appeared to have easy access to His Majesty's pockets. In the end however, Lawrence had failed on two levels:

---

[16] From 'Murphy's Laws of War', this is either Law #8, #10, or #23 depending on the version.
[17] His date of promotion was 12 March 1918.

first was his expectation that Zeid would have the same mature judgement as Feisul; second to supervise and control Zeid's appropriation from the fund.

Lawrence returned to Guweira and explained the situation to Joyce. Lawrence decided to throw in the towel. He had lost confidence in his own abilities and was deeply disappointed that he had misplaced his trust in Zeid. By camel with four of his Ageyl bodyguards, he travelled to GHQ to put himself in Allenby's hands. He wanted to request transfer to some job that required little responsibility. When he arrived at GHQ, he was quickly disabused of the notion. Allenby needed Lawrence and the Northern Arab Army.[18] The British War Cabinet had recently decided a victory was needed in the Middle East and that Allenby should, for once, receive priority. Allenby needed to begin his advance up the coast towards Beirut and wanted Feisul's forces to guard his flank. This, for the Arabs, meant taking Ma'an, the major railhead in the Hejaz between Amman and Medina. To assist the Arabs, Allenby would launch a diversionary raid towards the town of Salt, then move towards Amman to destroy a bridge and a tunnel to slow Turkish reinforcements from the north that might try to reach Ma'an. Lawrence was energized with the prospect of a new mission and completely dropped plans to move north towards Kerak. The new priority was Ma'an.

Returning to Akaba in late March, Lawrence and the other Hedgehog officers made preparations for the offensive. He then moved to the east of the railway to await news from Amman. When it came, he planned to raid the line while Feisul's regulars attacked Ma'an.

Allenby's early April raid on Salt did not go well. Weather slowed the force and gave the Turks ample warning of the intended targets, so that defences were amply bolstered. A strong Turkish counterattack forced the British to abandon the attack. Disappointed, Lawrence moved south to assist in the assault on Ma'an, which had already begun.

Contrary to Dawnay's meticulous plan which avoided the main Turkish defences, Feisul's sub-chiefs argued for an attack on the main defensive position, centred on Ma'an's train station. After much argument, it was decided the Arabs would attack in three columns, one each to the north and south to cut the rail line entering the town, and a third central column to attack the main defensive positions. The British advisors decided not to interfere: it was, after all, the Arabs' game.

Beginning on 11 April, the southern column under Nuri as Said with 350 regulars and 1,000 Howeitat irregulars, and Captain Pisani's four mountain guns took Ghadir al-Hajj station and destroyed a thousand lengths of track on the line before withdrawing to join with the central column. Meanwhile, Ja'far Pasha al-Askari with 600 regulars,

---

[18] The Arab Revolt in the south had not met British expectations. Despite 'Miralai' Davenport's best efforts, both Abdullah's and Ali's work was characterized by inertia. Any advantage achieved was attributed to a relative decline in Turkish strength through desertion, sickness, and the unreliable nature of the railway rather than any action claimed by the two leaders.

Arab cavalry under Mahlud al-Mukhlis. (Harry Chase, James A. Cannavino Library, Archives & Special Collections, Marist College, USA)

500 tribal warriors under Sherif Nasir, eight machine guns, and one 18-pounder artillery piece attacked Jerdun station, about 15 miles north of Ma'an, taking it and seizing its stores. That evening, Lawrence and Captain Hubert Young showed up in a Rolls-Royce tender with explosives to blow up a bridge just south of the station. Before they could carry out the demolition, there was a counterattack that the regulars repulsed after several hours of hard combat. They continued the demolition after that. Then, with the bridge blown and their work finished, the force turned south, destroying 3,000 lengths of track along the way, to join the main attack under Mahlud al-Mukhlis.[19]

Now concentrated to west of the station, Feisul's regular army, numbering around 3,500 men, attacked east towards Jebel Semna, the Turks' first line of defence. The ridge line was one of many defensive positions that ringed the all-important station and to approach it the attackers had to cross a low valley. On 13 April, the attack began. After three hours, the Arabs captured the first ridge line. Mahlud, probably Feisul's best general, was wounded in the fight and rendered *hors combat*. The next line of defence, the Hill of Birds, was 4,000 yards in front of the attackers and behind it lay the well-defended station and around 4,000 men from four Turkish regiments.

---

[19] The attack on Jerdun (Jardunah) station probably took place on 17 April.

Three attempts were made on the station over the next three days with sporadic bombing carried out by the aircraft of 'X' Flight throughout the battle. The first two times, the Arabs reached a point around 350 yards from their objective before deciding to retire to their original position to reconsolidate. Airdrops of Turkish-language leaflets urging the defenders to surrender had no effect and the garrison was successfully reinforced by an additional 3,000 men from Amman over the course of the battle.

On the 17th, the Arabs attacked again, finally penetrating the station's defences before being compelled to retire by heavy machine-gun fire from the high ground to the north. Emir Feisul decided to suspend his attacks and fell back on the ridge line at Jebel Semna where he reinforced his position and waited. The two forces faced off in what would be a long stalemate.

The good news was that the railway had been completely disabled and would not be repaired. To the south, in Medina, Fakhri Pasha would not receive regular resupply and would not be able to withdraw his troops. Moreover, Ja'far Pasha's regular troops had proved capable of conducting regular military manoeuvres while being heavily engaged by the enemy. They did not wither and retreat: their morale remained high despite the loss of around 90 men killed. It marked a sea-change in Arab capabilities from that of a purely guerrilla force conducting irregular 'tip and run' operations to a conventional force engaging a regular army.

To the south, Colonel Dawnay prepared for his raid. Joyce had fallen ill with pneumonia and been invalided back to Suez. Dawnay, the meticulous planner, would take charge of field operations – he wanted in on the action anyway, having been cooped up in Cairo for many months. On his orders, an advanced "aerodrome" for 'X' Flight had been built at Disi[20] and logistics bases (forward supply dumps) prepared at Abu Sawana, where the forces assembled on 16 April and at Jebel Sinn. The forces included the RFA 10-pounder section, the Rolls-Royce armoured cars and tenders, several small Fords with Hotchkiss machine guns, and 150 camel-mounted Howeitat irregulars under Sherif Hazaa. Also present was the newly formed 150-man Egyptian Camel Corps (ECC) commanded by Captain Frederick Gerard Peake. Captain Hornby, the senior sapper, would destroy as much of the railway as he could.

Peake was another interesting character. He was commissioned into the Duke of Wellington's Regiment in 1906, but found the social life a young subaltern was supposed to lead not quite to his liking and spent most of his time hunting and learning the local languages. Eventually he found himself a position with the Egyptian Army, considered an elite posting because of its continuing 'Kitchener' tradition. He spent the first months of the war trying to find a way into it from the now-isolated Sudan and ended up fighting Bulgarians in Salonika and the Senussi in the Western Desert before being called to the Hejaz as commander of the Camel Corps in April 1918. He arrived just in time for Dawnay's operation. He was met by Lawrence, who Peake initially thought to be an Arab, until he spoke.

[20] Also spelled Decie.

Captain Frederick Gerard Peake. (Public Domain)

"Well, Peake, so you have arrived at last. We have been waiting some time for you and your braves, and there is plenty of work for you up country."

Dawnay's operations order reads like the test solution for a classroom exercise at Sandhurst. Everything was ordered and placed by timings and numbers and phases, with each man, vehicle, camel, and aeroplane in their designated positions. It was a work of art, at least until someone asked Hazaa if he understood. He did, but he had a small problem. He didn't have a watch to synchronize with anyone else's. He said he would move when the cars did and then someone could relay the next order to him. Problem solved. Dawnay even specified that the Rolls-Royces would have their exhaust cut-outs closed, which ruined a favourite pastime of the drivers. Instead the cars would roll out of camp like the silent luxury cars they were originally meant to be.

The expedition moved forward to Tooth Hill, a promontory that lay several thousand yards west of the railway. They were joined around midnight by Lawrence, who had left Ma'an behind and decided he could be of good use to Dawnay who spoke no Arabic. He thought his intercession might be needed at some point if difficulties should arise between the Howeitat and the Egyptian troops, who hated each other. His concern was prescient, as it turned out.

The next day played out as Dawnay had specified. Chance in warfare is a given and tends to throw the most determined commander's plan into chaos, but that day wasn't the occasion for chance to rear its head. The only part of Dawnay's plan that didn't go as scheduled was when the Turkish defenders of one post surrendered ten minutes earlier than specified in the order.

On 19 April, at the appointed hour, Lieutenant Brodie, the RFA artillery section commander, watched as Gilman's three armoured Rolls-Royces silently passed his ready position, rolling east with the sun breaking over the foothills to their front. A reconnaissance done the previous day had provided each section with precise routes and bearings to follow. They followed those routes now as the 10-pounders covered their advance. The ECC trotted out on the armoured cars' flank towards their first objective, a Turkish guard post on a hill 1,000 yards west of the rail line.

The cars opened fire as they approached. The Turks opened fire and then realized what was coming. They quickly surrendered and three men were captured. Brodie shifted his guns to cover the larger post near a ten-arch culvert bridge on the railway. The ECC turned to attack it. Experience from January had taught that armoured cars and artillery were not enough to force the day: a ground force was needed to seize and hold territory. The ECC and the Howeitat were to fill that role.

Brodie, observing the troops advance, ordered his guns to fire. High-explosive rounds at 2,550 yards did the trick. Brodie was pleased: his guns were hitting the fortification dead on. The advance slowed and an armoured car moved in, its Vickers-Maxim chattering away at the post. The Rolls-Royce moved in a cloud of steam as the water-cooled gun heated up and the overflow spilled onto the car's hot bonnet. The advance resumed as a white flag appeared and more prisoners were taken.

It was 10.30 in the morning and the order to 'Stand easy' was given. Brodie loaded his guns back on the Talbot trucks and shifted them once more to cover Tell Shahm station, several miles to the south, and then told his men to take a lunchbreak. The Royal Air Force (RAF) planes weren't due until 4 p.m., so in the interim tea was brewed and biscuits with bully beef were the order of the moment.[21]

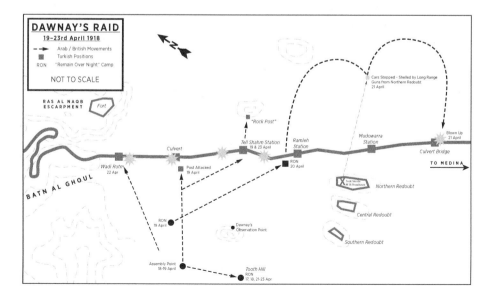

---

[21] The Royal Flying Corps became the Royal Air Force on 1 April 1918.

Turkish position near Tell Shahm that was attacked on 19 April 1918. (Gilman Family Collection)

While Brodie and his gunners waited, the armoured cars and tenders went seeking targets. Hornby had loaded the tenders to the gunwhales with explosives and rushed in to take out the first bridge, a stone culvert type. They enthusiastically proceeded to place 120 slabs of guncotton under it while the armoured cars stood guard.[22] Dawnay and Lawrence had come forward in the third tender to observe and were sitting, complacently watching, when Hornby fired the charge and nearly threw them out of the car. Lawrence went forward on the next bridge to teach Hornby economics: how to stuff the culvert's drainage holes and cut down on the explosive used. The next demolition required only 15 slabs. It was Lawrence's 'scientific method' of bridge destruction.

Hornby's Rolls-Royce tender ran up and down the line in the area, stopping only to let him blow up rails and culverts. There weren't any enemy for him to be concerned with; besides he was well covered by Brodie's guns and Gilman's armoured cars. Hornby had brought two tons of explosive and intended to use it all. The only untoward incident happened when a 20-pound rock thrown up by one of Hornby's blasts landed on the turret of an armoured car. It bounced off harmlessly but probably damaged the crew's hearing.

On schedule, two British BE2c aircraft appeared overhead. They had flown from Disi, a short 15-minute flight away, and dropped three bombs on Tell Shahm station. One aircraft circled overhead as the second strafed the station with its machine

---

[22] The slabs weighed 15 ounces each, which equates to around 112 pounds of explosive.

gun. The next phase of the attack was on. Brodie was in an observation position 800 yards in front giving direction to the guns by field telephone. When he gave the order to fire, the guns fired first on some trenches in front of the station before shifting to the station building itself. The armoured cars and the tenders employed their Vickers machine guns to spray the station liberally with .303 fire. As the two mounted groups approached the station, the Howeitat broke off to attack the 'Rock Post', a fortified redoubt on the slope of a hill to the east of the station. They charged the position and the outnumbered and outgunned Turks again quickly surrendered.

Returning west to the main objective, the Howeitat raced the Egyptian cameliers, who were coming from the north, pell-mell to get to the station and its booty first. Lawrence won the race in a tender and ran in to grab the station bell as a souvenir. Peake got the ticket punch. The Egyptians and Arabs met on the doorstep and bedlam ensued. Lawrence and the headmen mediated a solution: both groups came away happy – the Egyptians with food, the Bedu with nearly everything else. Among the other things captured were around 200 rifles and 20,000 rounds of ammunition. The Turks were bewildered by the scene and a bit miffed that their capture seemed secondary to the looting of the material goods. In one way they were right, as once the Bedu had finished loading their camels, they withdrew from the rest of operation and went home with their loot. Lawrence captured the scene in *Seven Pillars*:

> Then came the central act of the day, the assault upon the station. The armoured cars went forward snuffling smoke, and through this haze a file of Turks waving white things rose out of their main trench in a dejected fashion. We cranked up our Rolls tenders; the Arabs leaped on to their camels; Peake's now bold men broke into a run, and the force converged wildly upon the station.

The armoured cars herded 31 prisoners off to a holding area, while a cistern with 3,000 gallons of good water served to replenish the force for the rest of the operation. Then the force withdrew to a campsite in the desert northwest of the station for the night. The next day's action, according to Dawnay's plan, was to take the station at Ramleh six miles to the south.

Just before dawn, Lieutenant Wade took his armoured car south from the camp along with a second as back-up. He picked his way cautiously and approached the station which appeared quiet. He broke the silence with half a belt of machine-gun rounds into the windows and doors of the building. Nothing stirred. Wade got out and inspected the building to find it was evacuated. He returned to camp and the force moved forward to Ramleh where they spent the day refitting and resupplying from their forward base nearby at Tooth Hill. Hornby continued his work along the line to blow things up.

The RAF flew overhead and dropped several bombs on Mudowarra, the next station 12 miles to the south. The pilot saw that a Turkish train was stopped there. He scribbled a note and dropped it over the camp to inform Dawnay. The train came from the direction of Tebuk but there was no information on what it carried.

At dawn on the 21st, the force rolled out with the armoured cars providing security in front and on the flanks. They moved across the tracks and then southeast until they were about 6,000 yards from Mudowarra. This was the station Lawrence most wanted to destroy as it was a critical water stop for the trains, but two previous visits had shown it to be too well defended. The force stood easy while Dawnay, Peake, Hornby, and Lawrence went forward in one of the tenders (LC1105) to do a reconnaissance. Gilman accompanied them in one of the armoured cars. The cars crept to within 2,500 yards of the station in full view of the Turkish defenders sitting on a hilltop bastion that lay around 200 yards west of the railway. Dawnay ordered a halt and the officers took turns looking at the Turkish defences with their binoculars until a flash and a puff of smoke told them they were unwelcome. A shell exploded near them, a bit too close for comfort. The Turks had taken their time to lay their guns in accurately. They had four Austrian Škoda M.16 mountain guns that fired a 10cm (4in) shell to over 7,500 yards, meaning the British were well within the howitzers' range. The gun crews were experienced as their next rounds landed closer to the cars, but luckily still not close enough to do damage. Having confirmed the Turks had good artillery, Gilman yelled for everyone to load up and get out of the area. Everyone hopped in the cars and took off the way they had come. Gilman followed with his armoured car to provide a fig-leaf of protection, but it was nearly for naught. Gilman described what happened next,

> My armoured car was following the tender to act as a screen when I distinctly saw a shell land immediately in front of the tender now travelling at over 70 m.p.h. The shell was a dud and did not go off and I saw it sticking in the sand as I passed. Had this shell exploded it must have killed everybody in the tender. Had this happened 'The Seven Pillars of Wisdom' [sic] would never have been written nor many other books on Lawrence, and the film 'Lawrence of Arabia' would never have been shot. I do not suppose any of my crew noticed the incident and the occupants of the tender were not in a position to.
>
> Lawrence was so annoyed at having been caught by this wily Turkish trick he wanted to get back at them. So he guided the party by a detour to a many culvert [sic] bridge below Mudowarra, and out of range of all the Turkish guns, where we laid heavy charges and blew the whole structure sky high. I got a photo of it going up. This completed that day's work and we withdrew to a point some miles above Mudowarra and camped for the night. I slept alongside Lawrence that night and in a discussion on what we had done that day, I mentioned the incident of the dud shell. I do not think it made much impression on him for I never heard him mention the subject again or discuss it with others. We were both very tired and sleepy. After all, I had had quite a bit of experience of dud shells on other fronts. Don't anybody say you can't see a shell arrive, you can you know.[23]

Although Lawrence did not appear to be impressed with Gilman's tale, he did acknowledge the event in *Seven Pillars* saying, "We made off in undignified haste, through the dropping shells, into some distant hollows to the south-east."

---

[23] Quoted from Gilman's diary in Philip Walker's *Behind the Lawrence Legend: The Forgotten Few Who Shaped the Arab Revolt*, Oxford: Oxford University Press, 2018.

Colonel Dawnay stands next to Rolls-Royce Tender LC1105, the same car in which they were riding when nearly hit by a Turkish artillery round. (Gilman Family Collection)

A subsequent aerial recce of Mudowarra station by 'X' Flight aircraft reported the garrison had been increased to around 500 men and four howitzers. The station was too well defended to risk an attack.

But the artillery ambush had upset Lawrence and Dawnay a bit and they decided to let the Turks know how they felt. Taking the armoured cars and explosive-laden tenders south, nearly to Hallat Amar where Lawrence had destroyed his first train the previous year, they found a long ten-culvert bridge over a wash and blew it sky high. Satisfied with their accomplishment, they withdrew north to their camp. Lawrence left the camp that evening and returned to Feisul's headquarters now located at Aba el Lissan.

Dawnay was not yet finished wrecking the railway, however. The following day would be perhaps the most challenging of the operation. They headed north out of their overnight camp towards Wadi Rutm, a small station at the base of the Batn al Ghoul valley.[24] The valley opens to the south, but to the north, it quickly narrows beyond the station as the rail line snakes up several 'S' curves to reach the plateau above. The walls of the valley close in tightly on either side of the station. On the western side, the ancient camel caravan and pilgrimage route follows the base of the hills while on the eastern, the Ras al Naqb escarpment rises around 1,000 feet to a

---

[24] Batn al Ghoul means Belly of the Beast.

large rock-wall fortress and support base the Turks built to overlook and protect the station. The off-duty station guards and other support personnel stayed in tents within the fortress walls. As the British force approached, the guards withdrew from the station and headed up the escarpment's mule trails to reach the safety of the fort's walls.

The Egyptian cameliers approached the station first and got to within 400 yards before heavy rifle fire from the fort above forced them to back off. The armoured cars approached and poured fire into the station, then shifted to the fortress high above them. But they could not hit it effectively because their turret machine guns could not be elevated enough. Next, the 10-pounders came into play and Brodie ordered his guns into action at 3,700 yards. They fired round after round of HE at the station and up at the fortress works. The fire was so heavy that the Rolls-Royce tenders ran back to the Tooth Hill camp several times to pick up more ammunition for the guns. At the height of the exchange, Hornby and Dawnay took an armoured car loaded with explosives and ran it up the valley to within 50 yards of the buildings. Hornby jumped out and led Dawnay into the buildings to set charges. After laying out the explosives, the fuses were lit and they escaped to the safety of the armoured car just before the buildings went up in a flash of smoke and flying masonry. Dawnay called the main attack off at dusk and the force returned to its bivouac site for the night. On 23 April, the force occupied itself in more destruction before withdrawing to Abu Sawana and then back to home base at Guweira. When Dawnay got back to camp, he continued on to Cairo where he was needed. Joyce returned from his convalescence on 18 March.

Break in the action. RFA 10-pounder section shelling Wadi Rutm station, 22 April 1918. (John Pascoe & John Winterburn)

10-pounder recoiling during anti-aircraft firing practice. (John Pascoe & John Winterburn)

Dawnay's plan did not achieve all its objectives. That is not to say the plan was faulty – the push north to Kerak never materialized because of Zeid's poor judgement, while the assault on Ma'an faltered after Dawnay's concept of operation was changed by the Arab commanders. That said, Ma'an's Turkish garrison was fixed in its barrack fortress. But then, so too were Feisul's forces stuck on Jebel Semna.

Dawnay's southern railway-bashing, however, was a rousing success. He assembled and executed a large-scale combined operation in the enemy's rear. The use of forward supply points, aerial reconnaissance and bombing, mobile guns and armoured cars against strongpoints, followed up with mounted infantry to exploit their successes, delivered the Turks in the Hejaz a setback from which they would not recover.

Dawnay's after-action report detailed that the force destroyed three rail stations, over five miles of track, 18 bridges and culverts, and six miles of telegraph line and poles were burned. Essentially, the railway from Ma'an to within three miles of Mudowarra, a stretch of 65 miles, was under Arab and British control for five days, which resulted in the capture of over 500 Turkish soldiers. And, as Leofric Gilman noted, the Turks were never able to repair the railway again.

With the fate of Medina fairly well sealed, the question of the Turkish Army north of Ma'an came back to the fore. Feisul's forces were entrenched around that city and attention was turned again to the rail line. The damage done by Allenby's raid on Salt and Amman had been inconsequential and was repaired quickly. To worsen matters, Allenby had authorized another attempt on Salt in late April after Beni Sakhr tribal elders contacted him directly to propose a coordinated operation.

No one informed the BMM or Hedgehog; Lawrence was horrified to learn of the operation, knowing that although the Beni Sakhr promised to field 20,000 warriors in support, actually he had very little to offer.[25] The operation, which involved General Henry G. 'Harry' Chauval's Australian cavalry crossing the Jordan in flood and nearly being encircled, failed and cost Allenby 1,650 casualties. Both operations against Salt and Amman shook Feisul's confidence. The bright side, if any, of the operation was that it diverted the Turkish leadership from Allenby's next objective and the general staff resolved not to involve itself in rebel affairs. Lawrence, as usual, had an opinion on the matter, saying: "They [the General Staff] saw moving irregulars was an art." Allenby's staff realized that working with guerrilla forces required dedicated professionals who understood the nuances of the tribes, their strengths, weaknesses, and actual capabilities. It was not like controlling a dedicated national army, and thus they would leave handling the irregulars to the advisors who knew their charges.

In order to keep Ma'an isolated from the Turks, Captain Young was tasked with keeping up the demolitions on the railway north of Ma'an towards Dera'a. Young was relatively new to Hedgehog, initially chosen as a possible understudy for Lawrence.[26] He spoke Arabic fluently, probably better than Lawrence, and was experienced at working with indigenous soldiers, first as an artillery officer in India and then as an assistant political officer in Mesopotamia.

Young first met Lawrence at Carchemish in 1913, before the war when he was on leave from the army and travelling about the Middle East to learn Arabic. He stayed in northern Syria with Lawrence for a week learning about archaeology and being amused by the poor relationship Lawrence had with the Germans. Then the war began and Young went off to India and Mesopotamia. They had met again in Basra after Lawrence returned from his Kut expedition, but this time Young was less impressed by Lawrence's overt disdain for regular British officers. Young had heard vaguely of Lawrence's exploits in the Hejaz through military reporting and was surprised when he learned he (Young) had been assigned to the BMM. Upon meeting again in Cairo's Hotel Savoy in February 1917, Lawrence told Young that he had asked for him personally. The two sailed to Akaba from Suez on board the Egyptian steamer SS *Borulus* and spent the hours talking about the situation and Feisul. When Young arrived with Lawrence at the busy port, he met the other Hedgehog officers and it became clear that he was part of a great project – not just one man working alone.

Instead of being Lawrence's replacement, Young was immediately put to work as another advisor. With Feisul's troops firmly anchored so close to Ma'an, it was decided to expand operations and sabotage the railway south of Dera'a again to prevent

---

[25] Lawrence estimated the Beni Sakhr had no more than 400 capable men.
[26] Although Lawrence at first said no one could replace him, he recommended Young and Gertrude Bell as possible candidates. The High Commissioner, Wingate, thought Young the better choice.

reinforcements from coming down the line. But, in the middle of the operation, Young was pulled due to sickness after one abortive raid. Lawrence thought Young had pushed himself too hard and had tried to do too much on his own. Young was also impatient and often locked horns with the Arabs. Joyce concurred with Lawrence. Young was replaced by Hornby and Peake who continued to sabotage the railway with Sherif Nasir and his men. Young returned to Akaba in July to work as 'Q', the quartermaster or supply officer for the mission, just in time for the final push north. But Allenby's push was to be delayed once more.

An early April offensive in Europe by the Germans prompted the War Council to demand troops from the EEF. Twenty-four combat-experienced battalions would be replaced by native units from the Indian Army that were not combat ready. They would require training; the long awaited final push would have to come later. Feisul was extremely disappointed. The delay, coupled with the British failures at Salt, would try his own and his force's morale. Living as part of a rebellion in enemy-controlled territory was more dangerous and exhausting than coping with a general war. Additionally, public revelations of the Sykes-Picot treaty and news of what appeared to be a successful German advance in Europe were fraying the edges of the Arab-British alliance. The senior Hedgehog officers knew the next days and weeks would be crucial if the Arabs were not to drift away into the arms of the Turks. Lawrence was aware of and briefed Hogarth on the fact that Feisul was in secret contact with Djemal Pasha and was discussing the possibility of breaking with the British. Feisul's belief that the British would win the war had been shaken over the last months.

Lawrence spent much of the late spring travelling back and forth between Allenby's and Feisul's headquarters. When he learned the offensive would be delayed, he struggled to come up with a game plan to ensure Feisul stayed on the British side. While he was turning over ideas, he found that a reorganization of the Imperial Camel Corps would free up several thousand camels, which gave him an idea to mount a raid on Dera'a, which would put a great deal of pressure on the Turks and possibly even force them to remove troops facing Allenby to deal with the threat. He also felt the plan would occupy Feisul and allow him to move further north into Syria. The only problem was that Feisul didn't have the necessary transport animals to move the size force needed to do the job. So, he asked for some camels and Allenby gave him two thousand. In late May, when Feisul learned of the gift he was overjoyed, but his correspondence with Djemal would go for several more weeks until it became clear who was winning the war.

The raids north of Ma'an continued with such intensity that Peake's Egyptian Camel Corps was aptly renamed 'Peake's Demolition Co., Ltd.' The HACS War Diary recounts one such episode with Peake:

> Lieutenant Greenhill with 17 men, two Rolls-Royce armoured cars, one Rolls-Royce tender, and two Fords reported to Captain Peake. Made Tahouny [Tahuna] and our base of operations. Captain Peake, Lieutenant Greenhill, and one Sherifian officer proceeded on reconnaissance of

line between Ma'an and Jerdun. Was informed of an Arab outpost was on the railway but this proved untrue. Returned to camp. A plan was then formed to cross the line and operate from the eastern side. To this end, a guide was secured and the two armoured cars, accompanied by Captain Peake and a detachment of 12 ECC, to blow up rails to enable the cars to cross the line, proceeded to Wadi Jerdun. Here party halted to await approach of dusk, it being desirable that cars cross unobserved. At dusk, cars and ECC proceeded towards line at a place selected by guide. Suddenly heavy rifle fire opened on party at close range. Cars backed out due to exposed condition of personnel. I did not open fire on enemy as it was not advisable in view of forthcoming operations to advertise the presence of the cars and, it being dark, the enemy position was extremely uncertain. Party withdrew a distance of 3,000 yards and parked for the night with no casualties. It was decided that the cars should assist the Sherifian Army in an attack at dawn on the Red Fort [near Jerdun].

The next morning at 0430, two armoured cars moved off for attack formation in line at 200 yard intervals. LC336 took right flank. Hostile fire was encountered at 1,000 yards. From this time forward both cars were heavily engaged and were the target of enemy machine guns. Cars gradually moved forward and extended their flank until a range of 600 yards was reached. Targets engaged were enemy machine guns, one of which it is believed to have been put out of action, a supposed telephone post in communication with Ma'an, and infantry firing from parapets. No rounds were fired at any but definite targets and I have a good reason for believing enemies suffered considerably, as gunnery of both gun teams was excellent. About this hour, Sherifian troops were advancing at about 1,000 yards to our rear. At 0800, infantry was almost to our position. Cars moved forward and further extended their flank until a range of 400 yards was reached, but from this point the attack was not pressed. A general retirement of the infantry took place.

The cars remained in position for another half an hour expecting a second attempt would be made. We fired a considerable number of rounds to counter enemy fire, the cars being the sole remaining target. The mirage at this time on our objective was becoming intense and made the observation very difficult. We now received full effect of enemy fire and I could see no advantage to be gained by remaining in action longer, having on my car only one belt of small arms ammunition, which I kept in reserve in case of accidents or an enemy attempt to rush car. My pressure [fuel] tank, both front wheels, spare rear wheels, and oil tank were punctured and being uncertain also as to the amount of petrol left in my gravity tank, the engine having fed from this for some time, I gave the order 'Out of Action'. I would like to mention my appreciation of the splendid behaviour and work of crew of each car especially in the case of Private Ross, driver of armoured car LC336. Sergeant Grant also ably conducted LC340.[27]

As Lieutenant Greenhill reported, not all operations were entirely successful. His comments illustrate the general tactics used in attacking enemy strongpoints and demonstrates that the cars were not completely immune to the effects of enemy fire. Exposed tyres and tanks generally suffered greatly at close ranges. There were more small missions like this run against the railway; many more were successful, but by mid-July the Turks were beginning to gain on the destruction and repair the lines faster than they could be broken. Feisul's forces around Ma'an would soon be threatened, perhaps in as little as a month, if the Turks kept up the pace.

Feisul liked Lawrence's plan to take Dera'a but, although he now had the transport animals, he did not have the troops required for the operation. Many men were

---

[27] LC336 and LC340 were the military registration numbers of the two HACS cars.

needed to maintain pressure on the Turk garrison at Ma'an, and reinforcements from the south were not forthcoming. Grand Sherif Hussein refused to send Abdullah's and Ali's forces north as he needed their protection near Mecca. Hussein was greatly concerned not only with Fakhri Pasha's forces but also those of Abdul Aziz ibn Saud who, although an ally of the British, very much wanted to seize the Holy Cities from Hussein for himself and his tribe.[28] Tribal politics in Arabia, as elsewhere, trumped international agreements. Plans for the attack on Dera'a were, for the moment, frustrated.

The British, through wireless intercepts, knew the Turks were quickly repairing the damage on the Dera'a–Ma'an line.[29] It was only a matter of time before more reinforcements would be sent south to lift the 'siege' at Ma'an and something needed to be done to prevent that threat from materializing. The first step was to request air cover. General Geoffrey Salmond, Allenby's senior Royal Flying Corps officer, arranged to have aircraft from Palestine bomb the railyard at Amman and the railway line to the south, while 'X' Flight, flying from the advance landing ground at Guweira, would bomb the line from Ma'an north to Jurf el Derwish. The aircraft also provided invaluable reconnaissance data that allowed the BMM to monitor the Turks' strengths and movements. Coupled with agent reporting and wireless intercepts, the BMM's advisors had as complete a picture of the enemy's status and his intentions as they could wish. Additionally, as with its predecessor, 'C' Flight, the presence of 'X' Flight aircraft stiffened the Arab rebels' resolve on the battlefield. The threat the Turkish and German aircraft posed and which initially had frightened them badly, was diminished when the Arabs knew there was an aerial force to protect them.

Lawrence and Dawnay struggled to find a solution to the impending crisis. If the rail line was reopened, the 6,000 Turkish soldiers available in Amman could descend on Ma'an and then launch an offensive that could endanger Feisul's main force. With a shortage of men, however, there was little Feisul could do. Then Dawnay remembered that Allenby's reorganization had left one unit without a job: the Imperial Camel Corps (ICC). Composed of Britons, Australians, and New Zealanders, the ICC had been formed to fight in the desert. They had fought well in the Western Desert and had spent unbroken weeks on patrol in the Sinai. But when Allenby's force had reached the mountainous terrain of Palestine, their services were no longer required. The battalions were being reorganized into an Australian horse-mounted brigade and a New Zealand machine-gun squadron. Dawnay requested that two ICC companies be preserved and released to Hedgehog for the new mission. Under

---

[28] Ibn Saud was supported primarily by the British Government of India which believed in a divide-and-rule policy that supposedly balanced the aspirations of Hussein and ibn Saud.

[29] The Arab Bureau's reporting is filled with 'reliable intelligence' provided by sources named Agent 'Y, and others, in a crude attempt to cover the fact that the information came from wireless intercepts.

Dawnay's plan, the companies would be utilized to attack the station at Mudowarra and targets between Ma'an and Amman. The attacks were expected to confuse Turkish intelligence as to exactly how many troops Feisul had available and would make them think twice about launching a precipitous offensive, especially if they did not realize the attacks were carried out by the same unit.

Dawnay briefed the plan to General William H. Bartholomew, one of Allenby's staff, who supported the concept.[30] Allenby agreed to the request and Lieutenant-Colonel Robert Vere 'Robin' Buxton was ordered to take the remaining ICC companies to Akaba for an undefined task. Buxton, an Etonian, had served with the West Kent Yeomanry before being seconded to the ICC. He commanded the ICC's Second (British) Battalion and would now have the opportunity to lead his 300 men on one last mission. His force started out across the Sinai from the ICC base at Kubri on 23 July. They would arrive in Akaba on the 31st, nine days and 160 miles later.

Allenby had already moved up his plan to resume operations. The abortive British raids on Salt and Amman had convinced the Turks that the main thrust of Allenby's next offensive would continue in that same direction, an assessment confirmed by British intelligence sources. In reality he intended to attack in a different direction, up the Mediterranean coastline. The planned diversionary attack would serve his purposes perfectly. But Allenby stipulated a very precise timetable to support his upcoming move. Allenby's assault would begin on 19 September.

Before then, the Arab forces and their BMM partners had much to accomplish. There was one large objective that Dawnay and Joyce wanted to scratch off their list: Mudowarra. It had been visited by the Arabs and the BMM three previous times and during each 'visit' the target had proven itself too formidable and the attacks had either been aborted or not attempted. Mudowarra was the most critical station between el-Ula and Ma'an. Located over one of the largest aquifers in the region (today's southern Jordan), Mudowarra dispensed the water needed to keep the steam locomotives running. It also had a large Turkish garrison of around 300 men posted on three hilltop bastions. Lawrence had first seen the fortress on 18 September 1917 before the Hallat Amar train attack. Joyce had attempted an abortive attack on 22 January, which was followed by Dawnay's and Lawrence's encounter with the station's artillery in late April. By now, every senior BMM officer was intent on removing the thorn of Mudowarra from their side.

Situated 217 miles south of Amman, Mudowarra station sits east of three hills that guard its approaches. In addition to the ancient caravan and pilgrimage trail that ran parallel to the Hejaz railway, camel paths converged on the village like the spokes of a wheel. It always had been an important water source for the camel caravans and pilgrims. Its deep wells tapped into a huge underground aquifer that was (and remains today) important for local agriculture.

---

[30] General Guy Dawnay was reassigned to France in March 1918.

Colonel Buxton, commander of the Imperial Camel Corps. (Edward Metcalf Collection, The Huntington Library, San Marino, California)

Imperial Camel Corps troop past LC339. (Gilman Family Collection)

Akaba was the assembly point for the raid. Joyce would be leading the expedition, although he was somewhat miffed at being left out (as usual) of Lawrence's and Dawnay's planning process. Joyce appreciated Lawrence but complained that he always proposed great plans and left the details (and work) for others to complete. Dawnay apologized and explained that the tight schedule at Allenby's headquarters didn't allow him to discuss it with Joyce in advance.

Another officer had been selected to work with the BMM staff, Major Walter F. Stirling, who arrived on 18 July. Dawnay sketched out a proposed responsibility chart for Joyce:

> Yourself, directly in charge of the whole show.
>> Lawrence: running his peculiar brand of Lawrentian stunt, and carrying on as usual.
>> Young, i/c communications and administrative understudy to yourself.
>> Stirling, in charge of the travelling circus and doing the bulk of the reconnaissance work and so forth.

Stirling's personality would be a binding agent for the BMM in the field. He was a Sandhurst graduate and had served with the Natal Field Force in the Boer War. He retired in 1913, then rejoined the military when war loomed. He served first as an aerial observer and then with his original regiment, the Dublin Fusiliers, at Gallipoli before being medically evacuated. After his recovery, he served with Allenby during the Third Gaza offensive and was assigned to the BMM with Joyce in July 1918. He joined just in time to take part on the Mudowarra operation.

Major Walter F. Stirling, DSO, with his pet Saluki on 1 October 1918, the day he and Lawrence arrived in Damascus. (W. F. Stirling, DSO)

The ICC's 'cameliers' arrived in Akaba to a raucous reception and set up camp to await news of what would come next. What came next was a speech, not stirringly patriotic like one given on Saint Crispin's Day before the Battle of Agincourt so long ago, but a talk that explained the difficulties they would face, above all with their Arab colleagues, and the need to turn the other cheek. In comparison, according to Lawrence, the Turks at Mudowarra would not pose a problem. It was a motivational success according to Stirling and, with the idea implanted that they were the first European army to set foot in the region since the Crusades, the men went to sleep.

As a camelier, Geoffrey Inchbald described the scene:

> That night, Lawrence asked Major Buxton for permission to address the men and explain why he had sent for us – a most unusual experience during World War One, as it was only on very rare occasions for a commander to take the troops into his confidence. Illuminated by countless fires, he instilled in us how the Arabs thought we were the bravest soldiers in the world and he begged us to live up to the reputation he had built up for us.

The ICC left Akaba on 2 August with Lawrence guiding the column. He had given them a general idea of where they were going and what the target was, but had been especially careful not to divulge details to the locals: the attack had to be a surprise. It was the opening move of a two-pronged manoeuvre that, it was hoped, would divert the Turks from Allenby's true goal. The long column comprised 14 officers, 314 other ranks, four medical corps personnel, 411 camels, plus 22 men of the Egyptian Camel Corps with their 30 camels. Up through Wadi Itm, then a right turn towards Wadi Rum they marched. The ICC camped on 4 August and set off the next day towards Wadi Rum. There the corps watered their 400 camels, an endeavour that would take them over 30 hours. Lawrence left the column at Wadi Rum after they had linked up with their Arab guides and returned to help prepare the second phase of the campaign: Feisul's move north towards Dera'a. The Rolls-Royces would accompany him north.

Then it was on to Disi on 5 August where they met the 32 officers and men of the RFA 10-pounder Motor Section. The artillerymen would accompany the ICC, with their five Talbot tenders, one 10-pounder and a pom-pom gun.[31] One last participant was Captain E. Scott-Higgins, an engineer officer. Captain Young, in his new role as 'Q', had arranged for supplies to be forward-based at Disi, which was also an advanced landing ground for 'X' Flight. Everything required was stockpiled at a forward supply point there: food, fodder, water, petrol, ammunition, and explosives, although the Talbots were running through tyres too quickly. The Talbots also had problems with their wooden wheels. The dry air and heat caused them to shrink and become loose; several collapsed and had to be replaced.[32]

---

[31] A Vickers QF 1-pounder (37mm) rapid-fire gun that fired 300 rounds a minute.

[32] All the Rolls-Royces, save one called 'Blue Mist', were equipped with wire wheels that were more suitable for the desert and rarely required service. Even the older Blue Mist was eventually equipped with wire wheels.

"X" Flight advanced landing ground at Disi. (Gilman Family Collection)

Buxton, Brodie, Marshall, Stirling, in mufti, head out to reconnoitre Mudowarra in one of the RFA Talbots. (Edward Metcalf Collection, The Huntington Library, San Marino, California)

On 6 August the force camped about 12 miles west of Mudowarra. The following morning, two of the Talbots carried Buxton, Stirling, Brodie, and Captain Marshall, the force medical officer, forward to conduct a reconnaissance of the objective. The leaders were in mufti, dressed as Arabs. They dismounted from the truck and walked through the sand to a small hill about 4,000 yards away from the Turkish position, the same hill they had observed from in the abortive January attack. From this spot, called 'Observation Hill', they could watch the comings and goings of the three hilltop forts. Beyond they could see the water tower and station. Even the portly Turkish commander made an appearance riding on his donkey.

Buxton, who hadn't seen the area before, used an aerial photograph taken by one of 'X' Flight's pilots to orient himself and plan the operation. Before him, he could see the three promontories, steep rocky hills with manmade rock walls encircling the top of each. Inside the walls were tents and outside the main enclosure lay smaller sangars on the extreme ends and lower tiers of each hill. Each redoubt would be able to provide interlocking fire to protect the others. With an estimated 300 rifles defending the position, it would be a difficult target, but Buxton had his plan. Satisfied with what they'd seen, the team returned to camp to finalize preparations for the next day's attack.

The force moved closer, to camp within three miles of the Turkish post, and the troops were organized for the attack. There would be three main assault groups:

> against the southern redoubt: three officers and fifty men, including six bombers [grenadiers] and one Lewis gun,

> 1) against the middle or central redoubt: three officers and ninety-five men, including six bombers and two Lewis guns,
>
> 2) against the station, two officers and thirty men, including six bombers.

In addition, smaller parties would cut the telegraph lines and break the rails north and south of the station, and several parties would demonstrate on the far side of the northern redoubt and west of the other two.

The operation began at 0100 on 8 August, when the main assault groups moved into position between the southern redoubt and the station. The headquarters had moved closer to a small hill 500 yards to the west, while Brodie's guns were in position at Observation Hill. The medical personnel and field ambulance section was set up at an empty Turkish fort about 500 yards further west. The assaulters began to climb the steep sides of the hills – having taken off their boots to ensure silence. The attack was set to begin at 0330. The designated time passed without a sound. Another 15 minutes went by. Dawn was approaching and the command group began to get anxious. Finally at 0400 a report was heard from the southern redoubt as a Mills grenade went off. Then another, along with the chatter of a Lewis gun. A red flare was fired into the night sky – the southern redoubt had been captured. This was followed by a green flare – fired after the station fell. At the station

> Lieut. W. T Davies of No. 10 Company, and his party crawled around the stone buildings throwing Mills bombs through the windows before going in with their bayonets. The Turkish trumpeter was shot just as he was raising the instrument to his lips to sound the alarm. One of the casualties sustained by No. 10 Company during the attack was Lieut. J. W. Jones who was killed.[33]

---

[33] Davies was awarded the Military Cross for his actions that day. Geoffrey Inchbald, *Imperial Camel Corps.*

The northern redoubt at Mudowarra. (Edward Metcalf Collection, The Huntington Library, San Marino, California)

Turkish "sanger" fighting position on north perimeter of northern redoubt, Mudowarra. (Author)

As dawn began to break, the middle redoubt came into view and soldiers could be seen clambering up the slopes and over the walls and among the tents. Within minutes, a flare went up. It too was captured. Buxton moved forward to the southern redoubt and ordered the pom-pom gun to follow. Lieutenant Pascoe led the crew forward and they began to fire on the northern redoubt, the last remaining bastion in Turkish hands. Brodie set up the 10-pounder and began to engage the same target from the south. The Turks responded with their gun, but inaccurately.

By this time it was light, Captain Victor D. Siddons aircraft was overhead.[34] After some confusion – a junior officer would not authorize placing a prearranged signal on the ground without Buxton's verbal order – the aircraft were instructed to bomb the northern redoubt. Four 'X' Flight BE2e and BE12 aircraft dropped over 30 20-pound bombs and strafed the hill with around 500 rounds of machine-gun fire, while the artillery section kept up steady, accurate fire with shrapnel and HE rounds. The final phase began as the men of No. 7 Company under Lieutenant Rowan assaulted the hill, climbing up its rocky slopes, simultaneously firing rifles and lobbing grenades as they moved. The defenders hurled their own grenades and fired down into the attackers, but by 0700 it was over and the final defenders surrendered.

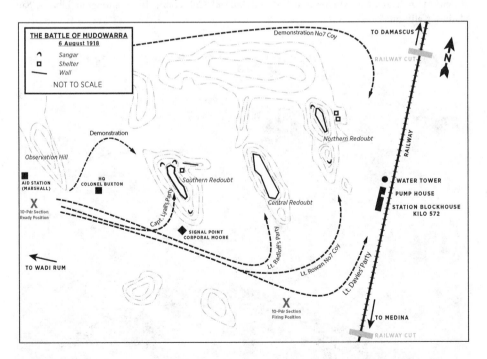

---

[34] Siddons took command of 'X' Flight on 12 May 1918.

Mudowarra. Looking at central and southern redoubts from northern redoubt. (Author)

The toll was four British killed and ten wounded. On the Turkish side 81 were killed and 151 captured, of which 34 were wounded. Two field guns and a number of rifles and machine guns were captured, along with ammunition and many horses, mules, and camels. Lieutenant Davies liberated a Turkish Army trumpet from the station which stayed with the ICC veterans and was used at their reunions for many years.

Consolidation of the objective began. Major Marshall and his medical team began the care and evacuation process using camel *cacolets* and the Talbots to transport the wounded, first to the aid station and then back to Guweira. More Turkish soldiers were captured as their patrols from the south approached the station without realizing it had been taken. Once the area had been cleared of prisoners and wounded, Captain Scott-Higgins began his work. The wells were filled with steel rails after all the needed water had been used to fill canteens and the ubiquitous 12-gallon *fantasses* filled. He then packed the wells with explosives and blew them and the pumps up. Then, as the ICC and the other units assembled on the plain, he finished the job by demolishing the water tower in one spectacular explosion, scattering its individual stones across the desert floor. A train, if it made the journey from the south and arrived at the station, would get no water at Mudowarra for its return.

The water tower and windmill pump being blown up at Mudowarra by Captain Scott-Higgins. (Edward Metcalf Collection, The Huntington Library, San Marino, California)

The water tower at Mudowarra after the station's capture. (Edward Metcalf Collection, The Huntington Library, San Marino, California)

Combining the essential elements of speed, surprise, and robust action, Buxton's combined operations force had travelled undetected over 70 miles behind enemy lines to overwhelm an enemy strongpoint with coordinated artillery and aerial fire and a well-trained ground force. Mudowarra was a classic special operation that integrated time-proven techniques, modern technology, and a touch of audacity.

When all was done Buxton eyed the good work his men had done and turned to his sergeant-major indicating it was time. The order 'Walk march!' was given and the force disappeared north into the desert towards their next rendezvous. Lieutenant Brodie took his men, cannon, and cars west, back to their base at Guweira.

CHAPTER EIGHT

Three Men and a Boy with Pistols

The Turks, not afraid in the least of enemy soldiers, stood helpless before a rebellion.

T. E. LAWRENCE, *SEVEN PILLARS OF WISDOM*

From Wadi Rum, Lawrence had gone north to begin preparations for the Great Raid. Allenby asked that Feisul's Northern Arab Army attack Dera'a and the railway to its north and south as a diversion for his main attack scheduled to commence on 16 September. Allenby thought that thousands of men a week early or a week late would not be as good as "three men and a boy with pistols in front of Dera'a" on the appointed day. Allenby didn't care if the mission was a tactical success as long as the Turks thought his main objective was Amman. Lawrence agreed with Allenby on that point, but he also believed the Arabs needed the victory to fortify their self-respect.

Allenby's requirement would mean moving the Arab base of operations to Azrak. Buxton's ICC would play a role as well. After their success at Mudowarra, they moved north through the desert, east of the railway, to the wells at Bair. It was hoped their presence would not be discovered until they reached Kissir, south of Amman. There they would attack a bridge on the railway. The Turks, having been unable to locate the mostly defunct Imperial Camel Corps (Buxton's force being what remained), would be alarmed and think the entire ICC Brigade was near Amman and reinforce the deception that it was the objective.[1]

Joyce and Young had already begun to make logistical plans to support the mission, but Lawrence and Dawnay saw that it would be too large and slow for the mission at hand. Lawrence had to convince them that a speedier option was required. Young was especially upset that his magnum opus of a plan was being trashed and conflict ensued. Dawnay had remained at Allenby's GHQ, perhaps wisely, so Lawrence was left alone to argue the point. Young would later write in his memoir, *An Independent*

---

[1] Again, wireless intercepts that accurately portrayed what the enemy knew helped shape Allied operational and deception planning. The Turks did not realize that the bulk of the ICC Brigade had been disbanded.

Arab, that the sight of the "little man sitting in the mess tent reading [*Le*] *Morte d'Arthur* with an impish smile on his face" unnerved him no end. Eventually, the resentment passed and the two, still somewhat sceptical, were won over to the new plan. The clock was ticking.

The force that would move to Azrak was large, although it had been cut back from the 2,000 men originally envisioned the previous spring. Along with 430 of Feisul's regulars under Nuri as Said, there were Pisani's artillerymen with four 65mm Schneider guns, 25 machine guns, a section of camel-borne Gurkhas, Peake's Egyptian cameliers, four Rolls-Royce armoured cars and two Rolls-Royce tenders, now commanded by Lieutenant Stanley G. Dowsett.[2] The column would total nearly 1,000 men. Even Brodie's Talbots, deprived of their guns, joined in, to carry supplies forward to the dumps. Two 'X' Flight's aircraft would join them at a prepared landing ground at Azrak as would Major Marshall, RAMC, and his medical *hamla*.[3]

This would be the Northern Arab Army's first direct contribution to Allenby's operations since the revolt was announced. Previously, the guerrilla raids, railway sabotage, and attacks on Turkish strongpoints were ancillary to EEF operations. The independent actions of the Arab Revolt had diverted Turkish assets away from the main campaign but never contributed to a specific objective. Dawnay's plan was

One of 'X' Flight's aircraft at an advanced landing Ground. (Gilman Family Collection)

---

[2] The HACS's first commander, Captain Leofric Gilman, was medically evacuated from the theatre in July 1917. Dowsett served in South-West Africa in 1914/15 with the Natal Carbineers and in East Africa with the 5th LAMB in 1916.

[3] *hamla* is Arabic for a caravan of mules and camels for transport and evacuation.

different. The Arabs were no longer acting as a flank guard, but would conduct a multi-pronged, special operation that combined mobile gun platforms, regular infantry, and aircraft, with indigenous, irregular forces to destroy Turkish lines of communication and fix their troops in place. The operation would prevent the Ottoman Fourth Army from moving north to confront Allenby's main offensive and hopefully deceive the Turkish high command as to his true intentions. Again, the Arabs would be aided by excellent intelligence information. The entire operation would take place behind Turkish lines.

Lawrence left Joyce and Young to logistics planning and flew from Guweira in a BE2e piloted by Siddons. He met Feisul in Jefer to play tribal politics. Nuri Shalaan had finally agreed to join the revolt, feeling reasonably confident of Feisul's support. For the next phase, Shalaan's support was needed at Azrak, which was in his territory. Despite his wariness over treating with the Allies, due in large part to what he had heard about the Sykes-Picot Treaty and France's future role in Syria, Nuri nevertheless accepted Lawrence's word and Britain's support for the rebellion.[4] Nuri would support Feisul. Lawrence would later say of him, "Nuri is quiet, and retiring, but a man of few words and great deeds, intelligent, well-informed, decisive, full of quiet humour, and the best Arab sheikh I have ever met."

Buxton's camel corps had reached Jefer and, on 11 August, Joyce and Lawrence took two of the Rolls-Royces, an armoured car and a tender, driven by SC Rolls and J. E. Sanderson and went out from Aba el Lissan to meet Nuri and his forces. Meanwhile, Buxton and his men would wait at Jefer for several days, replenished by one of Young's preplaced supply sites. As Buxton later wrote:

> It is not unlike an attempt on the part of the Huns to blow up Waterloo Bridge, as it is many miles at the back of their lines and within five miles of their [the Turkish] Army headquarters. But with the promise of Arab support, Lawrence's leadership and an element of surprise, the matter should not be difficult.[5]

Joyce needed to reconnoitre the route to Azrak to determine routes and calculate march times. Over the hard, flat plains the cars flew, their exhaust cut-outs open and roaring. At times the cars' speedometers touched 65mph. Through the wadis, the going was slower, passage over soft sand had to be reinforced with brushwood especially for the armoured beast that weighed in at nearly five tons. The cars were quieter as the drivers picked their way though the valley with exhausts closed. Occasionally, a covey of birds was flushed, bursting out of their cover like a bomb explosion, surprised by the strange intruders. Finally, they reached the old castle at Azrak. Lawrence had been there before, but this time he brought modern engines of war to a place that hadn't seen soldiers since perhaps the sixteenth century. Before

[4] Lawrence told Nuri he should believe whatever the most recent document stated, which at that moment was that the Arabs would keep all territory that they conquered in the war.
[5] Quoted from an unpublished letter written by Buxton in Jeremy Wilson's biography of Lawrence.

leaving the area, they located a suitable landing zone for the planes and then headed back to Buxton's camp which had been moved forward to Bair. Lawrence and Joyce raced back in the two cars – their return was a combination of struggle and pleasure, tyre changes and racing across the flats at high speed with the wind rushing through the cockpits of the cars.

Lawrence rejoined Buxton on 15 August and would stay with him because they were certain to encounter local tribes that required his negotiating skills. Joyce returned with the tender to Guweira to help Young and Dawnay prepare for the march to Azrak.

Over the next days, Buxton's men and camels were watered, loaded, and prepared for action. But, because their supply dump had been looted by local Bedu, Buxton was forced to reorganize and pare down his force, sending 50 men and 100 camels back to British lines. Accompanied by an armoured car, they then departed on their trek towards the target bridge at Kissir. By 20 August, they had reached a point very close to Amman when two German planes passed overhead. Buxton had to decide whether to go forward as planned or abandon the mission. If the planes had seen them, then surprise was most likely lost. There was a Turkish headquarters near their target and the cameliers would have to dismount and walk several miles to carry out the attack. If the camels were discovered by an enemy patrol or the force met resistance on target, Buxton thought he could lose up to 50 men. Lawrence sent out two Arabs to reconnoitre the area ahead. They returned with bad news: an unfriendly tribe sat astride their intended route and, further, strong Turkish patrols were in the area. Lawrence agreed with Buxton's assessment that the raid was not worth the risk and the mission was scrubbed. The ICC's presence had been noted and had put the Turks on alert, which reinforced the deception plan in any event. Disappointed, Buxton and the ICC turned east to make a long circuitous trip back towards Bair and then to their base in the Sinai. Their job in the revolt was finished.[6]

Lawrence returned with them to Bair and then hurried on with the cars to Aba el Lissan in order to accompany Nuri as Said and his regulars north. Joyce would follow several days later with Emir Feisul. But, before they could depart, Grand Sherif Hussein did his best to throw a spanner in the works. Hussein, seemingly jealous of his son Feisul's success in the north, made an extraordinary proclamation in his newspaper, *Qibla*, that Ja'far Pasha al-Askari did not hold the position of chief of staff in the Northern Army. After most of his officers resigned in protest, Feisul too felt honour-bound to resign, as did Zeid when Hussein appointed him to take Feisul's place. Buxton, upon reaching Aba el Lissan, summed up the situation saying everyone was acting childishly. The spat threatened the operation as any delay meant the Arab forces would not be in position in time to act as Allenby's diversion. After

---

[6] As noted in A. P. Wavell's *The Palestinian Campaign*, the ICC marched over 700 miles in 41 days during which their camels were watered 12 times.

Hejaz Armoured Car Battery at Aba el Lissan camp. (Gilman Family Collection)

several days of correspondence, an apology of sorts was wrung from Hussein and Feisul was persuaded to continue his mission.

The first caravan of camels left the base two days late, with the others following. The columns converged on Azrak over 11/12 September and were ready for operations. Dawnay's final version of the plan – written on 9 September – detailed the mission's objectives:

> Demolition party [Gurkhas and Peake's Egyptian Camel Corps] to attack the railway north and south of Mafraq.[7] Under cover of plane bombardment, the main force of Bedouin supported by French mountain battery and armoured cars will assault the train station at Dera'a. Feisul's regular troops to move to Tel el Shehab to destroy the bridge there. All forces must withdraw by dusk on the 15th.

The force was assembled; Feisul and Sherif Nasir had arrived as had Joyce, Marshall, and Young. Also on the scene were Nuri Shalaan with his 300 horsemen, Nuri as Said and the regulars, Auda abu Tayi and others with their Bedouin irregulars. The Arabs totalled over 1,000 men.

Major Stirling was there, leading his 'travelling circus' with Peake and his demolitions company, Hornby, Scott-Higgins and the Gurkhas, Dowsett with the armoured cars, and two new men, Lieutenant Alec Kirkbride, an intelligence officer, and Major Earl Winterton, who had been commandeered from Buxton's camel corps.

---

[7] A station between Amman and Dera'a at Kilometre 162.

Captain Siddons was able to dispatch two aircraft to Azrak, a BE12 and a Bristol F2, a relatively new and capable fighter. Their mechanics and tools had come overland with the caravan in a Crossley tender. The planes would provide the force with a modicum of protective air cover from German and Turkish aircraft.

On 11 September, Dawnay was informed that Allenby's aircraft would not be able to support the attack at the required level and they would have to rely on what aircraft 'X' Flight had available. Slight changes were made to the plan, but Lawrence was confident of success. Members of the Beni Sakr tribe reported that the Turks had moved to retake Tafileh again. The tribesmen were shaken but Lawrence, on the contrary, was ecstatic because it meant the Turks were acting on the deception and moving away from Allenby. Even the assembly of Feisul's army at Azrak was a deception inside a deception, as their gathering was meant to show they would attack Amman, not their true target of Dera'a further north.

On 13 September, the first action kicked off with the departure of Peake and Scott-Higgins leading their sapper elements. Two armoured cars and two tenders accompanied them to provide flank security when they rushed the line. Rualla guides from Nuri Shalaan's group guided them from Azrak to their objective near of Mafraq. It was hoped that the destruction of the line there would prevent reinforcements moving towards Dera'a from Amman.

They were followed on the 14th, when the main column departed towards Umtaiye to the north. As the column moved northwest, they could see the RAF swirling above the town and the splash of bombs and the smoke that told of destruction. It was more noise for the Turkish generals to process and make them conclude an assault was brewing.

Discussions with Feisul and Nuri Shalaan kept Lawrence for several hours at Azrak and then he too raced off in one of the Rolls-Royce tenders, 'Blue Mist', to catch up. He reached the group the next day at Umtaiye to find out that Peake's operation had failed because of a misunderstanding. Peake's guides had taken him to the wrong spot. They had encountered an Arab band who insisted their territory not be disturbed (the band was allied to Feisul's revolt on the condition its territory not be used for operations against the Turks for fear of retribution against their families). Instead of trying to find another location, the attack was broken off. Peake's force needed to move to their next rendezvous north of Dera'a.

Lawrence was, to say the least, upset. He had counted on the railway disruption, but knew the main body, Nasir's and Nuri's troops, Pisani's artillery, and Stirling with the remainder of the cars also needed to move the last 20 miles north towards Tell Arar, past Dera'a. So he decided to take care of the bridge himself, without infantry. That evening, he took a camel patrol forward on a reconnaissance and located a good spot with a four-arch culvert bridge near Jabir, about 15 miles south of Dera'a.[8]

---

[8] Located at Kilometre 149 on the railway.

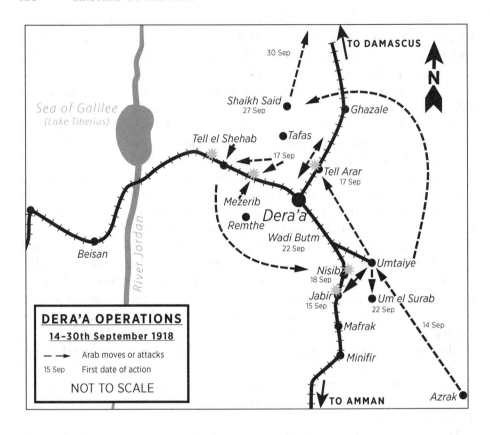

There was a small blockhouse nearby, but he felt the armoured cars could deal with it easily enough. The next morning, 16 September, with Joyce and Winterton, two armoured cars and two tenders, Lawrence headed back to the railway. It was a fine bridge that would take a week to repair. The convoy stopped on a ridge overlooking the point. Lawrence took some guncotton from 'Blast', the tender driven by S. C. Rolls, and loaded it into one of the armoured cars. The two armoured Rolls-Royces would approach the line, one covering the other, and Lawrence would place the explosives. The tenders remained to the rear on the ridge overlooking the area.

As they approached the target, one car crept stealthily down the wash towards the bridge while Lieutenant Grisenthwaite's drove straight at the blockhouse. The station's curious defenders came out of their trenches to see who their visitors were. A short burst from the Vickers dropped two Turks and compelled the remainder to surrender.

Lawrence went to work on the bridge with the bewildered Turkish prisoners watching. At about the same time, Rolls in his tender saw reinforcements coming down the line. Joyce and he drove forward to warn their comrades. Reaching the bridge, they were met by Lawrence who demanded more explosives. Back and forth they ran with bundles of explosives, cramming the drainage holes until they were fully packed.

Planting 'tulips' on the Hejaz Railway – preparing to destroy a bridge. (Gilman Family Collection)

While Lawrence attended to the bridge, Joyce and Winterton tried their hand at laying 'tulip' mines on either side of the culvert. Tulips, so called because of the shape of the railway track after the explosion, were small 30-ounce guncotton charges laid under the centre of the railway sleepers (cross-ties) so when they exploded, the upward force carried the sleepers and the attached rails upwards and inwards, twisting and rending them into a flower shape and that made repair difficult and reuse impossible.

While they worked, a dogfight was taking place overhead. Murphy was conducting a reconnaissance in his Bristol fighter when he encountered a German Rumpler two-seater. Murphy engaged the enemy and, after a long fight, brought it down. But Murphy's plane was badly damaged and he limped back to Akaba where it was declared non-operational. The Arab air force was down to one old, slow BE12.

Back on the ground, when the work was finished, the three prisoners were loaded into the tender with Rolls – the rest had fled into the brush. Lawrence and Joyce lit the fuses and the cars withdrew. The explosives went off in a massive blast as Lawrence had decided to go all out with 150 pounds of guncotton on the bridge. As masonry fell from the sky and the roar and smoke dissipated, Rolls manoeuvred his car away through the rough terrain as best he could. The tender had only made 300 yards from the track when there was a horrific crack and the car stopped dead: a rear spring mount had sheared off and the body dropped onto the wheel. They were stuck.

With enemy reinforcements approaching, the armoured cars returned to stand guard while Rolls assessed the situation; he was not about to abandon his car to the Turks. Throwing the cargo off the back of the car, Rolls saw he could temporarily repair it with a spare running board. He grabbed the long board and shoved it under the spring through to the other side while everyone levered the body up. With the board jammed between two side mounts and holding up the spring, the primary problem had been solved. But there was a new, smaller problem: an extra six feet of board protruded out the side of the car and would snag any obstacle they encountered. They didn't have a saw. It was now Lawrence's turn to be creative: he drew his pistol and fired several bullets through the board until it could be broken off. With that obstacle literally out of the way, the cargo was placed onto Joyce's tender and the four cars trundled off carefully to link up with the main force.

Throughout the day they pushed the cars beneath the desert sun. It was intolerably hot inside the armoured cars' steel shell, but the crews pushed on. The armoured cars kept cool – usually the radiators needed to be refilled once a day, the tenders every second or third, but on this trip it wasn't necessary.[9] At that night's camp, Rolls's car was bound up with much bailing wire and wood: there were no other repair facilities or options available.[10]

The destruction of the bridge cut Dera'a off from Amman, but it also held up reinforcements and supplies for the Turkish force situated at Tafileh. That force was scheduled to attack Aba el Lissan, but now it would have to wait. In the end, no Turkish attack would ever take place.

The next day, 17 September, Lawrence and the team caught up with the main force, just as it was deploying for the attack at Tell Arar. Feisul's army had crossed the railway that morning and began its attack at 0730. Nuri Said was in command and set his troops to flank the Turkish post that stood guard over the bridge and the all-important railway junction. The troops rushed the line and appeared to have captured it when another previously unseen post opened fire, scattering the troops. Pisani's guns were deployed and fired several salvos before the troops assaulted the position. Only one of Nuri's men was killed, but the junction was in Arab hands. Once demolitions were completed, all rail operations to the south would be effectively cut off, as well as to the west, the Jordan Valley and Palestine. Nuri set out machine guns in case of Turkish reinforcements.

Lawrence was suddenly struck by the quiet. Peake's demolition parties should have been active, but they were nowhere to be seen. Puzzled, he went to look for them and found them making breakfast. He was astounded that Peake would be taking a break but attributed it to the Egyptian Army's regularity. Later he would write, "It was like Drake's game of bowls," alluding to comment allegedly made by Sir Francis Drake while bowling in 1588. When told that the Spanish Armada was approaching Drake said, "Time enough to play the game and thrash the Spaniards afterwards."

---

[9] The Fords kept cool only with an added condenser, the Crossley and the Talbots boiled off continuously.
[10] 'Blast' made it through to the end of the campaign with Rolls's provisional repairs.

In good time, they returned to work, methodically destroying the rail line while Pisani's gunners, somewhat inexperienced at demolitions, practised blowing up the Wadi Arar bridge … twice. Peake intended to place 600 'tulips', the charge that he and Lawrence had developed, enough to take out six kilometres of track.

Nuri Said and Lawrence were observing the operation from a hill when they saw a plane take off from Dera'a airstrip to the south. It flew over the Arabs and apparently confirmed they were hostile, because the pilot returned to strafe them and generally upset operations. The aircraft then returned to base and got another eight aircraft up in the air, this time loaded with bombs. Peake's group continued working, moving further north and cutting rails and pulling down telegraph lines as they moved, while the Arabs scattered across two miles of plain to avoid making themselves a targetable group. As the bombs began to fall, Nuri opened fire with the Hotchkiss machine guns and Pisani optimistically opened up with shrapnel case from his Schneider guns. Slightly deterred, the planes flew higher and the bombs became less accurate. Suddenly, Lieutenant Hugh R. Junor showed up, flying the second British plane. Junor had heard of his comrades' troubles by radio and decided to take his place as sheepdog for the flock. In his obsolete BE12, he mixed it up with the Germans and drew them off, out of sight, which kept them from bombing the troops. But his fuel was running dangerously low and he returned to drop a message saying he would have to land. The ground troops rushed to prepare a small landing strip, but, as Junor came in, the wind caught the plane and rammed him into the rocks which sheared off his landing gear. Unharmed, Junor was pulled from the wreck and was able to extricate the machine guns before the wreck was blown up. He then commandeered a spare Ford and set off to do battle on his own. He blew a hole in the railway to the south before returning with the Turks on his tail. The Turks were dissuaded from further pursuit when they saw the Arab forces in front of them. All the while, the armoured cars were on flank guard, as the tenders dispensed explosives to the demolition teams. One of the Talbots was put out of action by a bomb and was abandoned, but its crew escaped injury.

Later that day, Nuri Said, Lawrence, Young, and Pisani with two of his guns went off to break the Palestine leg of the railway by attacking the station at Mezerib. They also intended to drop the Tell el Shehab bridge, the same one that had been attacked unsuccessfully the previous year. Approaching what was thought to be a lightly defended Mezerib station, a sharp engagement ensued. Pisani put his two mountain guns into action and reduced the Turks' will to resist with the heavy application of high-explosive shells. Twenty machine guns provided additional suppressive fire until the 40 survivors gave up. It was Nuri who went forward in front of his men to accept their surrender.

The station was looted by soldiers and the local peasants who had been closely following the action. Two German lorries were found on flatcars. They were filled with things strange to the Arabs but quite suitable to the Europeans and Egyptians,

Hugh Junor and his BE airplane. (Edward Metcalf Collection, The Huntington Library, San Marino, California)

including canned meats and some bottled asparagus. Nuri Said pocketed many bottles and offered the rest to the British (who could appreciate the bounty) after he had scared off the other Arab looters by telling them the bottles contained 'pork bones'.

The destruction at Mezerib was completed by cutting the telegraph lines on the station's roof which connected the Turkish command in Palestine with Dera'a. That made the Turks reliant on wireless and would cause them no end of confusion. Their indiscriminate use of radio would inform Allenby of the Arabs' success.

The plan to take down the Tell el Shehab bridge was thwarted by the arrival of a troop train from Beisan to the west. The Turks and Germans in the high command thought the threat to Dera'a more serious than Allenby to their front. It was their mistake.

Nuri and Lawrence discussed the risk and decided that the heavily reinforced bridge was not worth the loss of valuable lives as long as the railway between it and Dera'a was destroyed. Young and Lawrence emplaced more 'tulips' and Nuri's men set the station and the supply train ablaze. The fuel tanks of the lorries added to the fire which soared high into the night sky. That night, they worked their way beyond the Tell el Shehab bridge and placed several more charges on its far western side. The explosions kept the enemy troops awake all night. They would not be able to return to Palestine to assist against Allenby's upcoming offensive or move east; they were effectively marooned with the train. Pisani capped things off by placing a delayed charge on the station's water tower before they withdrew the following morning. Lawrence thought it unnecessary, but Pisani wanted to make a spectacular impression.[11]

To avoid the open plain of Tell Arar, Nuri Said drew off to the west of Dera'a, past Remthe and south to make a circle around the town and return to Umtaiye. There was one more bridge to blow, Lawrence's 79th, where they crossed the line south of Dera'a at Nisib. After another duel to drive off the defenders, large charges were laid at the base of the five-foot support piers of the 75-foot-long bridge. Once Nuri moved his column over the track and the men were well away, Lawrence fired the 800 pounds of explosive. In the process, he was nearly killed. He had, out of habit, used a short fuse and only escaped injury because he sheltered in a nearby abandoned Turkish dugout.

The Turks weren't finished shooting at them, however. As they moved towards Umtaiye, a repair train came north to attend to the damaged bridge at Jabir. Their forward progress was frustrated by the latest destruction at Nisib. But the train had a howitzer on board and, with the aid of a spotter aircraft, the field gun began to accurately shell the Arabs. They were able to move slowly out the gun's range, however, and took no casualties. As they were escaping, Lawrence observed the plane descend, apparently with some mechanical difficulty, and land near the rail line at Wadi Butm. He marked the spot in his mind and kept moving.

The armoured cars, Peake's demolition squads, Joyce and the Arab army returned to Umtaiye on 18 September. Nuri Said and his merry band, along with the Gurkhas, Pisani, Lawrence and Young, rode in on the 19th. The camp was besieged by locals and Nasir was given the task of explaining Feisul's revolt to them, some ecstatic, some angry or fearful of retribution.

The Englishmen counselled together the next morning to discuss the past days' work. Joyce explained that he had seen a group of Turks at work repairing the bridge at Jabir and sent Junor and Winterton to drive them off, but they too encountered an armoured train which spotted them and directed spirited gunfire at their car. Joyce explained that they had chosen the better part of valour and escaped. Lawrence then mentioned the plane he had seen land. An idea was hatched and a new sort of snipe hunt was about to begin.

Joyce asked for volunteers to go on the hunt but in the end he had to pick two drivers because everyone put their hands up. Lawrence and Junor each got an armoured car and, after a five-mile drive, they came to the mouth of the wadi and entered it with the exhaust cut-outs closed. The cars crept quietly down the valley until it turned and opened up onto a meadow. There they saw three machines parked on line 2,000 yards to their front, very close to the railway line. The crews

---

[11] Young was awarded a DSO for his gallantry during the attack at Mezerib.

sped forward anticipating the kill but the cars were checked by a deep ditch. Turning to parallel the ditch, they looked for a crossing point with no luck, but the diagonal route brought them closer. The pilots had seen or heard their approach and leapt to pull their propellors and start the engines for a quick escape. Two were successful, and the pilots hopped into the aircraft just as the cars reached their closest approach – about 1,200 yards – and began to fire. The British chased the planes with their guns roaring as the enemy made their take-off run, but the 'Huns' escaped unscathed. The third aircraft was not so lucky. It was still stationary and the armoured cars' gunners poured around 1,500 rounds of .303 ammunition from their Vickers into it while the pilot and mechanic sought cover in a nearby ditch. The enemy ground troops fired back – they didn't appreciate the British presence – but most of their fire pinged off the cars' ⅜-inch-thick steel plate with no effect. Junor stuck his head out of the turret to get a better view and took a round through his flying helmet, but suffered no apparent damage to his head. When the plane began to burn, the cars retired. The two planes that had taken off returned to try to drop their ordnance on the intruders. They only had four bombs each and the pilots hadn't perfected their techniques, so the cars, which were moving painfully slowly for the occupants, escaped with only minor damage from the near misses. Some shrapnel flew through the view ports and pinged around the interior, which added to the passengers' discomfort though. The only other damage was a shredded tyre.

The cars returned to Umtaiye somewhat bruised but still quite operational. The encounter made everyone worry about the Turkish air force's advantage. The Arabs were outnumbered nine enemy aircraft to zero of their own. An attack on the Dera'a airfield was ruled out as there were around 1,500 well-alerted Turkish rifles and machine guns defending the town. The solution lay in Allenby's direction and his air force. A messenger aircraft was due in to Azrak the following day and Lawrence thought he would hop a ride back to GHQ and ask for more air cover.

He left Umtaiye that night with one armoured car, one tender, and one Ford and returned to Azrak. They also planned to do some demolition work along the railway with Peake's crew and managed to shoot up a train before they headed to Azrak, but the quest ended when the armoured car took a round in its unarmoured pressurized fuel tank. With no pressure, the engine was instantly starved of fuel and quit.

After taking several hours to repair the leak, they continued on to Azrak, arriving in the early morning. Feisul was there with Nuri Shalaan. Colonel Joyce, who had recently arrived from Tall Afar, regaled the Arab princes with tales of the recent Arab army successes.

On 21 September, the scheduled messenger plane landed at Azrak. Lawrence hopped in to the back seat for a ride to GHQ, which left the original passenger stranded. With Stirling still bashing the line to the north, Lawrence flew off to see Allenby near Ramleh in Palestine. En route they did a quick reconnaissance for a potential target bridge at Zerga, 12 miles north of Amman. Lawrence thought that destroying it would help keep the Fourth Army in the south. He did not want any additional forces to possibly confront Allenby in the north.

Allenby's offensive at Meggido kicked off on 19 September. The Turks were fooled by the elaborate deception plan and thought he intended to attack towards Amman and concentrated their forces to the east. Allenby instead attacked north along the coast to the west.[12] The British XXI Corps blew a huge hole through the Turkish Eighth Army and kept moving. Around 9,000 cavalry and mounted infantry pushed up the coast and wheeled to the right as the Turkish divisions quickly collapsed. The success was stunning. It was the fourth year of the war and the Ottoman Army was exhausted. After 36 hours, elements of Allenby's forces had penetrated 70 miles beyond the Turkish front.

When he arrived at Allenby's office Lawrence was briefed on the unfolding situation. He was told that while the main thrust continued north along the coast, three other advances to the east were planned. One force (ANZAC Division) would cross the River Jordan towards Amman led by Major-General Edward Chaytor, the second (4th Cavalry Division) towards Dera'a by Major-General George Barrow and the third (Desert Mounted Corps) towards Kuneitra led by Major-General Henry Chauvel.[13] Chaytor would occupy Amman, while Barrow and Chauvel would pivot north towards Damascus. Feisul's Northern Arab Army was to cooperate and assist but not attempt to take Damascus without the Allies.

The lack of air superiority over Umtaiye was Lawrence's main focus. Allenby summoned his RAF generals, Salmond and Brigadier A. E. 'Biffy' Borton, and they promised two Bristols for air cover and a Handley Page O/100 bomber to ferry supplies. The Turks and Germans had been swept from the skies over Palestine and the generals and their pilots were enthusiastic to support the Arab Revolt.

The next day, a flight of two Bristols and an old DH-9 with Lawrence on board headed off for Umtaiye. Not finding the army there, they diverted to Um el Surab, the agreed alternate base, and landed on a strip that had been cleared under Young's supervision. Captain Ross Smith, who was also the Handley Page pilot, checked out the landing ground and declared it fit for the much larger plane. Before Ross Smith headed back to get his big plane, breakfast was served, only to be disturbed twice by enemy scouts. The crews rushed to their Bristols and chased them away, shooting two down, and declaring they wanted to remain with the Arabs as opportunities for hunting were better behind the lines. Finally the big plane was fetched, and Ross Smith returned to land his giant bomber in front of the amazed Arabs, who declared it the sire of the little Bristols. In addition to a great quantity of parts,

---

[12] Mostly due to Feisul's operations near Amman and Dera'a and the creation of a 'phantom' army in the Jordan River Valley.

[13] The designations for these units are simplified, as there were a number of units and nationalities involved.

The only known photo of the Handley Page O/100 at Um el Surab. (Joe Berton/Valerie Gilman)

fuel, and supplies, on board was Brigadier 'Biffy' Borton who wanted to see what the Arab Revolt was all about. The general was impressed with what he saw and promised to keep up a daily supply flight with the Handley Page. The RAF had its first self-supplied, forward aerodrome behind enemy lines.

Lawrence took the DH-9 to pick up the observer left at Azrak and sent him home with his pilot and machine. He then returned to Um el Surab with Feisul in the green Vauxhall car which Allenby had presented him. The force was together again.[14]

The pace had not slowed. Stirling took two armoured cars and a tender out on 22 September to support an Arab attack on the line north of Mafraq at Jabir. The Arabs attacked a strongpoint while the armoured cars attacked a nearby repair party that was endeavouring to build a replacement for the bridge that had been destroyed by Joyce and Lawrence. Trying to support the Arabs on their left flank the cars ran into bad terrain and then moved to the right where they found the going easier. The cars closed to within 500 yards of the line, as two machine guns opened up on them with very accurate fire. After enduring a hammering cacophony of 8mm machine-gun fire on their armoured cars steel skins, both crews had to retreat. Their tyres were completely shot away. Hiding behind a small hill, the crews changed the tyres in 15 minutes and then attacked again, firing single 250-round belts in turns to keep the guns from overheating. This time they penetrated all the way to the bridge and put the enemy machine guns out of action. The tender joined them at the bridge with its cargo of explosives and the crews jumped from their cars to finish the job. They placed explosives on the new wooden trestle and on the repair train and then

---

[14] Save Joyce who headed south towards Ma'an and Aba el Lissan with two armoured cars and a tender.

pulled back to a safe range as the charges went off. A short distance away, the Arab forces successfully assaulted the Turkish position, captured a number of soldiers, and destroyed the blockhouse before withdrawing. Once Stirling was satisfied with the results – the bridge was a smoking ruin and train was burning fiercely – the crews turned and headed back for Umtaiye, acting as rear security for the Arab forces. On the 24th, Winterton and Kirkbride conducted a small attack, ostensibly to ensure the rail line stayed broken. Lawrence mused that they did it just for the fun.

Ross-Smith returned that night piloting the big Handley Page. This time the bomber was carrying a deadly cargo and dumped 20 100-pound bombs on Mafraq, totally destroying the station. Shortly thereafter, Allenby issued an order to stop any more attacks on the railway. The rebuilding of infrastructure would be a priority once the war concluded.

Allenby's plan went well and led to the destruction of the Ottoman-Turkish Army on the coast. With their defeat, Djemal Pasha's Fourth Army at Amman and Ma'an began to dissolve and retreat north. Sitting directly on their line of retreat, the Arab Northern Army was confronted with a ragged but still dangerous group of around 10,000 Turkish, German, and Austrian troops trying to make their way north. A hot debate ensued among the British advisors present in Feisul's camp about whether to draw off and avoid confrontation or to harass the withdrawing enemy. Young, who understood himself to be in charge of military operations in Joyce's absence, wanted to avoid an entanglement with an enemy ten times their strength and advised moving east to Jebel Druse. Lawrence however, burdened by the implications of Sykes-Picot, knew the Arabs had to capture Damascus. After a somewhat acrimonious debate, Lawrence won out. It was decided to move to a somewhat secure area at Shaikh Said, 13 miles north of Dera'a. On 27 September they reached that location, exhausted from the past month's exertions, and set up camp. It wasn't long before the armoured cars patrolling the area reported the first strings of retreating enemy troops who were coming up the rail line by the hundreds.

While Chaytor's forces made their advance on Amman, Djemal hesitated to order its evacuation. General Liman von Sanders, the German army advisor to the Turks and commander of its armies in Palestine and Syria, had earlier warned Djemal to retreat, but he waited until 22 September. His delay ensured that his army would retreat in chaos. With Chaytor's forces in pursuit, the Fourth Army streamed north. The Turkish II Corps also abandoned their positions at Ma'an and fled. Directly to their front they encountered the Allies. After a lengthy negotiation to obtain guarantees for their safety from the Beni Sakhr Arabs, the Turkish commander surrendered his forces. The next day, Chaytor's ANZACs moved into Amman with around 11,000 prisoners.

Remnants of the Fourth and Seventh armies, the latter from Beisan in the Jordan Valley, continued to stream north pressured by the Allied conventional armies at their rear and Feisul's guerrillas pinpricking them on their flanks. Sometimes the pricks were substantial as the Turks paid the price for their oppression at the hands of vengeful Arabs, especially the locals who had joined with Feisul as his caravan penetrated their lands. Once they saw that the Turks had collapsed, it seemed all the locals had risen as one to make the enemy retreat north as dangerous and often as deadly as possible.

Venturing out of Shaikh Said on 27 September, the Arabs encountered a Turkish column. What happened is best told by Lawrence himself:

> Aeroplanes now dropped us a message that there were two columns of Turks advancing on us. One from Deraa was six thousand strong, and one from Mezerib, two thousand strong. We determined that the second was about our size, and marched the regulars out to meet it just north of Tafas, while sending our Hauran horse out to hang on to the skirts of the large column, and some unmounted peasants to secure the Tel el-Shehab bridge, which the Turks were mining. We were too late (since on the way we had a profitable affair with an infantry battalion) to prevent the Mezerib column getting into Tafas. They strengthened themselves there, and as at Turaa, the last village they had entered allowed themselves to rape all the women they could catch. We attacked them with all arms as they marched out later, and bent the head of their column back towards Tell Arar. When Sherif Bey, the Turkish Commander of the Lancer rearguard in the village, saw this he ordered that the inhabitants be killed. These included some twenty small children (killed with lances and rifles), and about forty women. I noticed particularly one pregnant woman, who had been forced down on a saw-bayonet. Unfortunately, Talal, the Sheikh of Tafas, who, as mentioned, had been a tower of strength to us from the beginning, and who was one of the coolest and boldest horsemen I have ever met, was in front with Auda abu Tayi and myself when we saw these sights. He gave a horrible cry, wrapped his headcloth

Bedouin sheik on horse (Talal El-Hareidhin of Tafas). (Harry Chase, James A. Cannavino Library, Archives & Special Collections, Marist College, USA)

about his face, put spurs to his horse, and, rocking in the saddle, galloped at full speed into the midst of the retiring column, and fell, himself and his mare, riddled with machine-gun bullets, among their lance points.[15]

What happened thereafter was retribution. With Auda leading the way, the Turkish column responsible for the massacre at Tafas was in turn cut into parts and then reduced systematically from 2,000 to very nearly none. Casually, Lawrence reported that "we turned our Hotchkiss on the prisoners and made an end of them, they saying nothing".

Major-General Barrow was at the same time pressing forward towards Dera'a from Beisan. His forces made contact with the Fourth Army's flank guard near Remthe on 26 September and then moved towards Dera'a which had been abandoned by the Turks who were streaming northward. Before Barrow's troops reached the town, the Arabs – Nasir's and Nuri's forces – had already moved in. Lawrence made contact with Barrow on the outskirts of the town and welcomed him as a guest to the town that the Arabs had just occupied.

[15] The headman of Tafas: Talal El-Hareidhin. *Arab Bulletin* No. 106, 22 October 1918.

CHAPTER NINE

Final Act and Curtain

Communicate the following to Sherif Feisul from Commander-in-Chief:

1. There is no objection to Your Highness entering DAMASCUS as soon as you consider that you can do so with safety.
2. I am sending troops to DAMASCUS and I hope that they will arrive there in four or five days from to–day. I trust that Your Highness' forces will be able to co-operate, but you should not relax your pressure in the DERA'A district, as it is of vital importance to cut off the Turkish forces which are retreating North from MA'AN, AMMAN, and ES SALT. Ends.

(SGD.) L. J. BOLS[1]

With the fall of Dera'a, the race to Damascus began. Bols's message released Feisul from any restraint and the Arabs plunged north.

The consolidation of the towns and countryside continued as fewer and fewer Turks, Germans, and Austrians moved north. Most had already been captured, many just disappeared. Feisul arrived and made temporary headquarters at Dera'a's train station. Barrow said that Chauvel was nearing Damascus and that he was getting ready to move north with Feisul's regulars.

Lawrence dallied a day in Dera'a while Nuri Said and the Arab troops marched north paralleling Barrow's troops. The next day, 30 September, Lawrence, Stirling and two drivers took 'Blue Mist', the smallest and lightest of the tenders and drove north. They caught up with Barrow and then continued on to Kiswe, south of Damascus, to meet Chauvel's forces. They stayed at Kiswe that night, the roads being too dangerous to continue on in the dark, and rose early to see Damascus burning. But it was not the whole city, which had been abandoned by the Turks and the Germans, it was the ammunition dump that had been set on fire.

Nasir and Nuri Shalaan took their horsemen and went ahead. Lawrence and Stirling followed, delayed temporarily by Indian troops who mistook them for a prize, capturing them. Once freed from their detention, they continued into

---

[1] WO157/738, message from Maj-Gen Bols to Lt-Col Lawrence, 25 September 1918

General Edmund Allenby and Emir Feisal. (Harry Chase, James A. Cannavino Library, Archives & Special Collections, Marist College, USA)

Feisul's standard bearer. (Gilman Family Collection)

The Hejaz Armoured Car Section and RFA 10-Pounder Motor Section in Wadi Rum. Mar–April 1917. (Harry Chase, James A. Cannavino Library, Archives & Special Collections, Marist College, USA)

Damascus. Although they had been preceded by Chauvel's Australians who had marched through the town, Lawrence immediately contrived to put a government in place and appointed Shukri Pasha Ayubi as temporary military governor until Feisul could arrive and assume leadership of the city. Chauvel, when he arrived, accepted Lawrence's appointments and work began to reinstate order and a new administration.[2]

Allenby arrived, driven in his Rolls-Royce, followed by Feisul from the south. The two men met for the first time and Feisul was given a telegram from the Foreign Office that stated the Arabs had been granted the status of belligerents. No one knew what that meant exactly but, for all intents and purposes, the Arab Revolt was over.

On 4 October 1918, at 1900 hours, Colonel Lawrence departed Damascus in Rolls-Royce tender LC1105. It was the same car in which he and Dawnay had

[2] Lawrence told Chauvel that Shukri had been elected. Chauvel did not think much of Lawrence at the time or after he had read *Seven Pillars*, in which Lawrence restated the falsehood that the Arabs entered the city first, before the Australians. Chauvel felt (rightly) that Joyce had done the most important work to support the Arab Revolt, although Cyril Wilson's role was singularly crucial to its success.

RFA 10-pounder mountain guns in action. (Harry Chase, James A. Cannavino Library, Archives & Special Collections, Marist College, USA)

been nearly hit by an artillery shell at Mudowarra the previous spring. He would not return. It had been almost exactly two years since Lieutenant Lawrence first arrived at Jeddah.[3]

Militarily, there was little more to be done. The political wrangling over the spoils of war now took centre stage.

The men of Hedgehog, aka the British Military Mission, were mostly dispersed to the winds. Many returned to England to retire and took up civilian careers, while a number, including Dawnay, Clayton, Wemyss, Boyle, Stirling, and Young, continued to serve in the military or diplomatic field.

Feisul bin Hussein bin Ali al-Hashemi, was crowned king of the Arab Kingdom of Syria in 1920, but was expelled by the French when he decided to rise up against his new colonial master. The British then installed him as King of Iraq on 23 August 1921. He died in France in 1933.

---

[3] Lieutenant-Colonel Lawrence was promoted to full colonel by Allenby after his return to Cairo in early October 1918.

Ja'far Pasha al-Askari continued to serve Feisul and became the Iraqi minister of defence under King Feisul's rule. He was assassinated in 1936 during a coup d'état that overthrew the Iraqi government.

Bimbashi Herbert Garland, MC took General Fakhri Pasha's surrender at Medina on 19 January 1919. He died in 1921, shortly after his return to England, his health compromised by his service in the Middle East.

Captain Raho was killed shortly after the armistice while fighting against the troops of ibn Saud. RFC/RAF pilot Major A. J. Ross was killed in a flying accident during the war.

The RFA 10-pounder Motor Section was disbanded on its return to Egypt. The RFC's 14 Squadron's 'X' Flight was also disbanded at Suez in late October 1918.

The Hejaz Armoured Car Battery became the No. 1 Battery, Light Armoured Cars, Lieutenant S. G. Dowsett, commanding. Dowsett's battery and others continued to serve in Iraq as part of Winston Churchill's and Chief of the Air Staff Hugh Trenchard's 'Air Control' plan to police British colonies with aircraft and armoured cars.

CHAPTER TEN

A Look Back

With the end of the war, Hedgehog disappeared, its specialized tasking completed.[1] It played a large part in the 'sideshow' that was Allenby's Palestinian Campaign and its legacy would affect British military thought, as well as that of other militaries, for years to come.

War is more than the science and art of disposing and manoeuvring forces in combat. It consists of continuous innovation, adaptation and modification of techniques, tactics, and procedures. It is a process of merging new with old. What works is kept, what doesn't is disposed of.

Hedgehog, from its inception, followed a continuous process of innovation and adaptation. Its mission to support the revolt stayed generally the same. But how it accomplished this task changed as the requirements and the strategic objectives grew larger and more ambitious. Evolving from the Arab Bureau and the British Military Mission, it used tactics that, individually, were not new to the battlefield, although many new technologies were employed for the first time. However, combined as they were behind the lines of the Ottoman-Turkish armies, they formed a new methodology of specialized, combined operations.

There were other instances of aerial reconnaissance, intelligence-driven operations, raids, mobile gun platforms, and guerrilla warfare used by the protagonists of World War I, but perhaps nowhere else were they adapted, modified, and used together on such a routine basis.

What the Arab Revolt was

Grand Sherif Hussein instigated and led an armed revolt, an insurgency, against the Ottoman Empire. His initial goals were to capture and control the Holy Cities of Mecca and Medina (al-Haramayn) and eventually to eject the Turks from all of Arabia. In this, Hussein was overly optimistic as he had done little planning and the

---

[1] For simplicity, I have chosen to collectively name the British Military Mission and the Arab Bureau as Hedgehog.

'armies' under the leadership of his sons were not trained or prepared for conflict with the Turkish Army.

Historically, revolutionary warfare progresses through several stages:

1. Organization phase: preparation and build-up of a base area from which the enemy can be attacked.
2. Insurgent or guerrilla warfare: limited attacks on the enemy, use of propaganda to gain support.
3. Conventional warfare leading to a decision: when trained and equipped in sufficient strength, attack the enemy's major formations to defeat them.

There are instances where these 'rules' are not followed but, generally, a successful insurgency will progress through all three stages. Occasionally, a stage may be skipped and, if the rebels are thwarted in one stage, they may return to the previous stage and begin again. Looking back to 1916, Hussein failed to account for any of them. He began with little preparation and committed his untested forces in conventional operations against Medina with little beyond a rudimentary plan of attack. No doubt it was because he had little military experience or training, but it was only due to the intervention of the British (and to some extent the French) that his revolt was saved. The subsequent months proved critical to the revolt's survival. It was as much Turkish inaction as the British guardianship of the crucial 'unassailable bases' (the coastal ports) that provided the time and resources that permitted the movement to survive.

That said, no one from Wingate and Clayton to Kitchener and Storrs seemed to have any concept or idea of how the revolt would unfold and what it should ultimately accomplish. The men of Hedgehog were crucial to the military success of the revolt but they made things up on the fly.

In some cases, plans and objectives were more political than military. For example, to Hussein, capturing Medina was primarily a political/religious objective. He needed to eject Fakhri Pasha's forces in order to claim that he controlled the Holy Cities. To some British and (especially) French officials, Hussein remaining in the Hejaz and tied down around Medina would also prevent him from making claims on the future French mandate territory of Syria. But to Lawrence, to capture Medina would be a wasted effort. It was only when Akaba was unexpectedly captured that the planners realized the operational landscape had changed and their strategy needed to be revised.

An uprising that had been localized to the Hejaz quickly became a Pan-Arab movement. It shifted from being a threat to one Turkish command at Medina, to threatening the entire southern Ottoman Empire. And after the 'crisis' at Rabegh passed, the Turkish Army was never able to counter the Arab Revolt effectively.

With the shift, Hedgehog's support also changed. Previously, the men of the BMM provided political advice, logistical support, training, and direct assistance in specialized skills like artillery and demolitions on a relatively limited basis.

After Akaba, Feisul began his move north with support from local tribal leaders. More and more logistical support from Britain was needed, as was aerial surveillance and intelligence. It was and is the classic conundrum that guerrilla leaders face: few insurgencies succeed without external support. It was at this point that the British military under Allenby became most heavily committed to the revolt, not for the revolt's sake, but to use it as an adjunct, 'complementary' operation to serve the Allies' overall purpose – the defeat of the Turks.

The Royal Navy continued to guarantee the sanctity of the coastal ports and provided the transport necessary for supplies and the gold needed to maintain the varied tribal interests, while the Royal Flying Corps' 'X' Flight provided the support needed to protect the Arab ground forces and the 'eyes on' tactical intelligence needed for operations. That support included photographic reconnaissance, mapping, and even delivery of supplies to the revolt. For an extra measure, 'X' Flight served as the courier link between Hedgehog's liaison and advisory staff and Allenby's headquarters, often delivering messages or the officers themselves, ensuring communications were continuous and effective. Hedgehog's direct connections to the intelligence departments in Cairo and at the army's forward headquarters were vitally important and kept it well informed about Turkish dispositions and intentions.

The terrain north of Akaba was open and permitted the use of vehicular forces and, although armoured cars had been used successfully in the Western Desert of Egypt, they were first used here on long-range raids behind enemy lines. Similarly, the ancient 10-pounders used by the RFA Motor Section were employed in ways never foreseen by their designers. When Dawnay wrote his operation plan for the April 1917 railway attack that integrated an aerial attack by 'X' Flight, along with a ground assault by armoured cars, mobile artillery platforms, an Egyptian camel unit, and a guerrilla force advised by Lawrence, he was breaking new ground in combined operations. Dawnay's raid was truly a special mission on a critical target.

There would be many other such operations, culminating with the great raid on Dera'a that incorporated all the elements listed above along with Ja'far Pasha al-Askari's Arab regulars who, advised by Joyce, were finally making significant contributions to the war effort. That raid is the epitome of revolutionary warfare's phase 3 operations.

The Turks never learned or understood how to effectively counter the Arab Revolt's use of irregular or *guerrilla* warfare. The Turkish solution was to employ a linear defence of the Hejaz railway that only provided a larger, more vulnerable target – an artery that was slashed repeatedly and bled the Ottoman Empire slowly and definitively dry. Lawrence said the Turks just didn't think hard enough.

Hedgehog's mission succeeded because men like Wilson, Clayton, Dawnay, Joyce, Garland, Gilman and others never let convention get in their way. They improvised, experimented, and developed techniques and tactics that worked for them. They also did not let a stated objective block them from another more lucrative one that

Lieutenant Wade and crewmen of the Hejaz Armoured Car Section in the Hejaz. (Joe Berton)

The officers of Hedgehog. Sitting: Grisenthwaite; L to R seated: Ramsey, Gilman, Joyce, Lony (?), Standing: Greenhill, Young, 'FlannelFeet', Bamford. (Gilman Family Collection)

may might been overlooked. Such was the case with Lawrence deciding to capture Akaba over Medina.

As previously stated, Hedgehog did not create guerrilla warfare, special or combined operations out of a void. For the most part, each of the constituent parts existed before. Wellington had used guerrilla bands in his Peninsula Campaign (albeit led by Spanish commanders without British advice) to confound the French. From 1899 to 1902, Boers fought the British in South Africa with their own version of irregular warfare, which would give the name 'commando' to later British units. The Boers invented the explosive trigger they used against British trains – the same design that Garland used against the Turkish railway. At least one of the Hedgehog team likened his camel-mounted raids behind the Turks lines to those of the flamboyantly effective U. S. Confederate cavalryman and raider James E. 'Jeb' Stuart. Of course, each of the British officers had studied the military masters, among them Jomini, Clausewitz, Foch, and Napoleon and integrated their thought into the operations of the Arabs. T. E. Lawrence was perhaps the lone Briton involved in the revolt who knew the theorists well but chose to disregard much of what they espoused. Instead he envisioned a course for the Arab Revolt that went against his superior officers' more conventional approach to operations.

The Arab Revolt was a synthesis of proven tactics that were modified and applied to its specific circumstances. New technologies were adapted to the effort as well, including aerial reconnaissance and photographic mapping to support ground operations, the employment of vehicles – both armoured and not – to conduct long-range raids both unilaterally and in support of mounted infantry. Another innovation was the aerial resupply of the Arab and British elements working behind the lines and the use of forward landing grounds and supply points. The Royal Navy was also a key element to the equation, especially in the early days of the revolt, providing naval gunfire support for the capture of the coastal ports, which became the revolt's 'unassailable bases', as well as providing supplies and moving troops all along the Red Sea. Without that support, the revolt would, in all likelihood, have withered on the vine. All of these elements worked together to make the Hejaz campaign both a combined and a special operation.

Of course, none of the success would have happened without the sanction of the British high command and, although Maxwell and Murray did permit the ball to begin its roll, it was Allenby and his staff who made the difference. As Lawrence explained in *Seven Pillars*, it was Allenby who conceived of "such unorthodox movements", who had broken the rules of "his administrative services to suit them, and support them with every moral and material asset, regular and irregular, military or political". Allenby was a general who understood and used "infantry and cavalry, artillery and air force, navy and armoured cars, deceptions and irregulars" to achieve the final victory.

The Allied victory over Germany and the Ottoman Empire was not a victory for everyone. The triumvirate of Pashas, disgraced by the capitulation, escaped Turkey by German torpedo boat after the armistice. Talaat and Djemal were assassinated soon afterwards for their role in the Armenian Genocide, while Enver was killed in a Russian ambush during the Basmachi uprising in Tajikistan. Shorn of its former territories, the reins of power were taken up Mustafa Kemal, the hero of Gallipoli who became known as Atatürk. Atatürk successfully resisted Allied attempts to further dismember Turkey and militarily ejected French forces from the homeland, troops that were ironically led by Colonel Brémond, back to Syria.

The question of whether the Arab Revolt was a success for the Arab is unfortunately easy to answer. The post-war Allied occupation of the region ensured Hussein's dream of a united Arabia under one ruler (himself) would never be realized. But his idea probably would not have long survived as many Arabs saw Hussein's forces as "just another colonial unit" and would not have submitted to his rule.[2] The growing power of ibn Saud would force Hussein from the Holy Cities soon after the war in any event.

The promises given to Hussein were as convoluted as the comment of Colonel Hugh D. Pearson:

"I feel sure we do not mean all that they mean and that we are letting them think we mean."[3]

[2] Fawzi al Qawuqji, quoted in *The Commander: Fawzi al-Qawuqji and the Fight for Arab Independence 1914–1948*, Laila Parsons, NYC: Hill & Wang, 2016.
[3] Pearson was a trusted member of General Wingate's staff; quoted in Philip Walker's *Behind the Lawrence Legend*.

Epilogue

How about some piracy on the high desert?

MAJOR RALPH ALGER BAGNOLD

The men sat in their trucks on the top of the hill and marvelled at what they saw. Before them lay a seemingly endless stretch of nothingness: the Great Sand Sea. They had just climbed a 300-foot sand dune with a patrol of Chevrolet 30-cwt trucks. The patrol had started out days earlier in Cairo, which now lay 200 miles behind them to the northeast. To get to this location, they had first driven to Ain Dalla, a spring deep in the Egyptian interior, and then motored on to the first sand dune to the west. The trucks were specially prepared and benefited from the experiences of two of the group's officers, Ralph Bagnold and Bill Shaw, both experienced desert explorers (Shaw was also an archaeologist and spoke Arabic). Both men had driven this area before when conducting surveys under the auspices of the Royal Geographical Society in the late 1920s and 1930s. Bagnold and Shaw had proven the impenetrable interior of Sahara desert could indeed be penetrated when they crossed the 150-mile barrier with three modified Ford Model-Ts.

The men sitting on their Chevys were the first training patrol of a British Army unit that would be called the Long Range Desert Group or 'LRDG'. Italy had just declared war on Britain and Bagnold proposed creating the unit based on his experiences in the desert. He was concerned that the Italians might use the Sand Sea to conduct a surprise attack on the Aswan Dam, which would give them control of Cairo's water supply. Many conventionally minded British officers thought Bagnold was crazy and believed the Sand Sea impassable despite the fact Bagnold had proven it could be traversed ten years earlier. He also knew the Italians had explored the region.

When no one believed it could be done Bagnold discovered the only passage through the Sand Sea in 1930. Later, in 1940, he was travelling to a posting in Kenya when his ship was diverted to Alexandria, a fortuitous arrival quickly noticed by the soon-to-be commander of British forces in Egypt, General Sir Archibald P. Wavell. Upon learning of his presence, Wavell decided Bagnold would be more useful to him in Egypt and arranged his transfer.

Wavell, whose forces were outnumbered ten to one at the outset of the war, also saw the danger and agreed with Bagnold. He interviewed Bagnold about his small reconnaissance unit proposal (after several other officers had pitched it in the rubbish bin) because he needed every advantage he could find. Bagnold knew he could deliver intelligence, but when Wavell asked what he would do if the Italians were inactive, Bagnold suggested "piracy" – in other words, to hit the Italians where they were most comfortable: on their own turf. Wavell liked the idea and dictated a letter that gave Bagnold carte blanche to raise, equip, and train a force to be ready in six weeks. Wavell knew his own staff would put up barriers as they generally opposed anything new or unusual.

But then Wavell was himself unusual. He had served with Field Marshal Allenby as one of his staff in World War I and was well acquainted with T. E. Lawrence, the British Military Mission, and their methods. He supported the Arab Revolt and, when he later wrote the official history of the Palestinian campaign, his assessment of it was clear:

> Its value to the British commander was great, since it diverted considerable Turkish reinforcements and supplies to the Hejaz, and protected the right flank of the British armies in their advance through Palestine. Further, it put an end to German propaganda in south-western Arabia and removed any danger of the establishment of a German submarine base on the Red Sea. These were important services and worth the subsidies in gold and munitions expended on the Arab forces.

After the war, Wavell stayed in contact with Lawrence and his biographer Captain B. H. Liddell Hart and wrote of Lawrence's contributions to the war in his book, *The Good Soldier*. He also corresponded with him after the war on the subject of irregular war *and its antidotes* [emphasis mine]. Wavell judged Lawrence as an "unwilling leader of a great adventure" and a man in an altogether "heroic but very human mould".

There can be little doubt that Wavell saw much in Lawrence's way of war and of those other British practitioners who fought the Arab Revolt with him. Among others, there were Reginald Wingate, the kingmaker; Clayton, the promoter; Wilson, the diplomat; Garland, the specialist sapper; Newcombe, the frustrated commando; Joyce, the leader and organizer, Young, the short-tempered logistician; Buxton, the straightforward cavalry officer; Gilman, the good-humoured machine-gunner; Brodie and Pascoe, the precise artillerymen; the irrepressible Stirling; and Dawnay, the Etonian planner and deceptionist. These men played different but equally important roles, all of which are important to successful special operations.

Wavell absorbed the lessons of the Arab Revolt and when he had need of such methods sought out another man with unique ideas to serve his plans: Orde Wingate, whose father was cousin to General Sir Reginald Wingate. Orde Wingate first served under Wavell in Palestine in 1937 where he organized the Special Night Squads (SNS) – Jewish counterinsurgency units that fought Palestinian rebels in the 1936–39 revolt. It was a collaborative effort where British advisors led patrols of indigenous Jewish settlers against the opposition Palestinian Arabs.

The SNS were 'an antidote' or 'counter-guerrillas' to the Palestinian rebels. The unit paralleled Hedgehog to a degree in its organization, if not its methodologies. Wingate directed the operation while British army personnel trained the Jewish soldiers and British Special Service officers provided the intelligence to drive operations. It was also a recipe that served the British in Malaya, Cyprus, Kenya, and Northern Ireland. The SNS were, however, extremely controversial as their operations were considered especially nasty and outside the law. This was the dark side of irregular warfare.

However similar their tactics, Orde Wingate thought little of T. E. Lawrence; he considered him an amateur. It is difficult to discern exactly why, other than Wingate was a professional military officer whereas Lawrence was anything but. Additionally and perhaps more importantly, Wingate was a committed Christian Zionist fighting the Arabs. He also thought the idea of paying soldiers for their loyalty to be wrong. There are as many disconnects between Wingate and Lawrence as there are similarities. It is possible that Wingate saw Lawrence as a competitor and chose denigration as a refuge for his ego. As it is said: opposites attract … verbum sap. Lawrence, however, seems to have been singularly unaware of Orde Wingate's criticisms.

Nevertheless, Wavell noted Wingate's extraordinary abilities in Palestine and called upon him again during World War II to fight the Japanese in the Far East using his talents in irregular warfare. Wingate formed the 'Chindits', a long-range reconnaissance and raiding force that harassed Japanese lines of communication, including destroying rail lines, in Burma during the Second World War.

Wavell, above all, was an unorthodox tactician and like Allenby knew best how to appreciate and employ the unique talents of his 'unusual' officers, despite being surrounded by large numbers of conventionally minded regular officers.

Similarly, when Wavell turned to Bagnold he knew with whom he was dealing: a man whose expertise in the North African desert exceeded that of perhaps any other Briton alive. Bagnold knew he would need all Allenby's authority and the time to prepare as, among other things, the trucks the British Army used were not suited for his concept. He would have to acquire and modify civilian vehicles for the purpose. That was innovation but innovation was anathema to the 'old' British Army in Egypt. Once Wavell took charge of British forces in Egypt that was no longer an obstacle.

Bagnold succeeded in his quest to build his little force, which collected intelligence on the Italian and later the German armies in North Africa. On one of their first 'recces' deep behind enemy lines, an LRDG patrol captured two Italian Army trucks and brought them and their cargo back to friendly lines. Among the cargo were documents which informed Wavell that no Italian offensive was imminent. He had time to prepare his defences and, more importantly, an offensive.

Before long, the LRDG went beyond its original mission and began to conduct direct-action missions against an unsuspecting enemy. The LRDG specialized in airfield raids and successfully put many enemy aircraft out of action on the ground.

Bagnold traced his ideas back to a fellow desert explorer, T. E. Lawrence: "Lawrence had lit the flame which fans the passion of those who lead guerrilla warfare."[1] Beyond that spark which pushed him into special operations, Bagnold imagined what he could do with "the special equipment and techniques we had evolved for very long distance travel, and for navigation".

When he first conceived of his long-range patrols Bagnold determined that the enemy had enough transport to conduct operations for a "radius of action of a paltry 100 miles". "The rest was his. Far from being impassable, hostile wilderness, the desert was a place that men with the right training and equipment, could cross and recross, navigate, watch, hide in and survive indefinitely."[2]

It was a statement reminiscent of what Lawrence said years before:

> I began idly to calculate how many square miles … perhaps a hundred and forty thousand … and how would the Turks defend all that … no doubt by a trench line across the bottom, if we were an army attacking with banners displayed … but suppose we were an influence (as we might be), an idea, a thing invulnerable, intangible, without front or back, drifting about like a gas? Armies were like plants, immobile as a whole, firm-rooted, nourished through long stems to the head. We might be a vapour, blowing where we listed. Our kingdoms lay in each man's mind, and as we wanted nothing material to live on, so perhaps we offered nothing material to the killing. It seemed a regular soldier might be helpless without a target. He would own the ground he sat on, and what he could poke his rifle at.

Bagnold was not alone in being influenced by the Arab Revolt and Lawrence. Colin McVean Gubbins was another, as was David Stirling. Stirling was a cofounder of the Special Air Service that, like Bagnold's LRDG, had its origins in North Africa. While many historians have stated that Stirling was influenced by Lawrence's adventures in World War I, a definitive connection has not been established, however logical it sounds. Nonetheless, Stirling's SAS adopted many of Bagnold's methods, making it an indirect legacy of Hedgehog at the least.

Gubbins, on the other hand, made liberal use of the lessons of the Arab Revolt. The son of a British diplomat, Colin Gubbins first experienced war on the Western Front during World War I. His experience was of a conventional nature as he was an artillery officer, but it was intense, extensive, and he was decorated for bravery. His next exposure was in the Northern Russia Expeditionary Force campaign in 1919 where he found himself as aide-de-camp to the British commander, Brigadier William Edmund 'Tiny' Ironside. He was then sent to Ireland during the Irish War of Independence of 1919–22. It was in these positions that Gubbins was exposed to the deleterious effects of "subversive and para-military warfare" on regular forces and that would mark the beginning of his systematic study of irregular warfare. During the interwar years, he received more practical education in India before landing a job

---

[1] David Lloyd Owen, *Desert My Dwelling Place: With the Long Range Desert Group in North Africa,* London: Cassell, 1957.
[2] Ben Macintyre, *SAS: Rogue Heroes,* London: Viking, 2016, p. 58.

directing operations and training in Britain's premier dirty tricks agency, the Special Operations Executive or SOE. One of his first tasks was to write two generic – that is applicable to any situation, anywhere – manuals on guerrilla warfare, *The Art of Guerilla Warfare* and *The Partisan Leader's Handbook*.[3] The inspiration and material to write these pamphlets came from Gubbins's study of several recent conflicts, significantly the Arab Revolt, as well as the Russian Civil War and the Irish War of Independence. The earlier Boer War and the campaign of von Lettow-Vorbeck in East Africa during World War I also influenced his writings, yet much of his writing was inspired by what he called "Lawrence's epic guerrilla campaign".

Some have called Gubbins's pamphlets the first codified examples of how to conduct guerrilla warfare. With the possible exception of Lawrence's *Twenty-seven Articles*, which deals with advising guerrillas, specifically Bedouins, this appears to be the case. According to Aaron Linderman, Gubbins's genius lay in synthesizing existing ideas into a brief and usable form.

Although Gubbins did not lead guerrillas in battle, the men and women of his SOE (he would become the SOE Director in 1943) did, using the techniques taught in his manuals. Even Orde Wingate benefited from Gubbins's work "applying Gubbins's recommended operational procedures faithfully … as shaped by his own experiences".[4]

But then, Wingate was more a commando than a guerrilla. Which brings up an important point of definitions:

– A guerrilla is a person who engages in irregular warfare especially as a member of an independent unit carrying out harassment and sabotage generally in his own country.
– Irregular warfare includes terrorism and guerrilla warfare.
– A commando is a military unit (or a member thereof) trained and organized as shock troops especially for unilateral hit-and-run raids into enemy territory.
– Special operations are small-scale, unconventional military actions against enemy vulnerabilities that are undertaken by specially designated, selected, trained, equipped, and supported units known as special forces. These operations include direct-action raids, assistance to foreign guerrillas or irregular units, long-range reconnaissance, counter-guerrilla or counterinsurgency operations.

Clearly, the Arab Bureau/British Military Mission/Hedgehog was an amalgam of all of these. Its influence, mostly remembered through Lawrence's writing of *Evolution of a Revolt*, *Twenty-seven Articles*, and *Demolitions Under Fire* demonstrates the

---

[3] Gubbins chose to spell guerilla with a single 'r'.
[4] Anglim, p. 102.

value of guerrilla warfare judiciously applied against a superior power, as well as the need for limited external support by a strong ally. Also demonstrated were the weaknesses and vulnerabilities of a guerrilla force in the face of technology – in this case weaponry – for which they had no counter.

With the support of a commander who understood the value of combined operations, Hedgehog was able to effectively provide advice and material aid to the Arab Army that enabled it to become the unconventional wing to the British Expeditionary Force's conventional front.

The Arab Revolt was indeed a sideshow to Allenby's campaign in that it never assumed the major burden of fighting. It did, however, exploit a vulnerability in the Ottoman-Turkish defences for which the enemy could find no effective counter. The Arab Revolt complemented the main force's operations by isolating the enemy in Medina and forcing him to divert men and material that could have been employed against the main threat in Palestine.

After the conclusion of World War I, the British Army was considerably reduced in size as a cost-saving measure. Specialized units that were created for special circumstances were disbanded and with them much of the specialized knowledge disappeared. The British Army retreated for the most part back into its 'regular' self; conventional officers took back control of a standing army. For the most part they were concerned with how to avoid the last war – the tactical morass that was the war in Flanders and France – and less concerned with preserving the lessons of the Arab Revolt that was, for them, mostly an aberration.

The people who needed the lessons most used them. Mao Tse-tung (also Mao Zedong) fought a war of liberation against the Japanese and referred often to Lawrence's *Seven Pillars*.[5] There are also unconfirmed accounts that Irish Nationalist Michael Collins wished to engage T. E. Lawrence as one of his Irish Free State commanders.[6] Collins allegedly thought highly of Lawrence's irregular warfare skills – after all, Lawrence was Irish.

It was only when a need for specialized units reemerged to counter the overwhelming superiority of the Axis forces that men like Bagnold and Gubbins reached back into history to find the way forward. They found the seeds for their special operations in the experiences and accomplishments of the men of the British Military Mission.

Somehow it is fitting that one poem runs as a common thread through the history of British special operations. From T. E. Lawrence who paraphrased it in *Seven Pillars,* to Ralph Alger Bagnold who often quoted it, to the Clock Tower in Hereford, England where its words honour the men of the 22 Special Air Service who gave their lives for their nation.

---

[5] Others who later relied on *Seven Pillars* were North Vietnamese General Võ Nguyên Giáp and Argentinian rebel Ernesto 'Che' Guevara.

[6] Michael Korda among others.

We are the Pilgrims, master; we shall go
Always a little further; it may be
Beyond that last blue mountain barred with snow
Across that angry or that glimmering sea.

JAMES ELROY FLECKER, 'THE GOLDEN JOURNEY TO SAMARKAND'

They had their dreams.

Order of Battle (as of 30 June 1917)[1]

Turkish Forces

HEJAZ EXPEDITIONARY Force (circa 9,000 men)[2]
Commander Fakhri Pasha

Medina
1 gendarmerie battalion
6 infantry battalions
1–2 battalions mule-mounted infantry (MMI)
12 Quick Firing (QF) Krupp mountain guns
2 Nordenfeldt guns
8 field guns
12 machine guns

COMPOSITE FORCE

Tebuk
1 cavalry squadron
1 gendarmerie battalion
4 mountain guns
4 machine guns
1 battalion (type & designation unknown)

Wadi Ethil
60 men of the railway battalion

---

[1] Drawn from TNA Kew FO 882/7.
[2] In November 1916, Lawrence assessed the Hejaz Expeditionary Force at around 13,300 troops.

Muadhdham
1 infantry company
2 machine guns
1 QF field gun

Khish Sana
1 squadron cavalry
1 infantry company
100 men MMI

Medain Saleh
Headquarters 162nd Infantry Regiment
1 infantry battalion
2 companies MMI
1 aircraft
2 mountain guns
2 field guns
2 batteries QF mountain or field guns

el-Ula
2 infantry battalions
1 company camel corps
1 cavalry regiment
2 field guns
1 aircraft

Ma'an – Garrison & Railway Protection Group – circa 5,000 men (?)
1 battalion, 161st Regiment
2 battalions, 129th Regiment
2 battalions, 130th Regiment

Arab Forces

Emir Feisul at Wejh
1,700 trained men
1,000 Bedouin (strength fluctuates on call)
1 × 5-in howitzer
2 × 15-pdr guns
4 mountain guns
12 machine guns

Colonel Newcombe near Medain Salih
130 trained men
Captain Bray and Indian machine-gun detachment (8 men)

Emir Abdullah at Wadi Ais
100 trained men
5,000 Bedouin
1 × 5-in howitzer
2 × 2.75-in mountain guns
1 × 87mm howitzer
6 × Maxim machine guns
7 × Hotchkiss machine guns

Emir Ali at Yenbo
1,200 trained men
1,500 Bedouin
4 × 5-in howitzers
2 × 10-pdr guns
2 × 70mm Turkish guns
12 machine guns
4 × French-Algerian guns

Emir Zeid at Rabegh
600 trained men
1,500 Bedouin
2 × 2.75-in mountain guns
2 × 10-pdr guns
1 QF mountain gun
8 machine guns

Ja'far Pasha
1,200 trained men (Meccan/Syrian levies)

Colonel Wilson at Jeddah
–   Senior Liaison to Grand Sherif Hussein
–   Chief, British Military Mission
–   Advisors included Newcombe, Lawrence, Garland, Davenport, Hornby

Colonel Joyce at Wejh
–   Officer Commanding Troops, Liaison to Feisul

Major Davenport
120 Egyptian Infantry
1 × 5-in howitzer
4 machine guns
Captain Stent – C Flight, 14th Squadron, RFC
circa 60 men
6 BE2c aircraft
Captain Gilman – Hejaz Armoured Car Section
circa 15 men
2 Rolls-Royce Admiralty Pattern cars
Colonel Brémond – French Military Mission & Trainers
Four MG sections circa 60 men
Infantry circa 40 men
Cavalry circa 40 men

Twenty-seven Articles: Memorandum by Major Lawrence, August 1917

Arab Bureau Papers, FO 882/7, HRG/17/74

The following notes have been expressed in commandment form for greater clarity and to save words. They are, however, only my personal conclusions, arrived at gradually while I worked in the Hejaz and now put on paper as stalking horses for beginners in the Arab armies. They are meant to apply only to Bedu; townspeople or Syrians require totally different treatment. They are of course not suitable to any other person's need, or applicable unchanged in any particular situation. Handling Hejaz Arabs is an art, not a science, with exceptions and no obvious rules. At the same time we have a great chance there; the Sherif trusts us, and has given us the position (towards his government) which the Germans wanted to win in Turkey. If we are tactful, we can at once retain his goodwill and carry out our job, but to succeed we have got to put into it all the interest and skill we possess.

1. Go easy for the first few weeks. A bad start is difficult to atone for, and the Aabs form their judgments on externals that we ignore. When you have reached the inner circle in a tribe, you can do as you please with yourself and them.
2. Learn all you can about your Ashraf and Bedu. Get to know their families, clans and tribes, friends and enemies, wells, hills and roads. Do all this by listening and by indirect inquiry. Do not ask questions. Get to speak their dialect of Arabic, not yours. Until you can understand their allusions, avoid getting deep into conversation or you will drop bricks. Be a little stiff at first.
3. In matters of business deal only with the commander of the army, column, or party in which you serve. Never give orders to anyone at all, and reserve your directions or advice for the C. O., however great the temptation (for efficiency's sake) of dealing with his underlings. Your place is advisory, and your advice is due to the commander alone. Let him see that this is your conception of your duty, and that his is to be the sole executive of your joint plans.
4. Win and keep the confidence of your leader. Strengthen his prestige at your expense before others when you can. Never refuse or quash schemes he may put forward; but ensure that they are put forward in the first instance privately to

you. Always approve them, and after praise modify them insensibly, causing the suggestions to come from him, until they are in accord with your own opinion. When you attain this point, hold him to it, keep a tight grip of his ideas, and push them forward as firmly as possibly, but secretly, so that to one but himself (and he not too clearly) is aware of your pressure.

5. Remain in touch with your leader as constantly and unobtrusively as you can. Live with him, that at meal times and at audiences you may be naturally with him in his tent. Formal visits to give advice are not so good as the constant dropping of ideas in casual talk. When stranger Sheikhs come in for the first time to swear allegiance and offer service, clear out of the tent. If their first impression is of foreigners in the confidence of the Sherif, it will do the Arab cause much harm.

6. Be shy of too close relations with the subordinates of the expedition. Continual intercourse with them will make it impossible for you to avoid going behind or beyond the instructions that the Arab C. O. has given them on your advice, and in so disclosing the weakness of his position you altogether destroy your own.

7. Treat the sub-chiefs of your force quite easily and lightly. In this way you hold yourself above their level. Treat the leader, if a Sherif, with respect. He will return your manner and you and he will then be alike, and above the rest. Precedence is a serious matter among the Arabs, and you must attain it.

8. Your ideal position is when you are present and not noticed. Do not be too intimate, too prominent, or too earnest. Avoid being identified too long or too often with any tribal Sheikh, even if C. O. of the expedition. To do your work you must be above jealousies, and you lose prestige if you are associated with a tribe or clan, and its inevitable feuds. Sherifs are above all blood-feuds and local rivalries, and form the only principle of unity among the Arabs. Let your name therefore be coupled always with a Sherif's, and share his attitude towards the tribes. When the moment comes for action put yourself publicly under his orders. The Bedu will then follow suit.

9. Magnify and develop the growing conception of the Sherifs as the natural aristocracy of the Arabs. Intertribal jealousies make it impossible for any Sheikh to attain a commanding position, and the only hope of union in nomad Arabs is that the Ashraf be universally acknowledged as the ruling class. Sherifs are half-townsmen, half-nomad, in manner and life, and have the instinct of command. Mere merit and money would be insufficient to obtain such recognition; but the Arab reverence for pedigree and the Prophet gives hope for the ultimate success of the Ashraf.

10. Call your Sherif 'Sidi' in public and in private. Call other people by their ordinary names, without title. In intimate conversation call a Sheikh 'Abu Annad', 'Akhu Alia' or some similar by-name.

11. The foreigner and Christian is not a popular person in Arabia. However friend-

ly and informal the treatment of yourself may be, remember always that your foundations are very sandy ones. Wave a Sherif in front of you like a banner and hide your own mind and person. If you succeed, you will have hundreds of miles of country and thousands of men under your orders, and for this it is worth bartering the outward show.

12. Cling tight to your sense of humour. You will need it every day. A dry irony is the most useful type, and repartee of a personal and not too broad character will double your influence with the chiefs. Reproof, if wrapped up in some smiling form, will carry further and last longer than the most violent speech. The power of mimicry or parody is valuable, but use it sparingly, for wit is more dignified than humour. Do not cause a laugh at a Sherif except among Sherifs.

13. Never lay hands on an Arab; you degrade yourself. You may think the resultant obvious increase of outward respect a gain to you, but what you have really done is to build a wall between you and their inner selves. It is difficult to keep quiet when everything is being done wrong, but the less you lose your temper the greater your advantage. Also then you will not go mad yourself.

14. While very difficult to drive, the Bedu are easy to lead, if: have the patience to bear with them. The less apparent your interferences the more your influence. They are willing to follow your advice and do what you wish, but they do not mean you or anyone else to be aware of that. It is only after the end of all annoyances that you find at bottom their real fund of goodwill.

15. Do not try to do too much with your own hands. Better the Arabs do it tolerably than that you do it perfectly. It is their war, and you are to help them, not to win it for them. Actually, also, under the very odd conditions of Arabia, your practical work will not be as good as, perhaps, you think it is.

16. If you can, without being too lavish, forestall presents to yourself. A well-placed gift is often most effective in winning over a suspicious Sheikh. Never receive a present without giving a liberal return, but you may delay this return (while letting its ultimate certainty be known) if you require a particular service from the giver. Do not let them ask you for things, since their greed will then make them look upon you only as a cow to milk.

17. Wear an Arab headcloth when with a tribe. Bedu have a malignant prejudice against the hat, and believe that our persistence in wearing it (due probably to British obstinacy of dictation) is founded on some immoral or irreligious principle. A thick headcloth forms a good protection against the sun, and if you wear a hat your best Arab friends will be ashamed of you in public.

18. Disguise is not advisable. Except in special areas, let it be clearly known that you are a British officer and a Christian. At the same time, if you can wear Arab kit when with the tribes, you will acquire their trust and intimacy to a degree impossible in uniform. It is, however, dangerous and difficult. They make no special allowances for you when you dress like them. Breaches of etiquette not

charged against a foreigner are not condoned to you in Arab clothes. You will be like an actor in a foreign theatre, playing a part day and night for months, without rest, and for an anxious stake. Complete success, which is when the Arabs forget your strangeness and speak naturally before you, counting you as one of themselves, is perhaps only attainable in character: while half-success (all that most of us will strive for; the other costs too much) is easier to win in British things, and you yourself will last longer, physically and mentally, in the comfort that they mean. Also then the Turks will not hang you, when you are caught.

19. If you wear Arab things, wear the best. Clothes are significant among the tribes, and you must wear the appropriate, and appear at ease in them. Dress like a Sherif, if they agree to it.

20. If you wear Arab things at all, go the whole way. Leave your English friends and customs on the coast, and fall back on Arab habits entirely. It is possible, starting thus level with them, for the European to beat the Arabs at their own game, for we have stronger motives for our action, and put more heart into it than they. If you can surpass them, you have taken an immense stride towards complete success, but the strain of living and thinking in a foreign and half-understood language, the savage food, strange clothes, and stranger ways, with the complete loss of privacy and quiet, and the impossibility of ever relaxing your watchful imitation of the others for months on end, provide such an added stress to the ordinary difficulties of dealing with the Bedu, the climate, and the Turks, that this road should not be chosen without serious thought.

21. Religious discussions will be frequent. Say what you like about your own side, and avoid criticism of theirs, unless you know that the point is external, when you may score heavily by proving it so. With the Bedu, Islam is so all-pervading an element that there is little religiosity, little fervour, and no regard for externals. Do not think from their conduct that they are careless. Their conviction of the truth of their faith, and its share in every act and thought and principle of their daily life is so intimate and intense as to be unconscious, unless roused by opposition. Their religion is as much a part of nature to them as is sleep, or food.

22. Do not try to trade on what you know of fighting. The Hejaz confounds ordinary tactics. Learn the Bedu principles of war as thoroughly and as quickly as you can, for till you know them your advice will be no good to the Sherif. Unnumbered generations of tribal raids have taught them more about some parts of the business than we will ever know. In familiar conditions they fight well, but strange events cause panic. Keep your unit small. Their raiding parties are usually from one hundred to two hundred men, and if you take a crowd they only get confused. Also their Sheikhs, while admirable company commanders, are too 'set' to learn to handle the equivalents of battalions or regiments. Don't attempt unusual things, unless they appeal to the sporting instinct Bedu have

so strongly, unless success is obvious. If the objective is a good one (booty) they will attack like fiends, they are splendid scouts, their mobility gives you the advantage that will win this local war, they make proper use of their knowledge of the country (don't take tribesmen to places they do not know), and the ga-zelle-hunters, who form a proportion of the better men, are great shots at visible targets. A Sheikh from one tribe cannot give orders to men from another; a Sherif is necessary to command a mixed tribal force. If there is plunder in pros-pect, and the odds are at all equal, you will win. Do not waste Bedu attacking trenches (they will not stand casualties) or in trying to defend a position, for they cannot sit still without slacking. The more unorthodox and Arab your pro-ceedings, the more likely you are to have the Turks cold, for they lack initiative and expect you to. Don't play for safety.

23. The open reason that Bedu give you for action or inaction may be true, but al-ways there will be better reasons left for you to divine. You must find these inner reasons (they will be denied, but are none the less in operation) before shaping your arguments for one course or other. Allusion is more effective than logical exposition: they dislike concise expression. Their minds work just as ours do, but on different premises. There is nothing unreasonable, incomprehensible, or inscrutable in the Arab. Experience of them, and knowledge of their prejudices will enable you to foresee their attitude and possible course of action in nearly every case.

24. Do not mix Bedu and Syrians, or trained men and tribesmen. You will get work out of neither, for they hate each other. I have never seen a successful combined operation, but many failures. In particular, ex-officers of the Turkish army, how-ever Arab in feelings and blood and language, are hopeless with Bedu. They are narrow minded in tactics, unable to adjust themselves to irregular warfare, clumsy in Arab etiquette, swollen-headed to the extent of being incapable of politeness to a tribesman for more than a few minutes, impatient, and, usually, helpless without their troops on the road and in action. Your orders (if you were unwise enough to give any) would be more readily obeyed by Beduins than those of any Mohammedan Syrian officer. Arab townsmen and Arab tribesmen regard each other mutually as poor relations, and poor relations are much more objectionable than poor strangers.

25. In spite of ordinary Arab example, avoid too free talk about women. It is as difficult a subject as religion, and their standards are so unlike our own that a remark, harmless in English, may appear as unrestrained to them, as some of their statements would look to us, if translated literally.

26. Be as careful of your servants as of yourself. If you want a sophisticated one you will probably have to take an Egyptian, or a Sudani, and unless you are very lucky he will undo on trek much of the good you so laboriously effect. Arabs will cook rice and make coffee for you, and leave you if required to do unmanly

work like cleaning boots or washing. They are only really possible if you are in Arab kit. A slave brought up in the Hejaz is the best servant, but there are rules against British subjects owning them, so they have to be lent to you. In any case, take with you an Ageyli or two when you go up country. They are the most efficient couriers in Arabia, and understand camels.

27. The beginning and ending of the secret of handling Arabs is unremitting study of them. Keep always on your guard; never say an unnecessary thing: watch yourself and your companions all the time: hear all that passes, search out what is going on beneath the surface, read their characters, discover their tastes and their weaknesses and keep everything you find out to yourself. Bury yourself in Arab circles, have no interests and no ideas except the work in hand, so that your brain is saturated with one thing only, and you realise your part deeply enough to avoid the little slips that would counteract the painful work of weeks. Your success will be proportioned to the amount of mental effort you devote to it.

APPENDIX 3

Demolitions Under Fire

This article appeared in *The Royal Engineers' Journal,* Vol. XXIX, No. 1, January 1919, Institution of Royal Engineers, and was signed 'T. E. L.'

We were interested in the Hejaz Railway, and spent nearly two years on it. The Turkish counter-measures were passive. They garrisoned each station (an average of 14 miles apart) with half a company, entrenched, sometimes with guns, and put in between the stations a chain of small entrenched posts, usually about 2000 yards. apart, and sited on small knolls or spurs within 200 yards of the railway, so that each post could see its neighbours and command all the intermediate line. Extra posts were put on one or other bank of any large bridge. The 15 or 20 men in the post had to patrol their section of line after dawn each day, and in the afternoon. There was no night activity on their part.

The Turks arrived at their system of defence after considerable experience of our demolition parties, but we were able, till the end of the war, to descend upon the railway when and where we pleased, and effect the damage we wished, without great difficulty. At the same time our ways and means had constantly to be improved. We began with small parties of ten or fifteen Beduins, and we ended with mobile columns of all arms, including armoured cars; nevertheless I believe that it is impossible for a purely passive defence, such as the Turkish, to prevent a daily interruption of the railway traffic by a decently equipped enemy. Railway defence, to be inviolable, would require a passive force, entrenched with continuous barbed wire fence, and day and night patrol, at a considerable distance from the line, on each side of it; mobile forces, in concentrations not more than 20 miles apart; and liberal air reconnaissance.

The actual methods of demolition we used are perhaps more interesting than our manners of attack. Our explosives were mainly blasting gelatine and guncotton.[1] Of the two we infinitely preferred the former when we could get it. It is rather more powerful in open charges in direct contact, far better for indirect work, has a value

---

[1] Guncotton is not as stable or powerful as gelignite 'blasting gelatine'.

of 5 to 1 in super-tamped charges, is quicker to use, and more compact. We used to strip its paper covering, and handle it in sandbags of 50 lbs. weight. These sweated vigorously in the summer heats of Arabia, but did us no harm, beyond the usual headache, from which we never acquired immunity. The impact of a bullet may detonate a sack of it but we found in practice that when running you clasp it to your side, and if it is held on that furthest from the enemy, then the chances are that it will not be hit, except by the bullet that has already inflicted a mortal wound on the bearer. Guncotton is a good explosive, but inferior in the above respects to gelatine, and in addition, we used to receive it packed 16 slabs (of 15 oz. each) in a wooden box of such massive construction that it was nearly impossible to open peacefully. You can break these boxes with an entrenching tool, in about four minutes slashing, but the best thing is to dash the box, by one of its rope or wire beckets against a rock until it splits. The lid of the box is fastened by six screws, but even if there is time to undo all of these, the slabs will not come out, since they are unshakeably wedged against the four sides. I have opened boxes by detonating a primer on one corner, but regard this way as unnecessarily noisy wasteful and dangerous for daily use.

Rail Demolition. – Guncotton in 15-ounce slabs is convenient for rail cutting. The usual method of putting a fused and detonated and primed slab against the web is quick and easy, but ineffective. The slab cuts a six-in. section out of the line, leaving two clean fractured surfaces (Hejaz rails are of a mild Maryland or Cockerill steel). The steel chairs and sleepers are strong, and the enemy used to tap the broken rails again into contact with a sledge, and lay in a new piece whenever the combined fractures were important enough. New rails were ten metres long, but the line worked well on unbolted pieces two or three metres long. Two bolts are enough for a fish plate, and on straights the line will serve slow trains for a mile or two without fish plates, owing to the excellence of the chairs. For curves the Turks, after we had exhausted their curved rails, used short straights. These proved efficient even on 120-metre curves. The rate of repair of a gang 100 strong, in simple demolition is about 250 cuts an hour. A demolition gang of 20 would do about 600 cuts an hour.

A better demolition is to lay two successive slabs on the ballast beneath the bottom flange under the joint and fish plate, in contact with the line. This spoils the fish plate and bolts, and shortens each of two rails by a few inches, for the expenditure of two slabs and one fuse. It takes longer to lay than the simple demolition, but also takes longer to repair, since one or other rail is often not cut, but bent, and in that case the repair party has either to cut it, or to press it straight.

The best demolition we discovered was to dig down in the ballast beside a mid-rail sleeper between the tracks, until the inside of the sleeper (iron of course) could be cleared of ballast, and to lay two slabs in the bottom of the hole, under the sleeper, but not in contact with it. The excavated ballast should then be returned and the end of the fuse left visible over the sleeper for the lighting party. The expansion of air raises the middle of the sleeper 18 in. from the ground, humps the two rails 3 in. from the horizontal, draws them 6 in. nearer together, and warps them from the vertical inwards by the twisting pull of the chairs on the bottom outer flange. A trough is also driven a foot or more deep across the formation. This gives two rails destroyed, one sleeper or two, and the grading, for two slabs and one fuse. The repair party has either to throw away the entire track, or cut a metre out of each rail and regrade. A gang of 100 will mend about 20 pairs an hour, and a gang of 40 will lay 80 an hour. The appearance of a piece of rail treated by this method is most beautiful, for the sleepers rise up in all manner of varied forms, like the early buds of tulips.

[Intelligence collected from wireless intercepts provided the information on repair times]

Simple demolitions can be lit with a 12-in. fuse. The fish-plate-flange type [bridges] should be lit with 30-in. fuses, since the fragments of steel spray the whole earth. The 'tulips' may be lit with a 10-in. fuse, for they only scatter ballast. If, however, the slabs have been allowed to get into contact with the metal of the sleeper they will throw large lumps of it about. With a 10-in. fuse most of these will pass over the head of the lighting man who will be only 15 yards or so away when it goes off. To be further is dangerous. We were provided with Bickford fuse by Ordnance. The shiny black variety causes many accidents, owing to its habits of accelerating or smouldering. The dull black is better, and the white very good. Our instantaneous fuse has an amusing effect if lit at night among friendly tents, since it jumps about and bangs; but it is not good for service conditions. The French instantaneous fuse is reliable. Detonators should always be crimped on to ready-cut fuses, and may be safely carried in the pocket or sandbag, since great violence is required to set them off. We generally used fuses for lighting.

Speaking as a rule rail demolitions are wasteful and ineffective unless the enemy is short of metal or unless they are only made adjuncts to bridge-breaking.

A pleasant demolition, of a hybrid type, is to cut both rails, and turn them over, so as to throw them on their face down the bank. It takes 30 men to start this, but a small gang can then pass up the line, bearing on the overturned part, and the spring of the rails will carry on the reversing process, until you have done miles of it. This is an effective demolition with steel sleepers, since you wreck the ballasting. We tried it once on about 8 miles of a branch line, with a preponderance of spiked wooden sleepers, and it made such a mess of rails and sleepers that the Turks washed their hands of it.

The Hejaz line carried a minimum of traffic, so that there was no special virtue in destroying the points of crossing places.

Bridge Demolitions. – The lightness of traffic affected the tactics of bridge demolition also, since a single break was met either by transport or deviation. As with the rails however, the methods we used are perhaps more important than why we did it. Most of the bridges are of dressed limestone masonry, in 80 to 100-pound blocks, set in lime mortar. The average spans were from four to seven metres, and the piers were usually 15 ft. wide and 4 ft. 6 in. thick. It is of course better to shatter a bridge than to blow it sky-high, since you increase your enemy's labours. We found that a charge of 48 pounds of guncotton, laid against the foot of the pier on the ground, untamped, was hardly enough, and that 64 pounds was often a little too much. Our formula was therefore about 1/5BT2 for guncotton charges below 100 pounds, untamped. In a pier 15 ft. broad, had the feet been marked off on it, we would have had no explosive between feet 1 and 3 and 12 and 15. The bulk would have been against 4, 5, and 10, 11, with a continuous but weaker band uniting and 10. Dry guncotton is better than wet for such work; gelatine is about 10 per cent. stronger for these open charges. With charges above 100 lbs. 1/6BT2 or 1/7BT2 is enough. The larger your object the smaller your formula. Under fire, the inside of the bridge is fairly safe, since enemy posts enfilade the line and not the bridge arches. It is however seldom leisurely enough to allow of tamping a pier charge by digging. When it is, a trench a foot deep is all that is possible, and this does not decrease a guncotton charge by more than 10 per cent. Gelatine profits rather more in proportion by simple tamping.

A quick and cheap method of bringing down the ordinary pier or abutment is by inserting small charges in the drainage holes that are usually present. In the Hejaz line these were in the splay of the arch, and a charge of 5 lbs. of gelatine, or 25 of guncotton, in these would wreck the whole line. The depth and small size of the drainage holes tamp the explosive to an extreme degree. Where the bridge was of many spans we used to charge alternate drainage holes on either side. In the ordinary English abutment where the drainage holes are small and frequent, it would be wise to explode several simultaneously by electricity, since the effect is much greater than by independent firing. Necklacing and digging down from the crown or roadbed are methods too clumsy and slow for active service conditions.

In North Syria, where we came to bridges of great blocks of basalt, with cement joints, we had to increase our charges for untamped work to 1/4 or even 1/3 BT2.

We found guncotton most convenient to handle when we knotted it up into 30-slab blocks by passing cords through the round holes in the middle of the slabs. These large bricks are quick to lay and easy to carry. An armoured car is very useful in bridge demolition, to hold the explosive and the artist. We found in practice that from 30 to 40 seconds was time enough to lay a pier demolition charge, and that only one man was necessary. We usually used 2-ft. fuses.

Girder bridges are more difficult. In lattice bridges where the tension girder is below the roadway, it is best to cut both compression beams. If the tension girder is overhead, it is better to cut both tensions and one compression. It is impossible to do a bridge of this sort very quickly. We had not many cases, but they took ten minutes or more each. When possible we used to wedge the gelatine in the angles of meeting girders. The only quick way is to lay an enormous single charge on the top of the abutment and root it all away with the holdfasts. This may require 1000 lbs. of gelignite, or more, and a multiplicity of porters complicates things. I never blew up a plate girder.

Mining trains pertains perhaps more to operations than to engineering, and is, any way, a special study in itself. Automatic mines, to work on rail deflection always sounded better than they proved. They require very careful laying and to be efficient have to be four-charge compound. This involves electrical connection. The best mine action we had was made for us by Colonel R. E. M. Russell, R. E., and we were about to give it extended use when the enemy caved in.

The ordinary mine was fired electrically by an observer. It is an infallible but very difficult way of destroying hostile rolling stock, and we made great profit from it. Our standard charge was 50 lbs. of gelatine. Guncotton is very little use.

However mining is too large a subject to treat of. The army electrical gear is good, but the exploder seems needlessly heavy. By using a single strand insulated wire (commercial) we fired four detonators in parallel at 500 metres; army multiple-stranded insulated cables will fire two at 500 metres. In series, I have never had occasion to fire more than 25 detonators (at 250 yards), but I see no reason why this number should not be greatly increased. The army electric detonators never failed us. A meter test might show that some of them were defective, but even the defective ones will fire on an exploder. It is usually unnecessary to insulate your joints. The exploder goes out of action quickly if knocked about in a baggage column, or slung on a trotting camel, so I usually carried two as reserve.

The Hejaz Armoured Cars

A Rolls in the desert was above rubies; and though we had been driving in these for eighteen months, not upon the polished roads of their makers' intention, but across country of the vilest, at speed, day or night, carrying a ton of goods and four or five men up, yet this was our first structural accident in the team of nine.

T. E. LAWRENCE, *SEVEN PILLARS OF WISDOM*

The above passage describes an incident that took place in September 1918, nearly two years after the Rolls-Royce armoured cars and tenders were introduced into the Hejaz. It is a telling statement of the reliability of the cars and the arduous circumstances in which they were used.

The 'armoured motors' of the Hejaz Armoured Car Battery (HACB) were officially designated as the 'Admiralty 1914 Pattern Armoured Car'. Each was built on a largely unmodified Rolls-Royce 40/50 chassis, known as the 'Continental' or 'Alpine Eagle' model.

Protection for the crew was provided by 3/8-inch-thick rolled steel-plate armour, which protected the mechanicals of the car as well. Extra spring leaves (13 total in front and 15 in the rear) and dual rear-wheel assemblies were added to compensate for the weight, but overall the cars were an 'off the shelf' Rolls-Royce chassis.

The Rolls-Royce 40/50 was introduced in 1907; after 1910, it was powered by a six=cylinder 7428cc engine that produced about 75bhp. From 1913, the cars had a four-speed transmission, with rigid front and rear axles that were suspended from the chassis by leaf springs front and rear. The car was stopped with the aid of rear-wheel-only brakes (four-wheel brakes only made their debut after the war). The power and reliability of the 40/50 was first proved in the gruelling Alpine Trial of 1913. The factory-modified 'Alpine Eagles' were copied and produced only for special-order sale thereafter and it was this version of the 40/50 that served as the foundation for the factory-produced Rolls-Royce armoured cars.[1]

---

[1] The special Alpine Eagle model was produced until about 1921.

Two of the HACB cars had served with the Royal Navy's (RN) No. 1 Armoured Car Squadron that were sent to help fight the Germans in the colony of South-West Africa, then with No. 10 Armoured Motor Battery in German East Africa.

The natives called them "the steel rhino that spit lead" and like their namesake, the heavy Rolls-Royces spent much of their time wallowing up to their chassis-rails in red mud. Unlike their namesake, however, they couldn't get out of the mud without hours of toil by their crews. When it was determined the cars were useless in swamps and rugged bush country against a fleeting enemy, they were sent to Egypt. There, the unit was disbanded and the cars turned over to the army to become part of the Machine Gun Corps (Motors). In early March 1917, two of the armoured cars were shipped to Wejh as the Hejaz Armoured Car Section (HACS) under the command of Lieutenant Leofric Gilman. After the capture of Akaba, the Arab Army moved there and the two originals were joined by three more armoured Rolls-Royces of the Egyptian Expeditionary Force's Light Armoured Motor Battery[2] and were redesignated as the Hejaz Armoured Car Battery (HACB).

Four other vehicles of the unit were called 'tenders'. In naval parlance, a tender is a support vessel and when the Royal Navy's Armoured Car Division went ashore, its support vehicles, or tenders, were assigned to carry supplies, fuel, and personnel that could not be accommodated in the cramped battle wagons. Initially, Wolseley and Ford cars were used in the role, which sufficed when distances were short and adequate roads

Talbot truck of the RFA 10-Pounder Motor Section. (Gilman Family Collection)

[2] The Duke of Westminster's RNAS No. 2 Squadron.

existed. No. 14 Squadron, Royal Flying Corps swore by their Crossleys and the Royal Field Artillery Motor Section needed their Talbot trucks (also called tenders) to move the 10-pounder guns they used so effectively. Not everyone was a Rolls-Royce fan.

In North Africa, however, neither Wolseley nor Ford was well suited for combat, although they were used in support roles. They could not keep pace with the Rolls-Royces on long missions across the harsh terrain and often broke down, only to be towed back to base by the armoured cars. The solution was found in the armoured cars themselves. Several cars from the Duke of Westminster's RNAS No. 2 Squadron were stripped of their heavy armour and fitted with simple metal and wood coachwork and a wooden bench seat. The rear of the vehicle consisted of an open bed with a tailgate that could be loaded with food, water, fuel, and all manner of items necessary for combat operations. Even fully loaded, the tenders could maintain 60 to 70mph across level desert terrain.

The Hejaz Battery initially had three Rolls-Royce and one Wolseley tenders. None of them were identical. Their bodies were constructed at the Ordnance Depot in Egypt and followed no plan, relying instead on the workers' ingenuity and the materials available. The Rolls-Royces retained the heavier springs of the armoured cars, as well as the double wheels (the Hejaz armoured cars ran double wheels front and rear). A wood cargo area was built behind the driver's area. At least one of the tenders was equipped with a folding fabric top and several had a door on the passenger side. Others were simply left open for ease, or speed, of entry and exit.

Despite being intended for logistics work, the cars were not defenceless. The driver kept a rifle within easy reach in a scabbard and carried his issued pistol. A Vickers machine gun on a tripod often sat in the back bed of the car for additional firepower.

The cars were the lifeline for the battery and Lawrence's operations. They picked up and delivered supplies from Akaba to the forward bases, which included thousands of Commonwealth of Australia gold sovereigns, offloaded from British ships to pay the rebel troops for their loyalty to the leader of the revolt, Sherif Hussein, and his son Emir Faisul, the commander of the Arab Northern Army. The tenders were also used to evacuate the sick and wounded back to Akaba, including Turkish prisoners of war, as, under the circumstances, they were the fastest and the most comfortable transport available.

But the Rolls-Royce tenders' most important job was to conduct reconnaissance and raids on the railroad line. The tenders carried the fuel, food, ammunition, and explosives required to destroy the bridges, blockhouses and tracks of the Hejaz railway. The system was the Ottoman Turks' main line of communication between Damascus in the north and Medina in the south, a distance of over 1,300 kilometres. They relied on it to keep their beleaguered forces in Mecca supplied and maintain their tenuous hold on the land between the two cities.

The armoured cars did not have the space to carry the large amounts of explosives (guncotton or gelignite) necessary to wreck miles of track, whereas the tenders did.

Along with the explosives, wire, and exploders, the demolition experts rode in the tenders. While the armoured cars secured the area, the tenders moved in close to the track to emplace explosives and retreat out of the area before all hell broke loose.

Lawrence's driver, S. C. Rolls (no relation to Charles Rolls, one of Rolls-Royce's founders), recounted a typical mission in his book *Steel Chariots in the Desert*. It did not end as peacefully as he had hoped. Lawrence was trying to destroy a long stretch of the rail line and after setting many blocks of guncotton, he sent everyone back to the cars and began to light the time fuses. Then he, too, ran back to 'Blast', which was theoretically now out of harm's way behind an embankment. But, before he reached the car, the charges began to explode and a section of rail that had been cut by the explosion came hurtling out of the sky to land on the front seat where Lawrence usually sat. The nine-inch piece of steel embedded itself in the wood under the cushion. Both men saw the incident for what it was: testimony to the near misses and escapes they had experienced in the desert thus far.

They didn't have much time to ponder their fate though, as bullets began to sing over their heads. The Turkish observation posts had finally noted their presence and responded with gun ire from hundreds of yards away. It was time to make an escape. With Lawrence gesturing wildly to the other cars, Rolls gunned his own car and shot away into the desert, past the armoured cars that were providing covering fire for the withdrawal.

The tenders were the fastest of the battery's cars, but all the Rolls-Royces had similar traits: the reliability to get their cargo to the target, a quiet engine useful for a silent approach, and the horsepower to get out of the area when the job was done. The known cars of the HACS/HACB were:

Armoured Car LC0808 before being stripped of its armour in August 1918. (Gilman Family Collection)

LC0808 stripped and converted to be a tender. (Gilman Family Collection)

ARMOURED CARS

LC336	Arrived Akaba November 1917
LC339	Arrived Akaba November 1917
LC340	Arrived Akaba November 1917; OC Lieutenant Leofric Gilman's car
LC0809	Arrived Wejh circa 4 March 1917; had served in South-West and East Africa
LC0808	Arrived Wejh circa 4 March 1917; had served in South-West and East Africa (converted to a tender in Akaba in August 1918)

TENDERS

LC341	probably 'Blast' driven by S. C. Rolls; model 1914 40/50, chassis no. 57 LB
LC1105	possibly known as 'Bloodhound'; model 1914 40/50
LC1298	'Blue Mist'; model 1909 40/50, chassis no. 60985
LC369	Wolseley

'Blue Mist'

There were a number of Rolls-Royce cars with the Hejaz Armoured Car Section (HACS) supporting the Arab Revolt. There were at least five armoured Admiralty 1914 Pattern armoured cars and four tenders.

There was one exception to the '1914' rule, however, and that was the car which subsequently became most associated with Lawrence of Arabia. The only photograph of Lawrence in a car during the campaign shows a tired man dressed in an Arab cloak and headdress sitting in the passenger seat of an equally tired car. It is 2 October 1918 in Damascus, Syria, the day after the city was captured by Commonwealth forces. The end of the Great War in the Ottoman Empire is near and the man is

Lieutenant Colonel T. E. Lawrence and driver Corporal J. McKechnie, Army Service Corps (ASC), sitting in 'Blue Mist', Marjeh Square, Damascus, 2 October 1918. (Courtesy: Rolls-Royce Heritage Trust)

Lieutenant-Colonel Thomas Edward Lawrence. The driver sitting next to Lawrence wears threadbare, dirty British khaki. They had arrived just behind the Australian Brigade to ensure that Feisul's Arab Army received credit for the city's capture.

If 'the car makes the man' then it is appropriate that the photograph shows Lawrence sitting in a Rolls-Royce. It was Lawrence, after all, who said, "A Rolls in the Desert is above Rubies." But the car depicted is not the elegant car it once was. It appears to be a common utility vehicle with open bodywork and all manner of supplies strapped to her. The fenders are bent, lights are missing, the paintwork sandblasted. In cavalry parlance, the car "has been run hard and put away wet". This was 'Blue Mist', a 1909 Rolls-Royce 40/50.

Blue Mist was described by one witness as "an older one than the others" unlike the other Rolls-Royce cars of the HACS, which were all 1914 'Alpine Eagles', a high-performance modification of the Silver Ghost developed for the 1912 Austrian Alpine Trial. The cars had four-speed transmissions and a 7428cc engine producing 75bhp. Blue Mist's engine was 7036cc and she had a three-speed transmission, which limited its torque and top speed compared to the Alpine Eagles. In effect, Blue Mist was the runt of the litter.

The official War Diaries of the HACS describe the cars only as tenders along with their military registrations. There were three tenders: LC341, LC1105, and LC1298. Two, LC341 and LC1105, were identified as 1914 models through photographs. They were used for heavy lift – to carry extra personnel, fuel, water, ammunition, and explosives for railway demolition operations – while LC1298 generally is noted as a courier vehicle, and was confirmed to be Blue Mist through a War Diary entry that states it "was broken down due to rear wheel collapsing". This was a common failure with wooden wheels in the extreme heat of the desert. Blue Mist was the only Rolls-Royce in the HACS with wooden wheels.

Near the end of the Middle Eastern campaign, in September 1918, the armoured cars and the heavy tenders were fully engaged with the Arab Army pushing north. Lawrence needed to get to Damascus quickly to ensure it was the Arabs who got full credit for its capture. Only one car was available, Blue Mist. In *Seven Pillars*, Lawrence wrote. "I made Blue Mist mine" before the final push on the city. Driven by Corporal J. McKechnie, Lawrence and Major W. F. Stirling dashed into Damascus on 1 October 1918, arriving just after the Australian Light Horse, which passed through the city. Lawrence quickly set up a "functioning" government to support Hussein's claim to the city and fulfil the terms of Sykes-Picot.

Lawrence was the man of the hour and Blue Mist was the car of the moment. Like the average sportsman who made the winning point in an otherwise lost game, Blue Mist was there when that iconic photograph was taken. It has become part of the iconography that is Lawrence of Arabia. Lawrence would resign from the army two days later.

Where did Blue Mist come from?

In his memoir, Safety Last, Stirling provided a clue that Blue Mist was "given as a wedding present to [Hugh] Lloyd-Thomas, who was the First Secretary [at the British High Commission] in Cairo. Then it was commandeered by Army."

According to Lloyd-Thomas's grandson, Blue Mist was his grandmother Aileen Bellew's car. She purchased it from the Earl of Clonmell for £400 in September 1916, shortly before she married Hugh. The Clonmell's letter of sale to "Miss Bellew" shows the chassis number as 60985. A final connection to Lawrence was only recently discovered. We know the car joined the HACS because of two messages recorded in a wartime radio log – one asks "Lawrence wants to know if Gilman can convert "Blue Mist" and the second states "Rolls-Royce 985" was in Akaba as of late December 1917.

The car began life as a Maythorn Pullman Limousine and was built in 1909 for Fletcher F. Lambert-Williams, who died in the *Titanic* disaster. The car was then acquired by Lord Clonmell. After its purchase, the car was shipped to Cairo where Hugh Lloyd-Thomas was First Secretary at the British High Commission.

Despite the war, the expatriate community still revelled in Cairo's nightlife. The family lore is that Aileen was out on the town at an elegant nightclub one evening when a man in flowing robes swept in and asked, "Whose Rolls-Royce is this outside?"

Aileen answered, "It's mine."

T. E. Lawrence introduced himself and announced, "I need to commandeer your car!"

With that, he drove away. Several weeks later, Lloyd-Thomas received a package that contained the car's solid silver and blue cloisonné enamel nameplate that stated simply: Blue Mist

The Lloyd-Thomases heard nothing of their car until after the Great War. In 1919, the car reappeared in Cairo. The family found her abandoned by the side of the road, hidden by a small sand dune. After digging her out, a new battery was connected and it started on the first try. Hugh and Aileen Lloyd-Thomas were posted to Rome in 1919. They decided to sell Blue Mist and, in late 1919, the car was sold to an Egyptian businessman in Cairo.

The car has long since disappeared; the family has only the name plate to remember the story.

Author's note: My thanks to Tom Clarke, Pierce Reid, Philip Walker and Richard Weston-Smith for their help in the research of Blue Mist.

APPENDIX 6

The Breech-Loading 10-pounder Mountain Gun

For you all love the screw guns –
The screw guns they all love you!
It's worse if you fights or you runs:
You can go where you please, you can skid up the trees,
But you don't get away from the guns!

RUDYARD KIPLING, 'THE SCREW GUNS'

Only a select few weapons merit their own ditty, but the 'screw gun', having earned its reputation on the North West Frontier of India in the late 1800s, inspired Kipling to write one. One observer noted that it had "proved most successful in dislodging unruly natives". The gun's role in later wars is almost unknown.

At nearly 900 pounds, the Breech Loading 10-pounder Mountain Gun (BL 10-pdr) was designed to be broken down and carried into battle on the backs of five mules (plus others for ammunition) and be unloaded and put into action relatively quickly – the manual called for 180 seconds for assembly. It was called a 'screw gun' because the gun barrel came in two pieces – a breech and a chase – that were screwed together before it could be fired. In ordnance terms it was called 'jointed'.

The BL 10-pdr replaced the Rifled Muzzle Loading 2.5-in Mountain Gun (2.5-in RML) and was deployed exclusively to India before the Great War, where it was declared obsolete almost as soon as it had been issued.

The improved gun had a maximum effective range of 3,700 yards and fired a heavier shell than its predecessor (2.75-in) because of its new loading mechanism. The guns were especially suitable in close quarters or difficult terrain where bigger guns could not be manoeuvred or deployed. A minor disadvantage was its reliance on a friction pull-tube igniter (Quill, Friction, Mark IV) to fire the gun. If the gunners ran out of these, there was no alternative way to ignite the charge.

At the beginning of World War I, the outdated BL 10-pdrs were sent to Europe with the Indian Mountain Batteries where their short range proved of little use. They were then sent to Mesopotamia and Egypt and from there they were used at Gallipoli and in East Africa. One element, the Royal Field Artillery's (RFA) 10-pounder

Motor Section was sent from the Western Desert to Akaba in November 1917 to join with the Hejaz Armoured Car Section to support the Arab Revolt against the Ottoman Army in the Hejaz.

Commanded by Lieutenant Samuel Brodie, the motor section consisted of six Talbot trucks that carried two guns and crews into battle. The guns were normally offloaded and fired from the ground, but they were also be fired directly off the rear beds of the trucks, making them one of the first mobile gun platforms.

The guns were first employed in attacks on Turkish positions along the Hejaz railway in early 1918 and most successfully in the August 1918 battles at Mudowarra and Wadi Rutm, where the section supported the Imperial Camel Corps' successful dismounted attacks that destroyed the railway stations. In concert with Rolls-Royce armoured cars sporting Vickers machine guns, the mountain guns would prove intimidating to the Ottoman defenders. In the words of Lawrence, despite their "inferior weapons" the RFA Motor Section "always prevailed".

Bibliography and Sources

Official and Archival Files

The National Archives, Kew.
FO 371 – Political Departments: General Correspondence, Egypt and Sudan.
FO 686 – Army Papers, Jeddah Agency.
FO 882 – Arab Bureau Correspondence and Reports.
WO 95/4415 – War Diaries.
WO 157 – Intelligence Summaries, First World War, Egypt.
WO 158 – Operations and military situation, Egypt and Palestine.

British Library
Notebooks, etc., of Lawrence, Colonel T. E., rel. to the Arabian campaign: 1916–1918, MS45914.

Imperial War Museum
Private Papers of Gubbins, Major General Sir Colin M., KCMG, DSO, MC; Documents 12618.

King's College
Papers of JOYCE, Lt Col Pierce Charles.

Collections
Edward Metcalf Collection, The Huntington Library.
George Pascoe Family Collection.
James A. Cannavino, Library, Archives & Special Collections, Marist College, USA.
Leofric Gilman Family Collection.
Richard Weston-Smith Collection.

Published Writings

Aksakal, Mustafa, 'Holy War Made in Germany? Ottoman Origins of the 1914 Jihad', *War in History,* Washington DC: American University, 2011.
al-Askari, Ja'far Pasha, *A Soldier's Story: From Ottoman Rule to Independent Iraq: The Memoirs of Ja'far Al-Askari* (1st English ed.), London: Arabian Publishing, 2003.
al-Sayyid-Marsot, Afaf Lutfi, 'The British Occupation of Egypt from 1882', *The Oxford History of the British Empire: Volume III: The Nineteenth Century,* Andrew Porter (ed.), Oxford: Oxford University Press, 1999.
Anderson, Scott, *Lawrence of Arabia: War, Deceit, Imperial Folly and the Making of the Modern Middle East,* New York: Doubleday, 2013.
Anglim, Simon, *Orde Wingate and the British Army, 1922–1944,* London: Pickering & Chatto, 2010.

Antonius, George, *The Arab Awakening: The Story of the Arab National Movement*, Ann Arbor: H. Hamilton, 1938.

Badcock, G. E., *A History of the Transport Services of the Egyptian Expeditionary Force: 1916–1917–1918*, London: Hugh Rees, Ltd., 1925.

Bagnold, R. A., 'Early Days of the Long Range Desert Group', *The Geographical Journal*, Vol. 105, No. 1/2 (Jan–Feb 1945), London: Royal Geographical Society.

_____, *Sand, Wind, and War: Memoirs of a Desert Explorer*, Tucson: University of Arizona Press, 1991.

Barr, James, *Setting the Desert Afire: T. E. Lawrence and Britain's Secret War in Arabia*, New York: W. W. Norton, 2008.

Beaumont, T. W., 'Rank and File', *Journal of the Society for Army Historical Research*, Vol. LVIV, No. 237, Spring 1981, London: Society for Army Historical Research, 1981.

Berton, Joe, *T. E. Lawrence and the Arab Revolt: An Illustrated Guide*, Madrid: Andrea Press, 2011.

Callwell, Charles E., *Small Wars: Their Principles and Practice*, London: HMSO, 1906.

Clayton, Sir Gilbert Falkingham, *An Arabian Diary*, Robert O. Collins (ed.), Berkeley: University of California Press, 1969.

Cowles, Virginia, *The Phantom Major: The Story of David Stirling and the S. A. S. Regiment*, London: Collins, 1958.

Cross, Cockade, et al, *Lawrence of Arabia & Middle East Airpower*, Woodhall Spa: Cross & Cockade International, 2016.

Daly, M. W., *The Sirdar: Sir Reginald Wingate and the British Empire in the Middle East* (Memoir 222), Philadelphia: The American Philosophical Society, 1997.

Erickson, Edward, *Ordered to Die*, Westport: Greenwood Press, 2001.

Faulkner, Neil, *Lawrence of Arabia's War*, New Haven: Yale University Press, 2016.

Fisher, John, 'The Rabegh Crisis, 1916–17: "A Comparatively Trivial Question" or "A Self-Willed Disaster"', *Middle Eastern Studies*, Vol. 38, No. 3 (July 2002), pp. 73–92, Milton Park: Taylor & Francis, Ltd., 2002.

Fromkin, David, *A Peace To End All Peace: The Fall of the Ottoman Empire and the Creation of the Modern Middle East*, New York: Avon, 1989.

Gordon, John W., *The Other Desert War: British Special Forces in North Africa, 1940–1943*, Westport: Praeger, 1997.

Hopkirk, Peter, *Like Hidden Fire: The Plot to Bring Down the British Empire*, New York: Kodansha, 1994.

Inchbald, Geoffrey, *Imperial Camel Corps*, Driffield: Leonaur, 2005.

James, Lawrence, *The Golden Warrior: The Life and Legend of Lawrence of Arabia*, New York: Paragon House, 1993.

Korda, Michael, *Hero: The Life and Legend of Lawrence of Arabia*, New York: Harper, 2010.

Lawrence, A. W., *T. E. Lawrence by His Friends*, Garden City: Doubleday, 1937.

Lawrence, T. E., 'Demolitions Under Fire', *The Royal Engineers' Journal*, Vol. XXIX, No. 1 (January 1919), Brompton Barracks: Institution of Royal Engineers

_____, *Oriental Assembly*, London: Williams & Norgate, 1947.

_____, *Revolt in the Desert*, New York: Garden City Press, 1927.

_____, *Seven Pillars of Wisdom: A Triumph* (The Complete 1922 Oxford Text), Salisbury: Castle Hill Press, 2003.

Lawrence, T. E., & Edward Garnett, *War in the Desert*, Salisbury: Castle Hill Press, 2016.

Linderman, Aaron R. B., *Rediscovering Irregular Warfare: Colin Gubbins and the Origins of Britain's Special Operations Executive*, Oklahoma City: University of Oklahoma Press, 2016.

Lloyd Owen, David, *Desert My Dwelling Place: With the Long Range Desert Group in North Africa*, London: Cassell, 1957.

Mcintyre, Ben, *SAS: Rogue Heroes*, London: Viking, 2016.

MacMunn, Lt-Gen Sir George & Capt Cyril Falls, *Military Operations Egypt and Palestine: From the Outbreak of War with Germany to June 1917*, London: HMSO, 1928.

Ministry of Information, *Combined Operations, 1940–1942*, London: HMSO, 1943.

Moh, Polly A., *Military Intelligence and the Arab Revolt*, London: Routledge, 2008.

Murphy, David, *The Arab Revolt 1916–1918: Lawrence Sets Arabia Ablaze*. New York: Osprey Publishing, 2008.

Murray, Archibald James, *Sir Archibald Murray's Despatches (June 1916–June 1917)*, London: Dent, 1920.

Nicholson, James, *The Hejaz Railway*, London: Stacey International, 2005.

Parsons, Laila, *The Commander: Fawzi al-Qawuqji and the Fight for Arab Independence 1914–1948*, NYC: Hill & Wang, 2016.

Pirie-Gordon, H. (ed.), *The Advance of the Egyptian Expeditionary Force Under the Command of General Sir Edmund H. H. Allenby: July 1917–October 1918*, London: HMSO, 1919.

Reinhardt, Charles & Prof Eric Ouellet, 'Ottoman COIN in the Arab Provinces: Modernization, Competing Nationalisms and World War 1914–1918', Defence Research & Development Canada, 2010.

Rogan, Eugene, *The Fall of the Ottomans: The Great War in the Middle East*, New York: Basic Books, 2015.

Rolls, S. C., *Steel Chariots in the Desert*, Driffield: Leonaur, 2005.

Schneider, James J., *Guerrilla Leader: T. E. Lawrence and the Arab Revolt*, New York, Bantam, 2011.

Stirling, Col W. F. *Safety Last*, London: Hollis & Carter, 1954.

Storrs, Ronald, *Orientations*, London: Ivor Nicholson & Watson Ltd., 1937.

Talaat, Mehmed, 'Posthumous Memoirs of Talaat Pasha', *The New York Times Current History*, Vo. 15, No. 1 (October 1921), New York: NY, 1921.

Walker, Philip, *Behind the Lawrence Legend: The Forgotten Few Who Shaped the Arab Revolt*, Oxford: Oxford University Press, 2018.

Wavell, Col A. P., *The Palestinian Campaigns*, London: Constable, 1932.

Wavell, FM Earl, *The Good Soldier*, New York: Macmillan, 1948.

Webber, Kerry, *In the Shadow of the Crescent: The Life and Times of Colonel Stewart Francis Newcombe, R. E., D. S. O.*, TBP.

Westrate, Bruce, *The Arab Bureau: British Policy in the Middle East, 1916–1920*, University Park: The Pennsylvania State University Press, 1992.

Wilson, Jeremy, *Lawrence of Arabia, the Authorized Biography of T. E. Lawrence*, New York: Atheneum, 1990.

Winstone, H. V. F., *The Diaries of Parker Pasha*, London: Quartet, 1983.

Winter, Brig H. W., *Special Forces in the Desert War: 1940–1943*, Kew: The National Archives, 2001.

Young, Maj Sir Hubert, *The Independent Arab*, London: John Murray, 1933.

Index